DEMOCRACY

Ernst B. Schulz

PROFESSOR EMERITUS OF POLITICAL SCIENCE

LEHIGH UNIVERSITY

BARRON'S EDUCATIONAL SERIES, INC.

Woodbury, New York

CONTENTS

PREFACE

Democracy, although the outcome of a trend of extended dura-
tion, is mainly a nineteenth and twentieth century phenomenon.
Except for occasional instances of "democracy" in earlier times,
authoritarianism of some type prevailed throughout the world
until after the American and French Revolutions of the late
eighteenth century. For several reasons, material pertaining to
ancient and medieval "democracies" has been excluded from
this monograph. The conditions of social and economic life in
the remote past differed greatly from modern ways of living;
"democratic government" occurred in only a few local communities, e.g., the Athenian city-state; and "democracy" was of the
direct rather than representative type. Moreover, judged by
modern criteria of democratic government, ancient and medieval
"democracies" were more authoritarian than democratic in nature.
In Athens, to cite a particular case, political liberty was confined
to Athenian "citizens" (males); these comprised roughly only
one-third of the total adult male population. A select minority
group monopolized the political rights associated with "popular"
government.

Determination of the presence or absence of democracy in
specific countries requires consideration of a variety of factors.
Among them are organizational arrangements and the nature and
extent of the freedoms enjoyed by individuals and groups. Particularly interesting questions arise with respect to the realities
of democratic government as distinguished from democratic
dogma. Time and again democracy is said to be featured by
majority rule. Is it? If so, in what sense? The purpose of this
monograph is to cast some light on these and other matters
pertinent to the subject of democratic government, including the
compatibility of democracy and various types of economy, the
arguments for and against democratic political institutions, and
democracy's prospects for the future.

Helpful comments during the preparatory stages of this publication were contributed by Professors R. J. Tresolini and D. D. Barry of Lehigh University. Mrs. Charles Hobson provided the expert stenographic service so necessary to an undertaking of this type.

E. B. S.

CHAPTER 1

THE NATURE OF

DEMOCRACY

More than two thousand years ago, Aristotle utilized two major criteria in classifying governments. One was the *number of persons* in whom governing authority is vested; the other the *primary purpose* toward which the exercise of governmental powers is directed.

In terms of the first criterion Aristotle distinguished three forms of government, viz., government by the one, by the few, and by the many. The second basis of classification, i.e., purpose, led him to differentiate "true" from "perverted" forms. True forms of government are characterized by the exercise of governmental authority for the benefit of all members of the body politic, whereas *perverted* types are featured by the use of governing power to promote the special and selfish interests of the ruling personnel. Government by the one for the benefit of all is *kingship* or *royalty;* government by the one for his private advantage is *tyranny.* Government by the few, if conducted for the purpose

1

of promoting the common welfare, constitutes *aristocracy*.[1] If the few rule in furtherance of their own selfish interests, the government is an *oligarchy*. The dominant few are likely to be men of property interested in increasing their wealth. Finally, government by the many (the citizens at large) for the benefit of all was identified as *polity* or *constitutional government*, whereas government by the many, usually the poor or the needy, for the purpose of promoting their selfish interests, was named *democracy*, a perverted form of government.

Unlike Aristotle, contemporary political scientists usually classify forms of government without introducing a test of purpose or motivation with respect to the use of governmental powers. Definitions of democracy, for instance, seldom include stipulations concerning the objectives to be attained by a government of the democratic type. However, an underlying assumption, even though unstated, seems to be that democratic processes of government probably will result in promotion of the common welfare.

Aristotle conceived of government by the many, whether of the true or perverted variety, as involving direct action by the body of qualified citizens in the formulation and adoption of policies. Hamilton and Madison, in their comments about democracy in the Federalist Papers, revealed a like conception of the nature of democracy. Thus Madison distinguished between a republic (representative government) and pure democracy. In his words a pure democracy is "a society consisting of a small number of citizens, who assemble and administer the government in person." [2] A distinction is still drawn between direct and indirect democracy, but emphasis now is placed on the latter form, that is, democracy of the representative variety. Although direct democracy survives in a few small communities, e.g., New England towns and some of the cantons of Switzerland, representative democracy prevails in communities of large size. Consequently, the term *democracy* as used today almost always signifies a democratic government of the indirect or representative type.[3]

Numerous definitions of democracy have been formulated. Some are extremely brief, such as "government of, by, and for the people," "a form of government characterized by the responsibility of those who govern to those who are governed," or "government by discussion." These definitions suffer from undue brevity but direct attention to some of the features commonly associated with democracy.

The longer definitions presented below are assignable to two categories: (a) those which include elements of classical democratic theory and (b) those which are designed to reveal the realities of the democratic process.

Examples of the first type are the following:

"Strictly speaking, a representative government is one whose officials and agents are chosen by an electorate democratically constituted, who during their tenure of power reflect the will of the electorate, and who are subject to an enforceable popular responsibility." [4]

"Where the will of the whole people prevails in all important matters, even if it has some retarding influences to overcome, or is legally required to act for some purposes in some specially provided manner, that may be called a Democracy. . . . a government in which the will of the majority of qualified citizens rules, taking the qualified citizens to constitute the great bulk of the inhabitants, say, roughly, at least three-fourths, so that the physical force of the citizens coincides (broadly speaking) with their voting power." [5]

The second and more recent type of definition places primary emphasis on the democratic method or process. Definitions by four authors are presented for consideration, viz.,

"The democratic method is that institutional arrangement for arriving at political decisions in which individuals acquire the power to decide by means of a competitive struggle for the people's vote.[6] . . . In a democracy . . . the primary function of the elector's vote is to produce government." [7]

"Conflict, competition, organization, leadership and responsibility are the ingredients of a working definition of democracy.

Democracy is a political system in which the people have a choice among the alternatives created by competing political organizations and leaders." [8]

"The people—do not and cannot govern; they control the government. In every live democracy they decide the broad march of politics." They decide issues "partly—and in the last resort—at the polls, and partly by the continuously manifested indications of public sentiment." [9]

"Since leadership—is the major characteristic of democracy, we might simply say that democracy is government by leadership. All other forms of government, differ as they may among themselves, have the one feature in common that they do not select the guardians of public authority in the competitive process which is an essential ingredient of true leadership. For the time being, they might all be grouped together under the designation of 'government by rulership.'" [10]

The last group of definitions, by stressing the realities of democratic government, is intended to counteract some of the misconceptions of democracy resulting from such phrases as "self-government by the people," "officials who reflect the will of the electorate," "the will of the whole people prevails," or "the will of the majority of qualified citizens rules." In a pure or direct democracy, policy-determination is a function that the people discharge directly, although not necessarily exclusively or without leadership, but in a democracy of the representative type, the people do not and cannot govern in the sense of deciding specific matters of policy and of undertaking the task of executing adopted policies. Policy-determination and administration are functions performed by elective and appointive officials in the name of the people to whom they are in principle responsible for what is done or left undone.

The broad march of politics is determined by the voters in choosing between competing leaders and programs on the occasion of an election. For example, by placing a liberal rather than a conservative party in control of the government, the voters have indicated the general direction in which they desire the government to move. After the election, decision-making becomes the task of the successful competitors for public office.

During the intervals between elections, public sentiment, expressed in various ways and through a variety of agencies, may influence the action taken by officials, just as the latter may play a significant part in shaping public opinion. Nevertheless, the role of the people in a representative democracy differs materially from that of the office-holding portion of the population. Legally speaking, those who govern are the office-holders who possess decision-making authority. The way in which they exercise this authority depends on their response to the social pressures of various kinds which may be brought to bear upon them.

Neither long nor brief definitions of democracy are adequate substitutes for an extended discussion of democratic political institutions and processes. All of the definitions quoted above, having been taken out of context, do an injustice to the scholars who have formulated them. An author's explanatory and supplementary comments require careful consideration in order to understand his views concerning the nature of democracy and the circumstances under which a particular country may be said to have a democratic rather than an authoritarian (non-democratic) government.

Before mentioning the features which, if present, warrant the conclusion that a governmental system is democratic in character, a few observations about the nature of authoritarian or non-democratic regimes seem advisable. Particular authoritarian systems usually differ from one another in various ways, but one characteristic, common to all of them, is the denial of significant political rights or privileges to most members of the body politic. As a consequence of this denial, minority rule prevails in the sense that ultimate as well as immediate control of the government is confined to a small proportion of the total adult population. Policies are decided on by officials who are neither legally nor politically responsible to the general public—only to the minority which enjoys a monopoly of governmental power. This minority may be the landowners, the wealthy, an hereditary nobility, a party with selective membership which is the only party permitted to exist, or some other comparatively small group. The door is closed to meaningful participation in the process of government by the people as a whole.

Some authoritarian governments are describable as autocratic because of the concentration of governing authority in a politically irresponsible ruler, such as an absolute monarch of the hereditary type or a leader like Hitler or Mussolini whose commanding position enables him to dictate the policies of government. An authoritarian government which is not dominated by one man may be identified as an oligarchy. Officials are responsible to a specially privileged minority group which ultimately determines the objectives to be attained through governmental action. Even authoritarian governments of the autocratic type almost always are actually oligarchical in character. The reason for this assertion is that an autocrat is unable to function without support and this needed support is usually provided by a minority group of some kind. In comparatively rare instances an autocrat is backed by the masses rather than by a select minority. The authoritarian character of the government is unaffected by this fact as long as the masses are denied appropriate ways of holding the autocrat to account for his actions, for instance, by removing him from his position and choosing his successor.

Democratic political institutions vary considerably from place to place and from time to time, but all of them involve recognition of certain fundamental principles. Stated differently, a governmental system is assignable to the democratic category if its *basic features* conform to the requirements of democracy.

In the first place, democracy requires a governmental organization which enables the people to exercise effective control over the principal policy-determining officials. This objective is ordinarily attained by providing for the direct election of these officials for limited terms of service. If this be done and the elected officers possess adequate means of controlling the appointed personnel, the governmental structure conforms to the democratic idea that those who govern shall be responsible to those who are governed. A supplementary requirement is that public service be open to all qualified persons regardless of their social status or family connections and that the voting public be free to choose among those who desire to occupy the all-important policy-determining posts. Open competition and freedom of choice are earmarks of the democratic process of government.

Another essential of democracy is a liberal suffrage in combination with the idea that each person's vote shall count the same as that of other individuals in determining the outcome of an election. Traditionally, "counting the same" has merely meant that no voter's ballot shall be assigned a greater value than that of other voters, e.g., twice as much, in determining the total support received by each of the candidates competing for election to a particular office. Weighted voting, in the sense indicated, is condemned as undemocratic. For reasons to be presented in a subsequent chapter, exactness as to the requisite degree of liberality in the matter of eligibility to vote is out of the question. Although voting qualifications are obviously necessary to prevent manifestly unfit persons from voting, e.g., children and insane individuals, highly restrictive requirements, which have the effect of confining control of the government to a small minority, are indicative of the existence of an authoritarian government of the oligarchical type. Consideration will be given later to the kind of qualifications consistent with democratic doctrines. Suffice it to assert at this point that voting qualifications should be of such a nature that most individuals, if they so desire, will be able to meet them within a comparatively short time after attaining maturity. This generalization may be considered too broad in one respect. It fails to cover the case of countries, commonly referred to as democracies, in which the voting privilege is denied to women. Liberal voting requirements, in those instances, is construed to mean universal manhood suffrage.

Certain other freedoms are as indispensable to democracy as the political rights mentioned in the preceding paragraphs. These are freedom of speech and of the press, freedom of assembly, freedom of association, and freedom from arbitrary arrest and imprisonment. Without these freedoms, the role of the people, except for occasional trips to the polls, is largely restricted to silent and passive observation of what public officials are doing.

The *free expression of opinion* concerning issues, parties, candidates, and the quality of governmental service is a means of providing and disseminating information on the basis of which both those who govern and those who are governed may decide on the action to be taken in specific situations. An adequately informed public is a presupposition of democracy, which is sometimes described as "government by discussion." Freedom to discuss any matters pertaining to government, to exchange views about public affairs in general, to praise or to find fault with governmental officials or aspirants to public office, is a freedom without which such political freedoms as the right to vote and to hold office lose much, if not all, of their value. The denial of freedom of speech closes the door to significant popular participation in the process of government. Once that door is closed it makes little difference whether elections are held or whether liberal voting qualifications are prescribed by law. Moreover, without freedom of speech, formal guarantees of freedom of assembly and freedom of association become meaningless. Why assemble, if people are prohibited from saying what they please? What are the chances of association, if people are unable to find out in what respect they agree or disagree about the policies which are, or ought to be, pursued by the government?

Freedom of assembly signifies freedom to gather together or to hold meetings for purposes concerning government. Some meetings may be held to discuss the issues of the day; others may be designed to bring about the nomination of candidates for public office; and still others may have the objective of winning support for proposed solutions of particular social problems. Meetings for these as well as for other reasons serve both as a source of information and as a means of securing collective or group action which is more likely to result in the gaining of an objective than the unaided efforts of particular persons.

Freedom of association for various purposes includes the right to organize political parties so as to compete for control of the government. If this freedom be denied, or seriously restricted, the result may be a no-party or a single-party body politic with an authoritarian regime of some sort. Political parties contribute to popular control of the government because like-minded individuals, by working together, stand a good chance of shaping the policies of government, either by placing their leaders and members in key positions or by furnishing an articulate opposition to the party or parties in power. Moreover, competition among parties provides voters with a choice among leaders and programs on election day. Freedom of association also permits the formation of organizations which favor or oppose the adoption of various policies without attempting to gain control of the government in the way that parties do. An example of an association concerned solely with public affairs in general is the League of Women Voters. Other associations having a primary purpose which may be religious, educational, or economic, for example, also contribute to popular control of government inasmuch as associations of this type may influence policy-determination by pressing for or against policies which they believe desirable or undesirable from the standpoint of their special interests.

Freedom from arbitrary arrest and imprisonment is requisite to the achievement of democratic government. Unless this freedom is insured, those in office at any particular time may silence or eliminate their opponents by sending them to concentration camps or by confining them to prison. In this way, free competition for control of the government, a feature of democracy, may be brought to an end.

Adequate sources of information are also necessary to democracy. Freedom of speech and of the press, of assembly, and of association contribute to the conveyance of information to the general public, but their value in this respect is diminished unless reliable knowledge concerning public affairs is obtainable. Dependable sources of information are needed to combat the spreading of misinformation. Secrecy in regard to the activities of government and the denial of access to governmental records and reports are a menace to democracy. Freedom of teaching, learning, and research is an indispensable means of ascertaining the truth about existing conditions and about the results or likely consequences of adopted or proposed policies. Unlimited freedom of inquiry is the best way of increasing the probability that reliable information will be made available to the public. In the absence of dependable sources of information, the people can easily be misled by leaders and parties who are more interested in exploiting the public than in promoting the general welfare. The problem of developing trustworthy sources of information is difficult to solve in any society, especially in one of a highly complex character.

Fulfillment of the foregoing requirements of democratic government, that is, appropriate organizational features, a liberal suffrage, the legal guarantee of certain basic freedoms, and adequate sources of information, may not justify the conclusion that a particular country qualifies as a democracy. Something more is needed. That additional something is consistent willingness to abide by the rules of the democratic process.

Elections, for instance, should be safeguarded against fraudulent and corrupt practices and conducted in an atmosphere free from intimidation. The rigging of elections by any means whatsoever prevents the voters from freely determining which leaders and parties are to be placed in control of the government. Furthermore, election results, however distasteful to the losers, must be accepted as conclusive and not be set aside by resort to revolutionary action.

As for legal guarantees of basic freedoms, these lose significance if denied in practice to dissenting and unpopular individuals and minorities. Fundamental freedoms for *all*, not merely for some, is a requisite of democracy.

Conformity to the rules of the democratic process also requires honesty in the presentation of information to the public. The withholding of facts and intentional misrepresentation on the part of officials, party leaders, the owners and editors of newspapers and periodicals, and persons in control of radio, television, and other channels of communication constitute serious threats to democracy. Freedom of speech and of the press may result in the spreading of falsehood as well as the truth. In the absence of high standards of integrity in the exercise of these and other freedoms, a disguised authoritarianism may prevail in a given country even though some of the formal features of democracy, e.g., a liberal suffrage and an elective legislature, are provided for by law. Standards of integrity depend on the moral code of a community. Attempts to establish them by law usually prove unsuccessful in communities which are tolerant of malpractices of one type or another in the field of politics.

A difficulty arises in passing judgment on the character of the political institutions of a particular country. Are its institutions democratic or authoritarian? The reason for difficulty in reaching a decision is indicated by the following question. What degree of conformity to the basic requirements of democratic government justifies the conclusion that a given country qualifies as a democracy? Complete conformity is unlikely. Organizational arrangements may be defective in some respects; qualifications for voting may come close to being unduly restrictive; the fundamental freedoms, nowhere absolute, may be limited to an extent which approaches incompatibility with democratic principles; sources of information may be of questionable adequacy; and the rules of the democratic process may at times be disregarded. No country commonly considered a democracy *fully* meets all of the requirements to which attention has been directed in this chapter. A typical shortcoming is inadequate provision of the information which, as a matter of democratic principle, is assumed to be available to the general public. Under the circumstances, a practical response to the question raised above is that a subtantial degree of compliance with the basic requirements of democracy warrants the conclusion that a particular country is assignable to the democratic category. How substantial? That is a matter of judgment. Borderline cases sometimes occur. In these instances about all that can be said is that the governmental system is neither wholly authoritarian nor entirely democratic in character. In subsequent chapters, more light will be cast upon the difficulties encountered in classifying particular governments.

An attempt to define democracy by including all of the specific requisites mentioned in the preceding paragraphs would result in an unusually cumbersome definition of great length. The definition which follows is neither short nor simple but it covers the essentials of democracy without being excessively detailed. Democracy is a process of government characterized by 1] freedom of opportunity for all individuals and groups to influence, if they can, the course of governmental action and 2] by organizational arrangements which provide for the making of final policy-decisions by officials chosen for limited terms of service, and therefore replaceable from time to time, by an electorate composed of persons able to meet liberal voting qualifications. The first part of this definition implies possession of the basic freedoms to which attention has been directed and also the availability of adequate sources of information. Both parts, by implication, signify the indispensability of willingness on the part of the public to conform to the rules of the democratic process. Of course, these implications may be far less evident than they are presumed to be.

The remainder of this book is devoted in part to a more detailed discussion of several of the various requisites of democracy which have been commented on briefly in the preceding pages. Such matters as different forms of democratic government, problems of representation, election methods, political parties, pressure groups, the relationship of liberty and equality to democracy, and the compatibility of democracy and different types of economy require consideration at some length to convey understanding of what democracy really means and to guard against misconceptions which, by giving rise to unwarranted expectations, may possibly endanger its survival. Concluding chapters deal with the arguments for and against democracy and with the outlook for its future.

STUDY QUESTIONS

1. What was Aristotle's classification of governments?
2. Compare Aristotle's definition of democracy with recent ways of defining democratic government.
3. What are the general distinguishing characteristics of authoritarian regimes? What are the two principal varieties of authoritarianism?
4. What are the fundamental features of democracy in the political sense?
5. To what extent is popular election of officials essential to democracy?
6. How liberal should voting qualifications be from the point of view of "democratic doctrine"?
7. Why are each of the following freedoms essential to democracy: (a) freedom of speech, (b) freedom of assembly, and (3) freedom of association?
8. Why is freedom from arbitrary arrest and imprisonment requisite to the achievement of democratic government?
9. Democratic government requires more than appropriate organizational arrangements, a liberal suffrage, and legal guarantees of basic freedoms. What are the additional requirements?
10. Why is it difficult to pass judgment on the character of the political system of a particular country?
11. Broadly stated, what are the two basic requisites of democracy?
12. How would you define democracy?

CHAPTER 2

ORGANIZATIONAL ARRANGEMENTS —VARIETIES

Organizational arrangements conducive to popular control of those who govern are essential to democracy. Different forms of government fulfill this basic requirement. Examples are the cabinet-parliamentary system, the presidential-congressional plan, the Swiss pattern of parliamentary government, and the council-manager type of organization.

Specific features of organization pertain to such matters as the methods of selecting and removing officials, terms of office, qualifications for voting and for office-holding, the composition of the legislature, the type of executive, the system of courts, the relationship of the component parts of a government to one another, and the powers and duties of the government as a whole. The character of many of these features is a matter of importance from the standpoint of effective popular control of the governing personnel.

In this chapter primary emphasis is placed on democratic requirements with respect to the methods of selecting and removing officials and the relations among the principal branches or organs of government. The next two chapters deal with the problem of representation and with election methods. Both of these aspects of organization have a direct bearing on the degree of correspondence between the actualities of government in a democracy and such democratic theories as "self-government by the people," "rule by the majority," or "each individual counts for as much as any other individual in the process of government."

Federal and Unitary Systems of Government

Democracy in the political sense is compatible with either a unitary or a federal system of government. These systems differ from each other in regard to the character of the relationship between the central government of a body politic and the units of local government included within its boundaries. The territorial distribution of governmental authority between different levels of government is a universal phenomenon. A central or national government deals with such problems of nation-wide importance as require uniformity of policy, whereas local governments handle matters of essentially local concern with respect to which diversity of policy is unobjectionable.

Under a unitary system of government the central authorities decide upon the extent to which a territorial distribution of power is desirable. The number and nature of units of local government, their governmental organization, and their powers and responsibilities are all determinable by the central government which is free to grant as much or as little local autonomy as it sees fit.

A federal system is characterized by an effective constitutional guarantee of the existence and powers of designated units of local government. The territorial distribution of power between the central government and local units, usually only the major political subdivisions, is incorporated in the constitution by the framers of that document. A redistribution of power requires a constitutional amendment or a reinterpretation of the constitution. Both the central government and the major local units derive their powers from the same source, viz., the constitution.

A country with a federal system may have political institutions of the authoritarian type. Such was the case in the German Empire of 1871 to 1918. Many democracies have unitary systems of government, among them Great Britain, the Scandinavian countries, Belgium, and the Netherlands. Some, such as the United States, Switzerland, and Canada, are countries in which federalism prevails. In the United States, the federal principle controls the relationship between the national government and the fifty states, but within each of the states, subject to minor exceptions, the unitary system is operative in regard to the relations between the state government and such minor units of local government as counties, townships, and cities.

The distinction between authoritarianism and democracy is based on the relationship between those who govern and those who are governed—not on a territorial distribution of governing authority. A particular government, national or local, may be either authoritarian or democratic in character—democratic if it is so organized and functioning that popular control of those who govern is a demonstrable fact; authoritarian if those who govern are controllable only by a privileged minority of some type. The pages that follow will be confined to a consideration of organizational arrangements which, in the case of a particular government, are compatible with the requirements of democracy.

The Selection and Removal
of Officials

The public officials and employees of democracies ordinarily attain their positions either through election or by appointment.[11] The vast majority are appointed. Although the election of certain officials, preferably by direct popular vote, is a requisite of democracy, the selection of a substantial proportion in this way is neither necessary nor desirable. Choice by election is commonly combined with a limited term of office, so as to afford opportunity, from time to time, to bring about a change in personnel. Democratic elections also involve liberal voting qualifications.

Which officials should be chosen by election? The answer to this question depends on several considerations. Probably the most important is the character of the function performed by an office-holder. Others are the effect of election on the relations among the several branches of government, on the quality of personnel, on standards of service, and on discharge of the responsibilities borne by the voting public.

Two primary functions are involved in the operation of any government, viz., policy-determination and administration. The former consists of determination of the ends to be achieved through governmental action and also of designation of the general ways of attaining them. For example, the objective may be a powerful military force; the preferred method of obtaining it—compulsory military service. Administration is the function of executing or carrying out whatever policies have been adopted. Apart from its routine aspects, the process of administration entails the exercise of discretion as to the most expedient way of executing an established policy. Questions of *administrative policy* require consideration. Policy issues of this type arise *after* decisions have been made concerning desirable objectives and the most appropriate means of gaining them.[12]

The only officials whose selection by election is indispensable to democracy are those invested with authority to settle basic questions of policy,[13] provided, however, that these officials possess adequate means of controlling the appointed personnel. Subject to this proviso, direct election of members of the legislature is sufficient to enable "the people" to decide who shall govern and broadly to what ends. Limited terms of office insure elections every so often and permit the electorate to change the composition of the legislature if dissatisfied with the policies it has pursued. This is one way of bringing about desired alterations in policy. Scheduling elections at appropriate intervals of time is a practical means of implementing the democratic idea that those who govern shall be responsible to those who are governed.

If election be confined to the choice of members of the legislature, effective legislative control of the administrative personnel becomes an imperative of democratic organization. Various controls have been devised. Among them are the power to appoint and/or to remove the chief executive; control of the purse strings; the power of investigation; the authority to create and to abolish administrative agencies and to prescribe administrative procedures; and the power to require the keeping of records and the submission of reports. Which of these or other controls should be provided depends on the particular pattern of democratic government.

If, for one reason or another, major limitations are placed on legislative control of the administrative branch, election of the chief executive, who heads the administrative services, may be advisable. This arrangement is characteristic of a governmental organization based on the doctrines of separation of powers and checks and balances. It is a favored method of providing for the mutual independence of the executive and legislative branches of a particular government. Another reason in support of election of the chief executive is the important part played by this official as a leader in policy-determination as well as in administration. Many proponents of democracy believe that the growing importance of the chief executive in the general process of government strengthens the case for election, even though this mode of selection is by no means essential to democracy. Whether election of the chief executive is preferable to appointment, or vice versa, remains a controversial question.

Experience indicates that the election of administrative officials other than the chief executive is, as a rule, undesirable. In the first place, the chief executive bears ultimate responsibility for administrative results. Election of administrators of lower rank than the chief executive divides both authority and responsibility and results in a disintegrated and cumbersome administrative organization. The chief executive should be authorized to select and remove his principal administrative subordinates, e.g., department heads. An elected official is accountable to the voters —not to the chief executive or to other officers of the administrative branch. Secondly, competent administrators are more likely to be chosen by appointment than by election. Success in winning voter support is hardly a reliable criterion of administrative capability. Another consideration which makes appointment preferable to election is that many able persons are unwilling to enter public service if initial entry and continued service depend on participation in drives for nomination and election. Election of administrators also tends to lower standards of performance. The desire to win an election by gaining and retaining the backing of powerful politicians and organized interest-groups frequently results in the subordination of sound administrative practice to considerations of political expediency. Multiplication of the number of elective offices is objectionable for still another reason, viz., the longer the ballot, the greater the burden of the voters and the greater the likelihood of "blind" voting.

Most of the objections to election of administrative officials also are valid with respect to the choice of judges. Their primary function is the administration of justice in accordance with the law of the land. Unlike prevailing practice in most of the states of the United States, the appointment of judges is the rule rather than the exception in other countries with democratic political institutions.[14]

Extension of the elective method to the selection of officials other than the legislative personnel and perhaps the chief executive, although seemingly consistent with democratic doctrine, increases the difficulty of attaining effective popular control over the agencies of government. The principal reason is that a division of authority among a multiplicity of elected officials results in a disintegrated organization. Responsibility for governmental action is divided among numerous officers who are individually accountable to the voters but not to one another. Ultimate responsibility for the total governmental result is *not* centered in one place. Consequently, voters experience difficulty in locating responsibility. It is comparatively easy for mutually independent officials with limited authority to shift responsibility for what has been done or left undone to one elected colleague or another. The voting public is unable to determine with certainty who is deserving of re-election and who is not.

For various reasons, as pointed out above, the *quality* of government may be lowered if administrative officials are selected by popular vote rather than by appointment. However, this adverse consequence is probably not as serious as the obstacle to effective popular control resulting from the dispersion of authority and responsibility caused by indiscriminate resort to choice by popular election.

The services of elected officials holding office for a fixed term may be terminated by refusal to re-elect them. In some bodies politic, removal of these officials before expiration of the term for which elected may be accomplished through such devices as *recall by popular vote*[15] or *impeachment, trial,* and *conviction* of the charges leading to impeachment. As for appointed officials, provision for their removal is commonly made. Although arrangements vary, removal by the appointing officer is generally considered an appropriate method. But removal of the appointed personnel by the electorate is usually deemed undesirable.

Branches of Government:
Principles of Relationship

Practically all forms of government involve the establishment of different branches or organs for the discharge of such functions as policy-determination, the execution or administration of adopted policies, and the adjudication of disputes which arise in connection with law enforcement. Belief in the advantages of specialization and/or the desire to erect safeguards against abuses of power[16] account for the fact that different persons are usually entrusted with the performance of each of these tasks. But the principle of functional specialization is seldom adhered to absolutely. The highest officials of a particular government are ordinarily participants in the discharge of more than one function. Nevertheless, different branches are identifiable under practically all forms of government, even though the same persons may be members of more than one branch or despite the fact that each branch may participate to a limited extent in the performance of functions which, for the most part, are assigned to other branches.

The relationship of the several branches of a particular government is indicative of the controlling principle of organization. If one branch is supreme with respect to the others, the basis of organization is the doctrine of integration. If the several branches are mutually independent of one another and consequently enjoy coordinate status, the form of government conforms to the separation of powers principle. This principle may be associated with an arrangement which enables each branch to exercise a limited degree of control over the others. In that event, the doctrine of checks and balances supplements the separation of powers principle of organization.

Different forms of government are operative in countries which qualify as democracies. Some are based on the doctrine of integration; others are characterized by a separation of powers in combination with checks and balances. In many, few officials

are chosen by popular vote; in some, the number of elected officials is comparatively large. In all cases, provision for the removal
of both elected and appointed officials is usually made. The remainder of this chapter will be devoted to a description of selected patterns of organization which are commonly considered
compatible with democratic doctrines.

Cabinet–Parliamentary Government

Cabinet-parliamentary government is based on the principle of
subordination of the executive to the legislative branch of government. Legislative supremacy is promoted in two ways, viz.,
by enabling the legislature to remove the executive at any time
and by providing that final decision on questions of basic policy
rests with the legislature. Ultimate popular control of the legislature is maintained by election of its members from time to time
by an electorate composed of individuals meeting reasonably
liberal voting qualifications. Different varieties of cabinet-parliamentary government have been devised but all of them are
based on the idea of popular control of the legislature and effective legislative control of the executive, primarily, although not
exclusively, by making the executive responsible to the legislature through the device of immediate removability of the former
at the pleasure of a legislative majority.

Cabinet-parliamentary government at the national level usually
is characterized by a chief of state, who is the nominal chief
executive; by a cabinet, including a prime minister, which is the
working or actual executive; and by a legislature composed of
one or two houses, to only one of which the cabinet, in most
countries, is responsible. Members of the dominant chamber of
the legislature, if there be two, are chosen by popular vote for a
designated term of years. The chief of state, either a president or
a king, may gain his post in various ways, among them direct or
indirect election, legislative selection, or, in the case of a king,
through operation of an hereditary arrangement. As a matter of

law, important executive powers are vested in the chief of state, but these powers are actually exercised by the cabinet which includes the prime minister or premier.

Cabinet ministers are chosen in the following manner. After election of the members of the dominant branch of the legislature, the chief of state invites the leader of the majority party in the legislature to become prime minister and to designate the personnel of his cabinet. The individuals so selected, usually prominent party members, are appointed to high-ranking administrative positions by the chief of state. If no party controls a majority of the seats in the legislature, the chief of state requests the leader of one of the stronger parties to form a coalition cabinet. In either case, cabinet ministers are usually, although not necessarily, selected from the legislature and retain their seats in that body.[17]

The cabinet, under the guidance of the prime minister, provides legislative leadership by presenting a policy-program to the legislature. It also functions as a plural executive and its members, individually, act as the political heads of the major administrative departments. Thus the initiative in both policy-determination and administration lies with the cabinet, although ultimate responsibility for what is done rests with the legislature as long as a majority of its members uphold the cabinet's leadership.

Resignation of the cabinet is in order once it becomes apparent that the support of a legislative majority has been lost. Lack of confidence in the cabinet may be indicated by the legislature in various ways, viz., by adoption of a motion of want of confidence, by passage of a motion of censure, by defeat of an important policy sponsored by the cabinet, or by the adoption of a policy despite the cabinet's opposition. In some bodies politic, the cabinet, on the occasion of withdrawal of legislative support, may dissolve the legislature and order an election within a short period following dissolution.[18] The outcome of the election determines the fate of the cabinet. If the election is won by the opposition, the cabinet necessarily resigns and the leader of the successful opposition is asked to form a new cabinet. Dissolution followed by an election enables the voters to decide whether a cabinet should remain in control or hand in its resignation.

The downfall of a cabinet may occur at any time. Consequently, the opposition party or parties must always be prepared to assume the responsibilities of leadership in policy-determination and administration. If dissolution of the legislature is ordered, as it may be in some countries, the groups in opposition to the cabinet stand little chance of winning the subsequent election without a known leader and a policy-program designed to appeal to the voting public. Whenever general elections are held, either at prescribed intervals of time or following a dissolution, the electorate is presented with a choice among the leaders and parties that are competing for control of the government.

Presidential-Congressional Government

Presidential-congressional government, sometimes referred to as the independent executive system, is based on the doctrines of separation of powers and checks and balances. The legislative and executive branches enjoy mutual independence in the sense that neither is legally or politically accountable to the other for the way in which it exercises its powers. An independent judiciary is also provided.[19]

The creation of mutually independent branches of government may be accomplished by establishing appropriate methods for the selection and removal of officials, by adequate guarantees of tenure of office, and by prohibiting persons from serving simultaneously in more than one branch. If no branch is permitted to select and/or to remove the personnel of the other branches and if no individuals may hold office at the same time in two or more branches, a firm foundation is laid for a separation of powers system, insofar, at least, as formal structural arrangements are conducive to that end.

In democracies, popular election of the chief executive and members of the legislature for fixed terms affords a simple way of promoting mutual independence, provided that the services of these elected officials may be terminated only by the voters. Under such an arrangement neither branch is placed in a position of subordination to the other. Independence of the judiciary may be secured in the same manner, but other means of promoting judicial independence may prove equally effective. Ordinarily, under any form of government, officials guilty of criminal misconduct may be removed from office prior to expiration of the terms for which elected or appointed. For this reason only, one branch of a separation of powers type of government may be authorized to remove members of another after the presentation of charges, trial, and conviction. Permitting it to make removals for other reasons would conflict with the separation of powers principle.

Mutual independence need not be absolute. Each branch may be given a limited degree of control over the others, although not to so great an extent or in such a way as to result in the type of subservience characteristic of an integrated organization. In other words, checks and balances may be associated with a separation of powers. The executive may be granted a suspensive veto[20] with respect to acts of the legislature; legislative approval of executive appointments may be required; and the courts may be empowered to pass judgment on the constitutionality of legislative and executive action. Other kinds of checks and balances may be established.

The national government of the United States exemplifies a separation of powers and check and balance type of organization. A brief description will reveal the organizational arrangements relied upon to prevent one branch of the government from dominating the others.

Members of Congress are chosen by direct popular vote:

representatives for two years and senators for six. Each house may expel its members by a two-thirds vote, but no other method of removal is available. Neither the President nor the courts possess authority to oust representatives and senators.

Nominally, the President is chosen by an electoral college. Actually, the selection is made by popular vote inasmuch as the voters choose presidential electors on a partisan basis and the latter cast their ballots for the known nominees of their parties. Choice by Congress is prohibited unless no presidential candidate obtains a majority of the electoral vote. In that event the House of Representatives selects one of the three highest candidates, subject to the stipulation that the delegation of each state may cast but one vote.

The President is elected for a four-year term. His removal from office prior to the expiration of this term requires conviction by the Senate following impeachment by the House of Representatives on charges of treason, bribery, high crimes, and misdemeanors. Congress may not remove him on grounds of lack of confidence or dissatisfaction with the policies he pursues. All he needs to do in order to complete his term is remain alive.

Judges of the national courts are appointed by the President with the advice and consent of the Senate. The appointments are for *good behavior* which has been construed to mean "for life." In this way judicial independence is promoted, because after appointment a judge may be removed only through the impeachment process upon conviction of treason or other criminal misconduct.

Another constitutional provision designed to contribute to both executive and judicial independence limits the discretion of Congress, in some measure, with respect to the compensation of the President and judges. The President's compensation may neither be increased nor decreased during the term for which he was elected. In the case of judges, a judge's compensation may be raised, but not lowered, after his appointment to the bench.

The constitutional allocation of powers among the three branches of the national government conforms for the most part to the distinction between legislative, executive, and judicial functions. "All legislative power" is vested in Congress, "the executive power" in the President, and "the judicial power" in the Supreme and inferior courts. However, because of the check and balance idea, a separation of powers along strictly functional lines was avoided by the framers of the constitution. Thus the President is authorized to recommend measures to Congress and to exercise a suspensive veto over its acts. His power to grant reprieves and pardons for offenses against the United States serves as a check on the judiciary. Congress possesses authority to create and abolish administrative departments and inferior courts; control of the purse strings is vested in Congress; and the advice and consent of the Senate is required in the exercise of the President's powers of appointment and treaty-making. The most important judicial check on the President and Congress is the power of the courts, inferred from the constitution, to refuse to enforce Presidential and Congressional acts on the ground of unconstitutionality. This power is exercised only if the constitutionality of governmental action is questioned in cases brought before the courts in the ordinary course of litigation.

The organizational features just described fail to reveal the actualities of the national government as a going concern. Political parties compete for control of the government and play an important part in its functioning. The President devotes much of his time to the advocacy of policies he favors and to the development of Congressional and public support for them. In the eyes of the people he is more of a popular and political leader than a chief administrator. The effectiveness of Presidential leadership in policy-determination varies with the man and the political situation. If his party controls both houses of Congress and if he commands the respect of the general public and the members of Congress, his role in the process of government comes close to being dominant. But a weak President who is unable to win public and Congressional support finds the going rough. His legal powers are not extensive enough to overcome persistent and widespread opposition to policies he favors.

This brief portrayal of the realities of national government in the United States will be concluded with mention of one more increasingly significant development that is common to *all* forms of government, not merely the presidential-congressional variety. The trend referred to is the growing influence of the expert personnel of administrative agencies in the process of policy-determination. This phenomenon is a consequence of the numerous problems requiring expert solution in the complex societies of the twentieth century. Large-scale and complicated governmental operations have become the order of the day.

Parliamentary Government: Swiss Type

The national government of Switzerland is neither cabinet-parliamentary nor presidential-congressional in character. It resembles each of these organizational patterns in some respects but differs from them in others.

The legislature or Federal Assembly is composed of two houses which are equal in law-making authority. Members of the lower house, the National Council, are chosen directly by popular vote for a four-year term. The cantons (major political subdivisions of Switzerland) are represented in approximate proportion to population. Members of the upper chamber, the Council of States, are commonly chosen either by direct popular vote or by the cantonal legislatures, but the constitution merely states that "each canton appoints two deputies," apparently in whatever way a canton prefers. Each canton also decides upon the term of service of its deputies. Terms vary from one to four years, with three- and four-year terms predominating. Equal representation of major political subdivisions in the upper house and representation according to population in the lower house is a feature of Swiss organization which corresponds to arrangements in the United States with respect to Congress.

The chief executive agency is plural in type. Its seven members are chosen for a four-year term by a joint session of the two chambers of the legislature. Each member of this plural executive, entitled the Federal Council, heads an administrative department. Departmental assignments are made by the Council. The President of Switzerland is selected annually by the legislature from the members of the Federal Council.[21] He serves as presiding officer of the Council but has no greater powers than the other members of this plural executive. However, as titular head of the state, certain ceremonial responsibilities are borne by him.

Although members of the Federal Council are prohibited from holding seats in the legislature, the Federal Assembly usually selects persons who are included in its membership at the time of appointment. The persons chosen are ordinarily leading members of the political parties which are represented in the legislature. A common practice is reappointment of Councillors willing to serve more than one term.

Legally, the Federal Council is the servant or agent of the legislature. Actually, it plays a leading role in the governmental process. Its executive responsibilities are extensive and its influence in lawmaking of policy-determination is great, largely because of the prestige of its members, their administrative experience, and their knowledge of public affairs gained through long periods of service. Another contributing factor is the fact that they are prominent members of the parties in control of the Federal Assembly. Federal councillors may speak in both chambers of the legislature and propose motions on subjects under discussion. Their recommendations to the legislature carry great weight. But it is their duty to act in accordance with whatever decisions are finally made by the legislature.

The Swiss executive council remains in office even if the legislature fails to follow its leadership or adversely criticizes its administrative record. No provision is made for votes of lack of confidence or for dissolution of the legislature if this body reacts unfavorably to the Council's recommendations. The fixed tenure of the executive and the legislature is a feature common to the

Swiss system and the presidential-congressional plan of government. An important difference between the two is legislative selection of the Swiss executive and legal subordination of the latter to the legislature. Legislative supremacy is the controlling principle of organization in Switzerland, just as it is in the case of cabinet-parliamentary government. However, the subserviency of the Swiss executive to the legislature is not combined with the insecurity of cabinet tenure which is a feature of the cabinet-parliamentary system.

The Council-Manager Plan

Another example of an organization that conforms to democratic doctrine is the council-manager plan. It is operative in nearly two thousand cities in the United States and is found at the local government level in a number of other countries.

Councilmen are chosen by direct popular vote for a fixed term of service. Ultimate responsibility for both policy-determination and administration rests with the council, even though councilmen are prohibited from engaging in administration either as department heads or, collectively, as members of a plural executive. The immediate responsibility for administration is borne by the manager and the administrative officials who are accountable to him. But the council's control over administration is assured by the simple expedient of authorizing the council to appoint the manager and to remove him at any time.[22] Since the manager continues in service only as long as the council chooses to retain him, his term of office is indefinite. Councilmen are responsible to the voters and the manager to the council.

The manager is administrative agent of the council, but he also plays a significant role in policy-determination. He participates in policy-determination as an adviser, consultant, and furnisher of information to the council. His policy-recommendations may be disregarded but his influence is likely to be substantial as long as the council's confidence in him remains unshaken.

Once the council loses faith, the manager's removal from office ordinarily occurs.

Another official provided for under the council-manager plan is the mayor. He is usually selected either by the council from its own membership or by direct popular vote. The mayor is a voting member of the council, presiding officer of that body, and official or titular head of the city government. He has no administrative responsibilities. The mayor and other members of the council are supposed to concentrate on the making of final policy-decisions and to furnish political leadership. Equally important is their function of keeping the manager under constant surveillance.

Concluding Observations

All of the patterns of government described above fulfill one of the requirements of democracy, viz., organizational arrangements conducive to popular control of public officials.[23] The voters, at election time, decide who shall govern. Between elections they observe and experience the effects of what is done, and their reactions are indicated by the results of each successive election. At all times, of course, the trend of governmental action may be influenced in some measure by the pressures brought to bear on "those who govern" by organized and unorganized interest-groups and, to a much lesser extent, by particular individuals.

Different patterns of government sometimes resemble each other in more respects than might be anticipated in view of differences in organizational arrangements. A comparison of cabinet-parliamentary and presidential-congressional government in regard to one feature illustrates the point.

Under the cabinet-parliamentary plan only the members of the legislature are selected by the electorate. However, if a two-party situation exists in a cabinet-parliamentary country, the voters, in effect, choose the prime minister because they know that the recognized leader of the successful party will serve in that capacity. To become prime minister requires prior attainment of party leadership. If no party is likely to win a legislative majority, as is the case in multiple-party countries, the voters merely know that one of several established party leaders will be invited to form a coalition cabinet.

In the case of presidential-congressional government, the voters choose the president as well as the members of the legislature. Candidates for the presidency may or may not be the leaders of their parties at the time of nomination. In the United States, for example, candidates are nominated, not because party leadership has been attained, but because the party conventions believe that the election chances of particular individuals are good. The primary aim is to pick a winner. Presidential candidates are referred to as the leaders of their parties. Why? Because they have been nominated. The candidate who becomes President continues to receive recognition as the leader of his party, whatever the realities of the situation may be; the beaten candidate's "leadership," at best nominal, rarely survives his defeat.

In a two-party cabinet-parliamentary country, the voters, knowing the identity of the leaders of the competing parties, may be said to "select" the prime minister. The President, under the Presidential-Congressional plan, is formally chosen by the voters. But resemblance in this respect does not negate an important difference, viz., that the attainment of party leadership precedes elevation to the post of prime minister, whereas a president's party leadership is usually acquired after, rather than before, nomination and election.

Various forms of government conform to the democratic idea that the "people" should be provided with appropriate means of deciding who shall govern and broadly to what ends. However, organizational arrangements, whatever their basic features, are insufficient in themselves to warrant the conclusion that the governmental system of a particular body politic qualifies as democratic. Other considerations are involved. These will be discussed after a survey of problems of representation and methods of election—two specific phases of organization.

1. What are "organizational arrangements"? Give examples.

2. Distinguish between federal and unitary systems of government. Which of these systems, if either, is essential to democracy? Give reasons.

3. Which officials should be elected in a democracy? Which ought to be appointed rather than elected? Under what circumstances is popular election of the chief executive desirable?

4. Distinguish between policy-determination and administration. What is meant by administrative policy?

5. What are the objections to popular election of administrative officials, such as department heads? Why is appointment of judges preferable to popular election of these officials?

6. Discuss the ways and means of promoting effective legislative control of the administrative personnel.

7. Explain each of the controlling principles of organization, viz., the doctrine of integration, separation of powers, and checks and balances.

8. What are the principal features of cabinet-parliamentary government?

9. Compare presidential-congressional government with parliamentary government of the Swiss type.

10. Why is the council-manager plan of government consistent with the principles of democratic governmental organization?

11. Show that organizational arrangements sometimes work out differently in practice than anticipated.

12. Why are organizational arrangements insufficient in themselves to warrant the conclusion that a particular body politic is assignable to the "democratic" category?

CHAPTER 3

REPRESENTATION

The prevalent type of democratic government is "representative" rather than "direct" in character. An elective legislature which represents the people is generally considered an essential of democracy. By choosing the members of this body, the voting public decides who shall govern.

Creating a legislature to "represent" the people involves difficulties. What specific principles of representation and which modes of apportioning representatives among the groups granted representation are compatible with democratic doctrine? How and by whom should representatives be chosen? What are the obligations of a representative? What kind and degree of representation is provided for in countries commonly recognized as "democracies"? These questions require an answer because of their pertinence to the classification of particular governments as democratic or authoritarian in character.

Representation and *representative government* are distinguishable. To "represent" means to take or fill the place of another in some respect or for some purpose. For example, an attorney represents his client. In the field of government the device of *representation* may be utilized for various purposes under both democratic and authoritarian systems. *Representative government* occurs when control over governmental policies is actually exercised by a representative body. Such a government may be either democratic or authoritarian in character. It falls in the authoritarian category if, for example, the choice of representatives is confined to a privileged minority, such as the large landowners or the members of a nobility. The difference between authoritarianism and democracy depends in large measure on who is represented and by whom representatives are selected.

Principles of Representation and Modes of Apportionment

All schemes of representation have one feature in common, viz., the representation of people. The differences among *principles of representation* arise from disagreement concerning the groups to be represented. A related problem, also controversial, is that of *apportioning* representatives among the groups receiving representation. How many representatives should be awarded a particular group? With one exception, these two aspects of representation are so closely connected that both necessarily require consideration in differentiating particular plans in regard to the composition of a legislative body.

The exception referred to occurs if all the members of a legislature are elected at-large, i.e., by the entire electorate of a body politic, if the nomination of candidates is open to all groups without restriction as to the permissible number of nominees per group, and if every candidate is placed in competition with all the other candidates who have been nominated. In that event no apportionment problem requires solution. At-large election of all members of a small local assembly or council is a fairly common practice, but the members of legislative bodies of large size are usually chosen by different groups of voters.

Identification of the groups accorded representation may be

in terms of class, of social function, of interests, of place of habitation, or possibly of some other common characteristic, e.g., age, wealth, or race. The allocation of representatives among groups ranges from an equal number per group to representation in proportion to the size of the groups to be represented. Factors other than size also may be taken into consideration, e.g., the comparative wealth of groups, or the relative importance of different group-interests.

Provision for representation of the inhabitants of different parts of the territory of a body politic receives widespread approval. People who live together in a particular place have certain interests in common by reason of that fact, even though their interests in regard to many matters may be diverse and conflicting. As a rule, local communities differ from one another in various respects. For example, some are urban, others rural. Moreover, differences exist among both urban and rural areas. Diversity in sectional interests, attributable to numerous causes, is a common phenomenon. This fact gives rise to the demand for a territorial distribution of the representatives comprising a legislative assembly.

Although the idea of geographical representation is popular, opinion is divided concerning the particular areas to be represented and the apportionment of representatives among these areas. The designated areas may be existing units of local government or districts created solely for the purpose of choosing representatives.

Equal Representation of Areas. Strict equality constitutes one solution of the apportionment problem. Each area is assigned the same number of representatives. No consideration is given to differences in population, wealth, social character, or other attributes. This statement holds true if the areas represented are units of local government; also, if districts created solely for the purpose of selecting representatives are laid out in disregard of social characteristics of any kind, including population. An example would be the creation of districts that are equal in square miles of area.

Equality of representation for territorial subdivisions is provided for in various bodies politic which are classified as democracies. Examples are Switzerland, Australia, and the United States. The upper chamber of the Swiss Parliament is composed of two members for each of the twenty-two cantons into which Switzerland is divided. These cantons are major units of local government. The Australian Senate consists of ten members for each of six states that differ greatly in population. In the United States, each of the fifty states is represented by two Senators in the upper chamber of Congress. Equal representation of counties in the state senate was provided for in seven states, e.g., New Jersey, at the time (1964) the United States Supreme Court ruled that state arrangements of this type are unconstitutional. In Vermont, to cite another example, the lower house was composed of one representative per town. Comparative size in terms of population had been disregarded in these and other instances. The decisions of the Supreme Court declaring that the states may no longer provide for strictly equal representation of areas without paying heed to population differences will be discussed briefly at the end of this chapter.

Representation of Areas According to Population. Another scheme of representation is based on the principle that the ratio of representatives to population should be the same in all of the areas granted representation. Thus, if the territorial units to be represented are political subdivisions like counties, a county with double the population of another receives twice as many representatives. Instead of designating existing units of local government as the areas to be represented, districts may be established for the particular purpose of selecting members of an assembly. If that be done, adherence to the principle of representation in proportion to population requires either the creation of districts with approximately equal numbers of inhabitants, or the allocation of representatives among districts in consideration of differences in population.

For purposes of representation, some bodies politic utilize a base other than total population. Examples are the number of citizens and the number of qualified voters. Whatever the base, application of the principle of proportional representation results in the same ratio of representatives to numbers in every area entitled to representation.

Exactly proportional representation is rarely, if ever, attainable. Its realization, if representatives are apportioned among units of local government, would occur only if a whole number and no fraction were obtainable as the quotient upon division of the population of each unit by the ratio of the entire population of the body politic to the total number of representatives. In political communities which establish special districts for the selection of representatives, the attainment of strictly proportional representation would require the creation of electoral districts with precisely the same population, or with the same number of whatever individuals comprise the selected basis of representation. Although exactly proportional representation is an impracticable ideal, representation in approximate proportion to numbers is comparatively easy to achieve. Even so, in view of population shifts that continuously occur, reapportionment among units of local government or the redrawing of electoral district boundary lines ought to be undertaken frequently, perhaps prior to every election and not merely, for example, once every ten years, if disproportionate representation is at all times to be avoided. Such is not the prevailing practice.

Modified Representation According to Numbers. Another scheme of representation makes allowance for differences in the number of persons but only in conjunction with limitations designed to safeguard sectional interests. The controlling idea is to provide representation for all parts of the body politic and also to prevent one section from dominating the legislature simply because it includes within its boundaries more than half of the individuals to be counted in connection with the distribution of representatives. Weight is attached to interests as well as to numbers. A guarantee of at least one representative per county, for example, regardless of population, precludes even approximately proportional representation if the number of counties is large and the size of the legislature small. Thus, if there be 70 counties and the legislative body includes only 100 members, no more than 30 seats are distributable among the counties in consideration of differences in population. The result is seriously modified representation according to numbers. Again, it may be provided that no part of the body politic may select more than a certain percentage of the total number of representatives, regardless of size in terms of number of inhabitants. A metropolis containing a majority of the population, for instance, may be allocated only 30 percent of the seats. The conviction prevails that the interests of the people comprising the metropolis are no more important than those of the persons residing in small municipalities and rural areas. Conflicts of interest due to sectional differences receive recognition and account for modified representation on a numbers basis.

Functional Representation. Functional representation means the granting of representation to groups of individuals engaged in the same occupation or sharing a common interest and collaborating in the pursuit of particular objectives. Relationship by function or purpose is distinguishable from relationship by place of residence. Examples of functional groups are labor unions, farmers, lawyers, doctors of medicine, and religious sects. Proponents of functional representation contend that each such group ought to be represented directly in the legislature by one or more persons chosen by its membership.

The point is made that failure to provide for functional representation leads to lobbying and other forms of pressure politics by the spokesmen, frequently unknown to the public, for special interest-groups. Although not holding seats in the legislature, these spokesmen or agents bring pressure to bear on public officials to promote the interests of the groups for whom they speak. Sometimes, of course, members of a legislature, even though elected by the voters of a district, are really the disguised agents of a pressure group. The advocates of functional representation believe that open and direct representation of distinguishable interest-groups is preferable to the indirect and behind-the-scenes activities of lobbyists and their sponsors, or to the deception of the voters that occurs when a person elected to the legislature is actually the spokesman for a particular special purpose group or bloc of some kind.

Under a scheme of functional representation an individual belonging to a labor union would participate in the selection of the union's representatives. As a member of a religious association, he also would be entitled to vote for persons desirous of representing the association in the legislature. His different interests would be represented by the representatives of each functional group to which he belonged rather than by a representative chosen by the voters of the area in which he lived. The representatives of areas, so it is claimed, are incapable of adequately representing the diverse interests of each of their numerous constituents.

Two problems require solution in connection with functional representation. Agreement must be reached concerning the groups to be represented. For instance, should all farmers be assigned to a single functional group or should distinctive groups of farmers receive recognition, e.g., wheat farmers, cotton growers, or tobacco producers? The other problem is that of apportionment. How many representatives per functional group? Among the answers to this question are equal representation, or representation in proportion to numbers, to social importance, or to some other criterion of comparative significance. Obviously, serious division of opinion is likely to arise concerning the proper solution of each of these major problems.

Few countries have experimented with functional representation. Examples are Ireland, Spain, and Italy during the period of Mussolini's regime.

Representation of Classes. The representation of classes in the social or economic sense was a common practice during the period of origin of modern parliaments. Social status was emphasized and gave rise to representation of the several estates of the realm, such as the nobility, the clergy, and the commoners. A surviving example of a legislative body based on class distinctions is the British House of Lords. This chamber possesses limited authority as compared to the House of Commons to which the cabinet is solely responsible.

Sometimes only one class receives representation. Such is the case, for instance, if a high property-owning qualification is required for both voting and membership in the legislature. Property owners enjoy a political monopoly. An arrangement of this type is provided for in the Constitution of Liberia.

Representation of the General Public. All of the plans of representation so far considered have been associated with the idea that a representative acts for or in behalf of some identifiable group comprising part of the population of the body politic. As a result the nature of these groups and the apportionment of representatives among them are considered matters of major importance.

A different point of view is that every member of a representative assembly represents the general public rather than the constituency by which he is chosen. That being the case, the character of this constituency and the number of representatives selected by it are rather unimportant considerations. Some arrangements for choosing representatives may be more expedient than others, but whatever the mode of choice, whether by the voters of an area or by the members of a functional group, the representative acts for or in behalf of the general public and not as a spokesman for the persons who selected him. Each legislator represents the entire population; not merely a part thereof.

This conception of the nature of representation is associated with election-at-large of all representatives. It may or may not receive recognition in politically organized communities which, for various reasons, provide for the selection of representatives by territorial or functional constituencies. Even if widely supported and stressed, it is unlikely to result in complete indifference to either the character of these constituencies or the apportionment of representatives among them. To a limited extent, the principle of representation of the general public is endorsed in most communities. Members of a legislature, no matter what the method of selection, are usually expected to keep "the general welfare" in mind in passing judgment on proposed policies.

Plans of Representation and Democracy

Of various controversial questions concerning popular government, one to which considerable importance has been attached is the appropriateness of particular schemes of representation. Some principles of representation and methods of apportionment are claimed to be in conflict with the requirements of democracy. If so, which ones?

Democracy as a form of government is defined in various ways,[24] but all definitions, either expressly or by implication, involve one general idea, viz., that the people decide, from time to time, who shall govern and that their freedom of choice is unrestricted, except for public service qualifications based on considerations of competence. Choice by the people, of course, means election by all persons who are able to meet voting qualifications of a liberal rather than a highly restrictive type.

Political equality is commonly considered a feature of democracy. One of its requirements is an effective guarantee that the privilege of voting be granted to every person possessing the qualifications prescribed by law. Another essential of political equality is that each individual's vote shall count the same as that of other persons in choosing among the candidates competing for a specific office. This requirement precludes the weighting of votes in the sense of giving some men two or more votes and others only one, for example, in the selection of a particular official.[25] A third necessity is that the same qualifications for office-holding apply to all individuals. No exceptions are permissible or justifiable in a democracy.

But what about schemes of representation? Does political equality require any particular plan? Do apportionment plans which disregard numbers, either entirely or in large measure, necessarily prevent fulfillment of the democratic idea? In dealing with these questions, separate consideration will be given to the alternatives of election-at-large of all representatives or election of representatives by different groups of voters.

At-large election obviates decisions about which territorial or functional groups are to be represented and to what extent. Its effect on the political complexion of a legislative body, e.g., on the number of seats per political party or other group of like-minded voters, depends on the mode of election which is used. Methods other than the list or single transferable vote techniques of proportional representation are unlikely to result in the representation of each competing party in proportion to the votes cast for its candidates on the occasion of an election. Single choice— plurality and majority choice election methods enable the strongest party to win all of the seats. For this reason, the advisability of election-at-large instead of election by districts is often questioned, even though each representative presumably represents the entire electorate. The combination of election-at-large with these election methods results, so it is claimed, in political inequality inasmuch as only those voters comprising the winning plurality or majority are represented by persons of their own choice. Voters who cast their ballots for defeated candidates are represented by individuals to whom they are opposed. However, with the election methods referred to, such is also the case, and unavoidably so, if the single member or multi-member district plan is used. Whoever voted against the winner or winners is "represented" by someone whom he hoped would be defeated. If this fact constitutes "political inequality," election-at-large is no more deserving of condemnation on this ground than election by districts, since the inequality complained of is due to reliance on either the plurality or majority choice rules for determining the outcome of an election. Particular methods of election may prevent realization of the avowed objectives of various principles of representation and plans of apportionment. The reasons why will be presented in the following chapter.

If representatives are chosen by various groups of voters, the question arises as to which plans of representation, among the many available, are compatible with the democratic process of government. Principles of representation as well as methods of apportionment require consideration in this connection.

Of the principles of representation discussed above, the granting of representation to territorial or functional groups is sanctioned by most proponents of democracy. Class representation is usually disapproved on the ground that any association of political rights with classes founded on social status runs counter to democratic doctrine. Even so, it may be argued that class representation is permissible in a democracy provided that all classes possess the same political rights.

Many people believe that strictly proportional representation according to numbers is essential to political equality, whatever the character of the groups granted representation. This plan of apportionment requires a decision concerning the persons to be counted. Among the bases used or suggested are total population, the number of citizens, the number of qualified voters, the male population, the adult population, the landowners, the payers of direct taxes, and the number of inhabitants of a designated racial group, e.g., whites. Exclusion of persons because of color conflicts with democratic doctrines, but the effect of such exclusion in a particular body politic depends on the proportion of the population included within the excluded category. Counting only landowners or direct taxpayers also is difficult to reconcile with the concept of political equality. Whether *all* of the other bases of apportionment mentioned above are consistent with the requirements of democracy is debatable. Some of them, particularly total population, number of citizens, and number of qualified voters are less likely to be challenged than the others. Of course, considerations other than serious thought about democratic principles may account for the selection of one base rather than another. Nevertheless, the character of the base, whatever the motive which led to its selection, is pertinent to the question of whether or not a particular government qualifies as democratic.

Proportional representation according to numbers, preferably total population, is commonly regarded as being in line with democratic requirements, but many advocates of democracy question the propriety of both the modified numbers plan of apportionment and the strictly equal representation of groups irrespective of their size, especially the latter. However, various matters ought to be taken into account before passing judgment on either plan. Among these matters are the great diversity of individual and group interests; the accepted view concerning whom a representative represents; the prevailing conception of a representative's duty as a participant in the decision making functions of the legislature; the method of election; the division of party voting strength among the groups which are granted representation; and the role of political parties and other associations of individuals in the process of government in a democracy.

The representation of different interests in legislative bodies is usually considered desirable, but no method of apportioning representatives among *territorial* constituencies assures representation for all of the various interest-groups found in modern society. Wth respect to many matters, the interests of individuals within particular areas differ greatly. Moreover, the membership of most interest-groups commonly includes residents of numerous geographical districts. All schemes of territorial representation are unsuitable for the purpose of providing representation for interest-groups of every type. That is why functional representation is proposed as a substitute for, or a supplement to, the prevailing practice of allocating representatives among geographical constituencies. As pointed out previously, however, the apportionment problem arises in connection with functional as well as with territorial representation. Strictly proportional represen-

tation of either functional or territorial constituencies on a numbers basis is open to the criticism that this plan is based on the
assumption that the size of interest-groups is a dependable
criterion of their relative social importance. Such is not the case.
The role of a small interest-group in the general social process
is frequently as important as, or more important than, that of
considerably larger groups. In view of this fact, equal or modified numbers plans of apportionment may fulfill the requirements
of equitable representation as adequately as the policy of allocating representatives among constituencies in close accordance
with numbers.

Another matter to be considered in evaluating apportionment
plans is whom a representative is supposed to represent. If every
representative, no matter how or by whom chosen, is considered
by himself and by the people in general, to be a representative
of the entire community, insistence on strictly proportional representation seems unreasonable. In bodies politic wherein such
a tradition has become established, neither the equal representation of areas nor some plan of modified representation according
to numbers is likely to be considered undemocratic. But in places
that subscribe to the view that a legislative member is first and
foremost a spokesman for his constituency, the demand for
strictly proportional representation on the basis of numbers may
very well receive widespread support as an essential of democracy.

A third consideration which has a bearing on the choice of a
plan of representation is the approved role of a representative in
the functioning of the legislature. Several theories have been advanced and gained support.

The *mandate* theory requires a representative to vote for or
against proposed policies in accordance with the desires of his
constituents. If he knows what policies are favored by the persons who elected him, he is duty-bound to support them. He also
is obliged to vote against measures to which the folks at home
are opposed. But he is free to vote as he pleases in the absence
of a mandate from his constituents. This situation arises when

the desires of the latter are uncertain or when marked diversity of opinion prevails. From the standpoint of the mandate theory a representative is a delegate who is bound to abide by the instructions of those whom he represents. Since unanimity of opinion in regard to an issue is unlikely, the mandated representative ordinarily carries out a mandate which conforms to the dominant opinion in his electoral district.

A different but related conception of the duty of a representative is that of adherence to the leadership and policy-program of the political party to which he belongs. The representative, having been elected as a partisan, is expected to favor or oppose policies in accordance with the party's platform. His choice by the voters was due primarily to his party affiliation rather than to his personal qualifications or convictions about specific policies. This special version of the mandate theory is based on the belief that a choice among competing political parties is the primary purpose of an election and that a party may, in fairness, be held responsible for results only if all of its members in the legislature collaborate in supporting the party's program. A representative elected as a partisan is guilty of deceiving the electorate if he fails to adhere to the party line.

Another view concerning the obligation of a representative is that he should be guided by his personal convictions in working for or against proposed public policies. The rational foundation of this point of view is that a candidate's election to the legislature is attributable to the electorate's faith in his integrity, intelligence, sound judgment, and concern for the general welfare. As a member of the legislature he is likely to be better informed than his constituents and, consequently, be better qualified to judge the merits and defects of policy proposals. If his constituency loses faith in him, he may be replaced at the next election. The representative is free to heed the desires of those who elected him and may, if he chooses, support the program of his party, but as a general rule his actions should be governed by his personal conclusions concerning the soundness of proposed policies.

In practice, none of the three theories of a representative's duty is likely to be adhered to consistently. But in a particular body politic, one theory rather than another may tend to prevail. In Great Britain, for example, members of the House of Commons are generally expected to support their parties and party leaders, and ordinarily do so. The behavior of legislators in the United States is characterized by a lack of habitual conformity to any of these theories. Party lines are frequently disregarded in voting on bills; mandates from the folks at home often account for the stand taken by particular representatives; and various legislators are apparently inclined to follow their own judgment. As for the attitude of the people, opinion seems to be divided, but perhaps the mandate theory receives more support than the others.

The compatibility of particular schemes of representation with democratic doctrine depends in part on the generally accepted theory concerning the duty of a representative. If the mandate theory predominates and representatives function as delegates of their constituents, the case for strictly proportional representation is strengthened. From a "democratic" standpoint, the decisions of a body composed of "instructed" delegates ought to represent the wishes of a majority of the voters rather than the desires of a minority. That being the case, the ratio of representatives to constituents should be the same, or as nearly the same as possible, for all of the groups, territorial or functional, granted representation. The plan of strictly equal representation, regardless of numbers, is difficult to justify in combination with the mandate theory. Political inequality, rather than equality, prevails. Modified representation according to numbers, if associated with the mandate idea, is also indictable as inconsistent with democratic principles, although to a lesser extent than the strictly equal plan.

The objections to "strictly equal" or "modified representation according to numbers" lose weight if a representative's obligation is understood to be either support of the party or exercise of the representative's judgment. Arguments against these plans also are weakened if every representative, no matter how or by whom chosen, is looked upon as representing the entire body politic and not merely a particular group of persons.

The party-support theory of a representative's duty may, of course, be said to require proportional representation according to numbers, on the ground that control of the legislature by one party rather than by another depends, in some political situations, on the apportionment plan. However, the method of election and the distribution of party voting strength among the groups or areas granted representation are factors which usually count far more in determining the outcome of an election than the plan of apportionment in effect. Strictly proportional representation according to numbers sometimes proves advantageous to a minority party.

Suppose, for instance, that representation is apportioned in strict proportion to numbers among ten districts and that four of these districts contain sixty percent of the population and therefore select sixty percent of the representatives. If either the single choice—plurality or some majority choice mode of election be used, Party A may win all of the seats in these heavily populated districts by a narrow margin over opposition Party B. It might, for example, be supported by only 51% of the voters. Assuming 60,000 votes to have been cast in these districts, Party A's vote would amount to 30,600 as compared to a vote of 29,400 obtained by Party B. If the total vote in the other six districts amounted to 40,000 and Party B won out in every district and was supported by 75% of the voters, Party B's vote in these districts would be 30,000 and that of Party A 10,000. The nation-wide total for Party A, winner of 60% of the seats in the legislature, would be 40,600. Party B, although polling a nation-wide vote of 59,400, would possess only 40% of the legislative seats.

Insofar as the requirements of democracy are concerned, what has been said above indicates that a variety of considerations have a bearing on the importance of attaching weight to numbers in the apportionment of representatives among constituencies. The factors so far mentioned include the method of election, the distribution of party voting strength, the relative social importance of different interest-groups, the correlation between interests and place of residence, the prevailing conception of a representative's duty, and the generally accepted view concerning whom the representative represents—the group which selected him or the body politic as a whole. For these reasons, as well as for others to be discussed later, neither the strictly equal representation of groups, regardless of their relative size, nor modified representation according to numbers is necessarily indicative of the existence of authoritarian rather than democratic government.

Among the various countries commonly recognized as "democracies," few, if any, would be assignable to the democratic category if representation on the basis of numbers were an indispensable requisite. As previously mentioned, strictly equal representation is provided for in the upper chambers of such democracies as Switzerland, Australia, and the United States. In Canada, another democracy, "some eight million Canadians living in big-city areas with populations of 100,000 or more elect 99 M. P.'s, or about one per 81,000 people; three million in middle-sized cities elect sixteen, or one per 188,000; while seven million on farms or in towns averaging less than 12,000 population elect 150, or one per 47,000. An extreme example of urban versus rural discrimination in the ratio of eight to one is noted in Ontario."[26]

Many similar cases of marked discrepancy between the size of areas in terms of numbers and the representation accorded them exist, or have existed, in various bodies politic classified as democratic, including most of the states of the United States. Generally speaking, the legislative assemblies of these states have been characterized by under-representation of urban areas and over-representation of rural communities. Such has been the case for a long time. The latest rulings of the Supreme Court, to be considered shortly, mark the beginning of a change in this respect.

It may be argued that plans of apportionment which disregard comparative numbers are unfair. However, even if no other standards of fairness deserve recognition, the existence of "unfair" arrangements does not necessarily justify the conclusion that a governmental system is undemocratic. Too many other factors require consideration in passing judgment on the character of political institutions.

In 1964,[27] decisions of the Supreme Court were based on the contention that our Constitution's plain objective is that of making equal representation for equal numbers of people the fundamental goal. In *Wesberry v. Sanders,* the Court ruled that the constitutional test for the validity of congressional district schemes is one of substantial equality of population among the various districts established by a state legislature for the election of members of the Federal House of Representatives. This decision was based on the Court's interpretation of the stipulation in Article I of the Constitution that members of the House of Representatives are to be chosen by the people of the several states. Later, in the *Reynolds v. Sims* case, the Court asserted that the Equal Protection Clause of the 14th amendment requires that the seats in *both* houses of a bicameral state legislature must be apportioned on a population basis. Mathematical nicety is not a constitutional requisite, according to the Court, but a state must make "an honest and good faith effort to construct districts, in both houses of its legislature, as nearly of equal population as is practicable." Divergences from a strict population standard are constitutionally permissible if based on legitimate considerations incident to the effectuation of a rational state policy, but neither history alone, nor economic or other sorts of group interests, nor considerations of area alone are permissible factors in attempting to justify disparities from population-based representation. The Court deemed it inexpedient to attempt to spell out any precise constitutional tests and remarked that "developing a body of doctrine on a case-by-case basis appears to us to provide the most satisfactory means of arriving at detailed constitutional requirements in the area of state legislative apportionment." This invitation to further litigation will probably be accepted by persons dissatisfied with the details of particular apportionment plans.

One matter is clear. Unless the Supreme Court reverses itself or until the Constitution is amended, the national judiciary will pass final judgment on the appropriateness, ostensibly from a constitutional standpoint, of the composition of state legislatures. In all likelihood, it will also decide upon the constitutionality of particular arrangements concerning the structure of local assemblies, e.g., city councils. Whatever the eventual consequences of the Court's recent interpretation of the equal protection clause, the asserted requirements of "equal protection" in the United States are inconclusive in deciding whether a particular government, in the United States or elsewhere, is democratic or authoritarian in character. More than one feature of a governmental system is determinative of its essential nature.

At the beginning of this chapter, the following question was raised: "What principles of representation and what methods of apportioning representatives among the groups granted representation are compatible with democratic doctrines?" A partial answer, characterized by various qualifications, has been given. Further comment will be postponed until other subjects have been discussed, viz., election methods, the general character of the democratic process of government, and the part played therein by political parties and other associations of individuals. These matters have a significant effect on the relationship between results and the expectations or claims of the sponsors, in the name of democracy, of particular schemes of representation.

STUDY QUESTIONS

1. Distinguish between "representation" and "representative government."
2. Why is the assumption that "representative governments" are always democratic in character unwarranted?

3. Explain the difference between principles of representation and methods of apportionment.

4. What is meant by strictly equal representation of areas?

5. Explain "representation of areas according to numbers."

6. Why is "modified representation according to numbers" a compromise plan?

7. What is the nature and purpose of functional representation? What problems require solution in connection with functional representation?

8. Explain "representation of classes" and "representation of the general public."

9. What are the requisites of political equality?

10. Discuss the question of whether political equality requires any particular plan of representation.

11. What is at-large election? Give examples.

12. Why may particular election methods prevent realization of the avowed objectives of various principles of representation and methods of apportionment?

13. What bases other than total population are sometimes used in connection with representation according to numbers?

14. What matters ought to be considered before passing judgment on the appropriateness of different plans of apportionment from the standpoint of the requirements of democracy?

15. Why are all schemes of territorial representation unsuitable for the purpose of providing representation for all varieties of interest-groups?

16. Discuss the question of whom a representative is supposed to represent.

17. What are the different theories concerning the proper role of a representative in the functioning of a legislature?

18. Why may strictly proportional representation according to numbers sometimes prove advantageous to a minority party?

19. What may be said for and against the contention that "unfair" methods of apportionment are evidence of the existence of undemocratic government?

20. Discuss the decisions and opinions of the Supreme Court in
    Reynolds v. Sims and *Lucas v. The General Assembly of
    Colorado* (see the Appendix for the opinions and dissenting
    opinions in these cases).

CHAPTER 4

ELECTIONS

Democracy, as a governmental system, involves elections. Elections, in turn, necessitate the establishment of voting qualifications, procedures for the nomination of candidates, methods of election, and rules for conducting elections to prevent dishonest practices and the intimidation of voters. The outcome of an election determines who shall govern, but the result often depends on the nature of the established mode of election. Analysis of election returns has shown, in various instances, that the winning political party or candidate would have lost if a different election method had been used. This fact is understood by persons who have made politics their business and acquired considerable political know-how. That is why controversy commonly arises over the selection of an election method. Also, as observed in the preceding chapter, methods of election have a bearing on attainment of the ends sought through establishment of a particular scheme of representation.

Generally speaking, direct rather than indirect election prevails in democracies. The voters decide which candidate, among those competing against one another, is to hold a particular elective office. Under the indirect plan, the voting public merely chooses the persons who, thereafter, select the officeholders. Nominally, the President of the United States is chosen in this way, but the electoral college no longer exercises the unrestrained discretion contemplated by the framers of the Constitution. The discussion which follows, unless otherwise stated, pertains to direct rather than to indirect elections.

Voting Qualifications

Democracy requires liberal voting qualifications. Just how liberal is difficult to say, but the controlling idea is to establish minimum standards of competence for voting which will enable most persons to qualify at a comparatively early age.

Among the qualifications for voting seldom challenged as being in conflict with democratic principles are citizenship, age, residence within the body politic, and literacy, provided that adequate opportunty to overcome illiteracy is available to practically all persons. The conformity of tax-paying and property-owning requirements to democratic ideas is open to question. Race and sex qualifications are difficult to justify for at least two reasons. One is that neither race nor sex is a dependable criterion of competency. The other is the impossibility, through individual effort, of overcoming disqualification by reason of sex or race. Opportunity to qualify is permanently denied. Some countries today, e.g., Switzerland, and many in the past, e.g., the United States and Great Britain, have been classified as democracies despite denial of the suffrage to women, but the incompatibility of democracy and a sex qualification seems indisputable as a matter of principle. Justification for either a sex or race qualification requires conclusive evidence that the disqualified category of persons is unfit to discharge political responsibilities. Among the criteria of incompetence sometimes advanced are indifference to politics and absence of the desire to be enfranchised.

Citizenship as a qualification for voting meets with general

approval. Aliens owe permanent allegiance to another body politic. No matter how long their period of residence they might
exercise their voting privilege with a view to promoting the interests of their own country rather than those of the country in
which they reside. Usually, too, aliens constitute a small fraction
of the population of a body politic. The case for conferring the
voting privilege on aliens, in the name of democracy, seems weak,
even though it may be argued that aliens pay taxes and are
affected by the policies of the country wherein they dwell, in
some cases, permanently.

An age requirement is designed to prevent the immature from
voting and the stipulated age ordinarily falls somewhere near
twenty years, either slightly above or below. The lower the age,
the larger the electorate. If eligibility were related to a considerably higher number of years, e.g., forty-five or more, the
governmental system would be more authoritarian than democratic in character.

Residence qualifications are justifiable on several grounds.
Residents experience the results of elections, have a lasting interest in the policies of the government of their place of habitation, and bear the greater part of the tax burden. Moreover, residents are more likely to be better informed concerning issues and
candidates than transients or persons who have recently arrived
in a community. An appropriate residence requirement, if strictly
enforced, also prevents certain fraudulent voting practices, such
as colonizing and repeating.[28] Most persons are able to meet
reasonable residence qualifications. Consequently, their establishment and enforcement is not considered "undemocratic."

Literacy tests of a simple type disqualify comparatively few
persons in communities which provide adequate educational
facilities, such as a free public school system. Reading and
writing are skills that most persons can acquire rather easily. A
literacy qualification is defensible, if for no other reason, on the
ground that individuals who are unable to read, if permitted to
vote, need assistance at the polls, and the persons giving it may
abuse their responsibility with the intention of affecting the out-

come of an election. Educational requirements of a kind which comparatively few persons can meet, such as a master of science or doctor of philosophy degree, by confining control of the government to a minority, would result in the establishment of an authoritarian governmental system. Simple standards like literacy are unlikely to give rise to minority rule, except in extremely backward communities.

The effect of either tax-paying or property-owning qualifications on the size of the electorate depends on the type and amount of tax payments required or on the nature and value of the property which an individual must own. Comparatively few persons would be disqualified in many communities if the required tax payment were trivial; likewise, if ownership of a small value of property, either real or personal, were sufficient. But the effect of even trifling amounts is contingent on the distribution of wealth in a particular body politic, on the number of persons to whom a specific tax applies, and on the proportion of the population owning the stipulated kind of property, for instance, land. Obviously, tax-paying and property-owning qualifications, if made sufficiently severe, constitute a means of so reducing the size of the electorate that ultimate control of the government rests with a privileged minority.

Tax-paying and property-owning qualifications are objectionable for other reasons, especially from the "democratic" standpoint. The policies of government affect the interests of all persons, directly or indirectly, not merely those of tax-payers and property-owners. Horeover, the tax burden is borne by all persons even though many may pay no taxes *directly* to the government. Proponents of a tax-paying requirement admit this to be the case but argue that the only tax-conscious group consists of individuals who pay directly rather than indirectly. Another objection to the qualifications under consideration is that neither is a reliable indicator of competence for voting. This claim is rejected by those who favor these qualifications.

From the point of view of democratic principles, the arguments against tax-paying and property-owning qualifications seem more convincing than those in favor. Unlike racial and sex requirements, however, qualifications of this type, if not too severe, may be met by most persons desirous of doing so.

Disqualifications for voting may include mental incapacity (insanity, idiocy, feeble-mindedness); conviction of serious crimes and various specified offenses, e.g., bribery in elections, ballot-box stuffing, and desertion from military service; the holding of a title of nobility; pauperism; and active membership in the armed forces. Of these, the last two are likely to be challenged in a democracy. Many persons question the reliability of pauperism as an indication of political unfitness. Denial of the voting privilege to active members of the armed forces is partly due to fear of a politically powerful military personnel. It is also defended on the ground that men in service, being away from home, are unlikely to be well-informed concerning candidates and issues. But in these days of universal military service and better means of disseminating information, objections to permitting voting by persons in uniform have lost weight. Generally speaking, the various disqualifications have less effect on the size of the electorate than the positive qualifications for voting.

Nominations

Nominating methods are as important as election techniques. Ordinarily the choice available to voters on election day is confined to the candidates who have been nominated by the method or methods established by law. The quality of the persons elected to office depends on the calibre of the nominees. A thorough discussion of nominating methods would include consideration of various matters, including the probability that some methods will result in the selection of better candidates than others. However, the concern here is solely with the freedom or ease with which nominations may be made. Presumably, the greater the freedom, the greater the degree of political equality.

Self-announcement is the simplest and most liberal of all methods of nomination. Anyone desirous of becoming a candidate merely announces his candidacy by notifying the proper authority and filling out such forms as may be required for this purpose. Sometimes the sponsorship of a few qualified voters may be necessary.

Next in order of maximum opportunity to become a candidate is the petition plan. A person's name is placed on the election-day ballot if he files a petition signed by a designated number of signatories, usually qualified voters. The degree of difficulty in securing nomination depends on the number of supporting signatures required. In some jurisdictions a money deposit is necessary, and some candidacies may be discouraged if the stipulated amount is substantial.

The non-partisan primary resembles the petition plan in one respect but differs fundamentally in another. To compete for nomination in the primary merely requires the filing of a petition. Therein lies the resemblance. The basic difference is that the outcome of the primary election determines whose names will appear on the regular-election ballot. Usually, the contenders for office at the final election are the two persons who polled the most votes in the primary. All others are eliminated. In some bodies politic, a competitor who is supported by more than half of the voters in the primary, i.e., by a majority, is forthwith declared elected.

Nomination by partisan direct primary differs from the non-partisan primary in that the qualified members of each party, voting separately but usually on the same day and at the same polling places, select the party's candidates for public office. Competition among parties occurs at the regular election, not at the primary. Since an individual desiring to become his party's candidate for an elective office need only file a petition to have his name placed on the primary ballot, this mode of nomination provides freedom of opportunity in this respect for the members of particular parties. But if no other method of nomination is available, independents, i.e., persons not affiliated with a party, are denied the opportunity to enter competition for an elective position. Joining a party is their only recourse. Persons eligible to compete for a partisan candidacy must win the primary election to become the party's nominee. The rank and file of a party's members do the choosing.

Other devices for nominating party candidates are a caucus of party members, a party committee, and a convention of party delegates. In these cases, any individual may seek the party nomination, but the chances of success largely depend on obtaining the support of the established leaders of the party organization. Their wishes usually prevail. These modes of nomination, like the partisan direct primary, keep independents out of competition for elective offices unless alternative modes of nomination are sanctioned by law.

None of the methods of nomination described above conflicts with the requirements of democracy. As indicated, some are characterized by greater opportunity to become a nominee than others. The various methods have been described in an order determined by the degree of freedom provided, beginning with self-announcement which secures maximum freedom and ending with such partisan devices as nomination by party caucus, party committee, and party convention.

In deciding on an appropriate mode of nomination, factors other than maximizing the opportunity to become a candidate need to be considered. Among them are the probability of obtaining high quality candidates, the number of candidates likely to be placed in competition, the effect on party responsibility, the method of election, and the cost in terms of dollars and inconvenience. But if democracy is preferred to authoritarianism, the appropriateness of different modes of nomination relative to the goal of political equality ought to be taken into account.

Election Methods

The first paragraph of this chapter contains a statement to the effect that the outcome of an election often depends on the method of election in use. Analyses of election statistics have shown that in many instances different methods would have produced different results. An understanding of this fact requires knowledge of the primary features of various election methods.

The features referred to are the latitude allowed the voter in marking his ballot and the rule for determining which candidates are the winners. Other factors to be considered in connection with the choice of an election method are the character of the office to be filled and whether, in the case of a legislative body, its members are to be elected at-large or by districts.

The Single Choice-Plurality Method. Many bodies politic use the single choice-plurality method of election. The single choice feature of this method means that the voter may express but one choice for each position to be filled, presumably his first choice among the nominees in competition. According to the plurality rule, the candidate supported by the most voters, regardless of the proportion of the total vote cast, becames the winner. He may be the choice of only a minority of the voters but, despite this fact, he wins if his support exceeds that of any of his competitors.

This method of election, if used in conjunction with the at-large election of all members of a legislative body or of all the members, two or more, to be selected by the electorate of a designated area, enables the largest group of like-minded voters to win all of the seats. If combined with single-member as well as with multi-member districts, a political party will obtain a legislative majority if its adherents are so distributed, geographically, that it receives plurality support in a sufficient number of districts— more than half if all districts select the same number of representatives. The losing party may have polled a majority of the nation-wide vote, but to no avail if it commanded plurality backing in too limited a number of districts.

Single choice-plurality elections are unlikely to result in representation in strict or approximate proportion to the voting strength of different groups of like-minded voters. As a rule, one or more parties may be over-represented, others under-represented, and some receive no representation at all. Persons who favor the apportionment of representatives among constituencies on a numbers basis should realize that single choice-plurality elections may produce results which conflict with their apparent concern over what they insist constitutes "equitable" representation. If political equality requires the apportionment of representatives *among constituencies* in close accordance with population, why not, also, representation in proportion to voting strength for every group of like-minded voters, such as the adherents of a particular political party, *within each constituency?* What is considered a satisfactory response to this question may depend on one's conception of the role of a representative, or on one's conclusions concerning which of two alternatives is preferable, viz., placing one party in control of the legislature or getting along with coalition government as a consequence of the proportional representation of parties, if no party is supported by a majority of the voters.

Majority Choice Methods. Majority choice election methods are often favored by persons who contend that majority rule is fundamental to democracy. The desires of a majority should prevail in the selection of officials as well as in the determination of public policy.

Several majority choice systems have been devised but some of them are defective in that they fail to insure the desired result. A practical and reliable method is the alternative vote. More dependable, but less practical, are the Hallett and Nanson systems.[29] Two of the defective methods are the second ballot and Bucklin plans.

The second ballot method involves two successive elections if no candidate wins by a majority at the first election. In that case the first balloting serves the purpose of eliminating all but the two highest candidates. The second election permits the voters to choose between these two survivors and one or the other will win by a majority, except in the unlikely event of a tie. The defect of this method is that the eventual winner may not have been preferred by a majority to each of the candidates originally in competition. Since voters are not allowed, under this system, to rate all of the candidates in order of preference, evidence concerning preferences other than first choices is unavailable.

The Bucklin plan involves a preferential ballot with provision for the expression of first, second, and third choices.[30] If no candidate obtains a majority of first choices, second preferences are added to the first choice totals, and a candidate then obtaining the backing of a majority of the voters (not choices) is declared elected. If no one has received majority support, third choices are added to the total of firsts and seconds and the candidate with the highest total becomes the winner.

The Bucklin method is defective for two reasons. A voter's expression of lower preferences may injure the election chances of his higher preferences. Furthermore, if a candidate wins by a majority composed of first and second choices, the result merely indicates that the voters consider him one of the two best candidates.

The alternative vote system is free from these defects. A preferential ballot enables the voter, by using numbers, to rate all of the candidates in the order of his preference. First choices are counted and a candidate obtaining a majority wins the election. If there be no first choice winner, the next step is to declare the lowest competitor defeated and to transfer every ballot he received to the next available preference expressed by the voter. Totals are determined and if no candidate now has a majority, the lowest candidate at this stage of the count is eliminated. All of the ballots obtained by him are transferred, as before, to the next available preference indicated by each of his supporters. This process continues until the choice of a majority of the voters is ascertained.

Under the alternative vote plan a lower choice is never counted until the voter's higher preferences have been eliminated. Consequently, the full expression of preferences by the voter cannot injure the election chances of his favorite candidates. The chance that an eliminated candidate might have emerged as the winner has been shown, by an analysis of election returns, to be negligible. Eliminating the lowest candidate at successive stages of the count is based on the assumption, almost always warranted, that a majority of the voters prefer some other candidate.

If an office, such as that of chief executive, be held by one man, choice by majority vote seems more in line with democratic doctrine than choice by a plurality. The same observation applies if members of a legislature are chosen by single member districts. In practice, however, the plurality rule is preferred to the majority requirement.

Majority choice elections are as open to criticism as the single choice-plurality method, if used to select the members of a presumably representative legislature by election-at-large or by multi-member districts. In either case voters other than those comprising the winning majority or plurality are "represented" by persons whom they voted against. The strongest party or the majority party, if there be one, wins all of the seats allotted to a multi-member district or all of the seats in the legislature if the entire membership is elected-at-large, provided that voters cast their ballots on a party line basis.

The desire to prevent this result in connection with either plurality or majority elections has led to limited voting and cumulative voting plans. Under limited voting, the voter may vote only for fewer candidates than the number of seats to be filled, thus increasing the chances that more than one group of like-minded voters will receive representation. Cumulative voting is featured by giving each voter a number of votes equal to the number of seats to be filled and allowing him to concentrate all of these votes on one candidate or to distribute them among different candidates in whatever manner he prefers. This method, too, ordinarily results in the representation of more than one group of voters.

Proportional Representation Election Methods. Proportional representation methods of election are designed to provide representation in proportion to the comparative voting strength of groups of like-minded voters. They have proved to be effective means to this end. If a party commands the support of more than half of the voters it will win a majority of the seats. Minority groups will receive about the same proportion of seats as their voting support bears to the total vote cast in the election. The percentage of seats corresponds as closely as possible to the percentage of votes obtained.[31] Obviously, these methods of election are usable only for the purpose of selecting the members of a collegial body, such as a legislature.

Two systems of proportional representation have been devised, viz., the list system and the single transferable vote plan. The former is more widely used than the latter.

The list system is so named because each political party's list of candidates appears on the ballot. Voters cast their ballots for a party list and seats in the legislature are allocated to the parties on a proportional basis. A party supported by 60 percent of the voters wins the same percentage of seats; a party polling 20 percent of the total vote obtains 20 percent of the seats; and so on.

If a voter may vote for a list and also for a candidate on this list, the seats to which the party is entitled are assigned to those individuals among its candidates who obtained the most votes. However, if the voter may only vote for a list, the candidates on that list, up to the number of seats won by the party, are declared elected in the order in which their names are listed. This order has been determined by the party leaders.

The single transferable vote method of proportional representation operates differently. No party lists are placed on the ballot. The names of all candidates nominated by petition are arranged in a vertical column, usually, although not necessarily, without designation of their party affiliation. A space is provided next to this column for an expression of the voter's preferences. A voter may rate *all* of the *candidates* in the order of his preference by using numbers, 1 for first choice, 2 for second, 3 for third, and so on to the extent that he desires to give a rating.

To be elected a candidate must obtain the support of a designated quota of voters. What is known as the simple quota is calculated by dividing the total number of valid ballots by the number of seats to be filled. Another technique is to divide the number of ballots cast by one more than the number of seats to be filled and then to add *one* to the quotient, disregarding fractions. The resultant figure, known as the Droop quota, constitutes the size of the vote needed for election.

The initial step after establishment of the quota is ascertainment of the first choice total of each candidate. Any candidate with first choice support equal to or greater than the quota is declared elected. If a candidate receives first choice votes in excess of the quota, this surplus is distributed among the other candidates according to the next available preference indicated on each of the candidate's surplus ballots selected at random for distribution.[32] Totals are determined and any candidate now having the quota is elected.

The next step, if seats remain to be filled, as usually is the case, is to declare the lowest candidate defeated and to transfer all of the ballots so far distributed to him to the next available preference indicated on each ballot. After totals have been determined, any candidate who has reached the quota is elected. This process of eliminating the lowest candidate and transferring the ballots he received is continued until all seats are filled.

The single transferable vote method, like the list system, is a reliable way of securing proportional representation for the various groups of like-minded voters participating in an election. Like-minded voters, whether or not organized as political parties, obtain the representation to which their voting strength entitles them. The list system merely provides representation for political parties.

Proponents of proportional representation believe that apportionment of representatives, according to numbers, among the groups granted representation, is insufficient in itself to provide fair representation. It is equally essential that like-minded voters within each of these groups be represented in accordance with their voting strength. The controlling conviction is that the composition of a legislature, to be truly representative, should correspond as closely as possible to divisions of opinion within the electorate—the relative importance of each opinion group to be determined by the size of the vote it casts. Otherwise, political inequality rather than equality prevails.

Opponents of proportional representation contend that its advocates lay far too much stress on numbers and on conflicting interests. They argue that election methods resulting in proportional representation encourage people to divide rather than to unite, to exaggerate the significance of differences and to overlook, or at least to minimize, the importance of common interests. Uncompromising attitudes develop and give rise, so it is claimed, to a multiplicity of parties.

The primary purpose of an election, according to those who oppose proportional representation, is to place one party in control of the government so as to permit effective action to be taken without undue delay and bickering and to avoid the division of responsibilitiy among several parties for what is done. Representation of the principal opposition parties is desirable, but the existence of democratic government does not depend on the granting of one or more seats in the legislature to every group of like-minded voters. Nor does it require that the percentage of seats held by a party closely approximate the ratio of the vote it polls to the total vote cast at an election.

The Safe-Guarding of Elections

The purpose of elections is defeated unless proper measures are taken to prevent unqualified persons from voting, to protect eligible voters against intimidation, and to safeguard elections against various fraudulent and corrupt practices, such as bribery, ballot-stuffing, tampering with ballots, and the falsification of returns. It may be necessary, also, to limit the nature and amount of campaign expenditures in behalf of candidates and to exercise control over the sources from which candidates and parties obtain funds.

The registration of voters prior to an election is an effective way of preventing unqualified persons from voting, provided, of course, that registration laws are strictly enforced. Registration policies differ. In some jurisdictions provision is made for permanent registration; in others periodic registration is required. Some bodies politic provide for official registration, an arrangement under which designated officials are charged with the duty of compiling a list of qualified voters. Others prefer what is known as personal registration. This procedure requires each individual desiring to vote to appear before registration officials and present evidence of his eligibility. Under either system a high standard of integrity on the part of both registration officials and those in control of the polling booths is necessary. Another essential is the use of appropriate ways of identifying persons who appear at the polls and claim to be the individuals whose names appear on the list of registered voters.

Although it is difficult, if not impossible, to provide absolute protection against intimidation, a major step in that direction is the establishment of a secret ballot. Among the means of promoting secrecy in voting are the preparation of ballots by governmental officials at public expense, the handing out of ballots only at the polling place, the barring of assistance in voting, the prohibition of distinguishing marks on a ballot, and adequate arrangements for voting in seclusion. Some of these means pertain only to paper ballots. Others, such as voting in seclusion, are equally pertinent if voting machines are used. Additional ways of curtailing intimidation are the maintenance of order at the polling place and the prohibition of electioneering within this place or within a specified distance therefrom. Some intimidating practices are difficult to prevent. One example is forceful prevention of appearance at the polls. Another is the threat of dire consequences, such as loss of employment, if a particular candidate or party should win the election. Various subtle modes of intimidation, which cannot be dealt with effectively by law, may be resorted to by persons who want to win an election and believe that the desired objective justifies any and all means of attaining it. Such an attitude is certainly a menace to the democratic process of government.

The safeguarding of elections against fraudulent and corrupt practices is accomplished in large part by the two devices already discussed, viz., the strict administration of an appropriate voter registration system and adequate provision for secrecy in voting. Satisfactory registration systems, by preventing unqualified persons from voting, serve as a deterrent to such frauds as impersonation, colonizing, repeating, and the casting of votes for fictitious or dead individuals. Of the steps taken to promote secrecy in voting, the administration of elections by public officials, including the provision of paper ballots, if used, and the custody and handling of voting machines, also tends to prevent such trickery as ballot-box stuffing, tampering with ballots or machines, falsification of returns, and a variety of other frauds too numerous to mention. Another means of discouraging fraudulent and corrupt practices is to make specified acts criminal and to provide appropriate punishment. Among the various acts commonly included in the "election crimes" category are bribery, ballot-box stuffing, tampering with ballots or machines, intimidation of voters, and interference with the functioning of election officials.

In recent times the phrase "rigged elections" has gained currency, largely because of the purpose served by elections in various twentieth century dictatorships. A rigged election is one that is conducted in such a way and under such circumstances as to produce a desired result. It is a manipulated election. Fraudulent election practices of the type referred to above are not necessarily involved, although they may be. The principal means of manipulation include intensive propaganda drives, the intimidation of voters in various ways and, above all, serious restrictions on the freedom of choice exercisable by voters in an election. This freedom is commonly curtailed by prohibiting the functioning of more than one political party or by arrangements which result in but one candidate for each office to be filled. In one way or another the voter is denied a real choice among competing candidates or parties. If the appearance of a choice exists, the desired objective may be attained through propaganda, intimidation, and disregard of the principle of secret voting.

Democracy and Elections

What kind of elections meet the requirements of democracy? An answer based on the practices of democratic countries is likely to differ from the response of persons who conceive of democracy as "majority rule." Since conceptions of the nature of democracy vary, it is not surprising that proponents of democratic government disagree concerning the appropriateness of different election methods. About the only election feature which meets with general approval is that voters should be granted freedom of choice among candidates and parties, regardless of the particular mode of election which is used.

In filling an office held by one person, either a plurality or a majority vote may be required for election. The majority rather than the plurality rule seems more consistent with democratic ideas inasmuch as the winner in a plurality type of election, if there be more than two candidates, may be considered the best man by only a minority of the voters. However, the plurality mode of election is widely used in democracies. Its simplicity contributes to its popularity. Moreover, it does not prevent the will of the majority from prevailing if a majority of the voters are in agreement as to which candidate is the best. The candidate with the most votes may have obtained a plurality amounting to more than half of the votes cast. Barring a tie, such is necessarily the case if only two candidates compete for an office. With the exception of the alternative vote, reliable majority choice techniques are considered too complicated to be prac-

ticable. The simpler methods are defective in various respects
and fail to achieve their intended purpose. This fact strengthens
the case for plurality elections.

Popular selection of legislators, a typical feature of democracy, raises the question of which modes of election, for this
purpose, conform most closely to democratic requirements. Factors other than a particular election method have a bearing
on the response to this query. Among them are the principle of
representation in effect, the method of apportioning representatives among groups, and the prevailing conception of a representative's duty as a member of the legislature.

The list and transferable vote systems of proportional representation seem clearly in line with such democratic doctrines as
political equality, majority rule, and minority representation. In
fact, if, as some persons contend, the apportionment of representatives among constituencies in proportion to numbers is an
essential of political equality, then these modes of election are
the most appropriate of all, at least from the standpoint of logic.
A proportional representation method of election is the logical
companion of an apportionment plan based solely on the comparative size of groups. It provides for proportional representation of the various parties and groups of like-minded voters
within the territorial or functional groups which serve as constituencies for the selection of representatives. Consequently, the
combination of apportionment according to numbers with either
the list or the single transferable vote methods of proportional
representation comes closer than other arrangements to realization of the idea of strictly equal representation for all persons, or,
as sometimes expressed, to possession, by everyone, of an equal
share of a representative in the legislature.

Proportional representation methods of election are compatible
with various principles of representation and modes of apportionment, provided that several representatives are to be chosen by
each constituency. The constituency may be the entire electorate
of the body politic, as when all members of an assembly are
elected at-large, or it may consist of the qualified voters of

either a territorial or functional group entitled to select two or more representatives on the occasion of an election.

The usual arguments in favor of proportional representation election methods lose weight if every representative, no matter how or by whom chosen, is looked upon as a representative of the entire community and not merely of a part thereof. As for the various theories of a representative's duty in voting on proposed policies, none precludes the use of either the list or the single transferable vote systems of proportional representation. However, in the case of the list system, since representatives are elected as partisans, the voting public is likely to subscribe to the view that a representative is duty-bound to support the leaders and program of his party. But this conception of a representative's obligation often prevails in connection with any election method which provides for a ballot designating the party affiliation of all candidates for elective offices.

Limited and cumulative voting methods of choosing representatives are reconcilable with democratic principles. So are single choice-plurality and majority choice elections, more convincingly, perhaps, under some circumstances than others. One such circumstance is widespread acceptance of the view that every representative represents the general public. Another is prevalence of the belief that a representative should follow his own judgment in favoring or opposing particular governmental policies. A third circumstance is general support for the contention that the primary purpose of an election is to produce a government which, during the intervals between elections, will be able to function effectively. Majority and plurality election methods for the choice of representatives are looked upon, by many persons, as more likely to achieve this objective than proportional representation techniques. Therefore they should be given preference.

Different methods of election are used in the various countries commonly included within the democratic category. Many of them have been attacked by various persons as obstacles to the attainment of democratic government. But it probably would be difficult to convince the inhabitants of "democracies" employing these methods that their use is indicative of non-democratic organizational arrangements.

An impressive reason for contending that democracy does not require any particular method of election is that the democratic process of government involves much more than the specific way in which key officials are elected. As long as certain basic freedoms are guaranteed, among them freedom of speech, freedom of assembly, freedom of association, and freedom from arbitrary arrest and imprisonment, every individual has the opportunity, acting alone or in association with others, to influence the course of governmental policy. For this same reason, too much significance should not be attached to other single features of organization, such as the established principle of representation, the method of apportionment in effect, or the character of the relations among the several branches of government. These matters are by no means trivialities, but their importance tends to be exaggerated because of disregard of additional factors which have a bearing on the functioning of popular government. Different means may promote the attainment of a desired end, in this case a democratic governmental system. Some devices may be more appropriate than others, but the use of any particular means, e.g., a specific mode of election, should not be condemned outright without considering the totality of arrangements and practices which determine the essential nature of the political process.

STUDY QUESTIONS

1. Why is the method of election a matter of importance in democracies?

2. How liberal should voting qualifications be to satisfy the requirements of democracy?

3. On what grounds are residential qualifications justifiable; literacy tests?

4. What are the objections to tax-paying and property-owning qualifications for voting?

5. Enumerate typical disqualifications for voting.

6. Describe each of the various methods of nominating candidates for elective offices. What are the claimed advantages of each?

7. Why are methods of nomination at least as important as modes of election?

8. Explain each of the following election methods: (1) single choice-plurality; (2) the Bucklin plan; (3) the alternative vote majority choice method; (4) the list system of proportional representation; (5) the single transferable vote system of proportional representation; (6) limited voting; (7) cumulative voting.

9. What are the arguments for and against (a) plurality elections; (b) majority choice methods, and (c) proportional representation of either the list or the single transferable vote varieties?

10. What are the various devices commonly resorted to for the purpose of safeguarding elections?

11. Which modes of election, if any, conform most closely to democratic requirements (a) for filling an office held by one person and (b) for selecting members of a legislative body? Give reasons.

12. Apart from the selection of officials, what is accomplished by elections in a democracy?

CHAPTER 5

POLITICAL PARTIES

AND

PRESSURE GROUPS

The discussion so far has been confined for the most part to a consideration of the organizational requirements of democracy. Attention has been directed to the compatibility of different forms of government with democratic standards, to controversial questions concerning the appropriateness of various plans of representation, and to the requisites of democracy in regard to voting qualifications and methods of election. Such conclusions as have been drawn suggest that considerable flexibility in matters of organization is permissible on the democratic side of the line of demarcation between democracy and authoritarianism. Of course, the premises from which one starts, premises incorporated in the definition of democracy, affect the judgment that is passed on particular organizational arrangements.

If democratic government is defined as a system under which the people decide, from time to time, who shall govern and broadly to what ends, the conclusions reached are likely to differ from those drawn from a definition that equates democracy with majority rule. In the former of these definitions, the "people," with respect to elections, signifies the individuals composing an electorate based on liberal voting qualifications. The "broadly to what ends" phrase involves a more comprehensive meaning of "people," inasmuch as all of the inhabitants of the body politic have the opportunity to influence the course of governmental action through the manifestation of opinion concerning what those who govern should or should not do. As for the definition of democracy as majority rule, the usual implication is that the will of the general public prevails in matters of policy and that the will of a majority of the electorate or of those voting determines the outcome of elections.

This majority rule conception of democracy is largely mythical. It is doubtful that majority rule *commonly* occurs in countries classified as democracies, although there are occasions on which a decision is made by a majority vote of some type. An example is the choice of an official through the alternative vote system of majority preferential voting. But this mode of election is rarely employed and other majority choice methods are either defective in various respects or too complicated for use in large-scale elections. Under the widely used single choice-plurality election method, candidates who win by a plurality frequently obtain majority support even if more than two candidates are in competition. However, with this type of election a majority vote is unnecessary and many a winner is placed in office under the plurality rule despite the fact that only a minority considered him the best man. Another instance of decision by a majority of voters is afforded by popular voting on proposed policies or constitutional amendments.[33] To be adopted a proposal must be favored by a majority of those voting thereon, sometimes by a majority of the total vote cast at an election to choose officials as well as to vote on propositions, and in some bodies politic by a majority of the qualified voters.

As a rule policy-decisions are made by legislative bodies. Legislatures ordinarily reach decisions in accordance with the will of a majority of their members present and voting, provided that a quorum has been assembled. Sometimes a majority of the total membership is required.[34] In either case a legislative majority rarely represents a majority of voters unless apportionment of members among constituencies according to numbers is combined with either the list or the single transferable vote methods of proportional representation in selecting the members of the legislature. Even then, it is unlikely that a majority of the voters have a "will" concerning most proposals brought before the legislature for consideration. Moreover, many qualified persons fail to register or to vote and consequently the number of voters participating in the choice of legislators may constitute a minority of the electorate. A surprising example of voter apathy occurred in Michigan in 1961 in the election of delegates to its constitutional convention. Of a total of approximately 3½ to 4 million registered voters, only 839,000 were sufficiently interested to cast ballots.[35]

It may be contended that in the long run the policies that prevail in a democracy receive widespread public support. Unpopular policies, so it is argued, are eventually altered or abandoned. Even if this be the case, the initial and subsequent policy decisions are made by those who govern—not by a majority of the voters or by a majority of the people. And should a particular policy prove popular and receive general support, the development of its popularity after adoption hardly warrants the contention that its initial establishment represented an expression of the will of a popular majority. Nor is the modification or repeal of policies that prove unpopular accomplished by action of the voters or the people. Those who govern make the changes, possibly in response to reactions of the general public, but not necessarily so.

The majority rule conception of democracy, for the reasons

just presented, is misleading. It gives rise to misunderstanding concerning the institutional arrangements that are compatible with the democratic process of government.

Democracy in the political sense is a process of government which has two primary characteristics. One is freedom of opportunity for all persons to influence, if they can, the course of governmental action. The other is the existence of organizational arrangements which result in the making of final decisions by key officials chosen for limited terms of office, and therefore replaceable from time to time, by an electorate composed of persons able to meet liberal voting qualifications. Latitude in the matter of detailed features of organization seems unavoidable inasmuch as no specific supplementary organizational means of implementing the democratic idea have been proved to be indispensable. But the freedom of opportunity mentioned above is essential. Participation in the social process which culminates in decisions by officials directly or indirectly responsible to the electorate must be open to *all*.

Ample opportunity for everyone to influence the course of governmental action necessitates effective guarantees of freedom of speech and of the press, freedom of assembly, freedom of association, and safeguards against arbitrary arrest and imprisonment. In this chapter, the significance of freedom of association will be the subject of discussion. This freedom permits the formation of political parties and other purposive associations which enable individuals, acting collectively, to press for the adoption of desired policies.

Political Parties

Political parties are associations of individuals organized for the immediate purpose of gaining control of the government by placing their own members in the public offices through which basic policy decisions are eventually made. Their ultimate goal is to bring about the adoption of programs of governmental action favored by their leaders and the other individuals comprising the party membership. A particular party may be unsuccessful in its effort to gain control of the government but even so it strives for representation in the legislature because direct participation in the law-making process is preferable to the indirect action which is the only recourse of unrepresented parties. Of course, defeat at one election may be followed by victory in the future, and parties which have never succeeded in achieving control, or in obtaining a significant number of legislative seats, have nevertheless, through persistent agitation, brought about the adoption of policies which they have advocated.

In democracies, political parties discharge a variety of functions. They nominate candidates for elective offices and recommend persons for the holding of appointive positions. Activities in relation to elections include efforts to persuade persons to register for voting and to go to the polls on election days, the conducting of election campaigns, and the provision of information about candidates and issues. At least as important as these functions are the formulation of policy proposals, agitation for their adoption, and the provision of leadership in the political field. Furthermore, victorious parties assume the responsibility of running the government and the losers keep a watchful eye on what is being done and provide a critical opposition.

Individuals acting alone are unable to accomplish what parties can. A group of individuals, united behind candidates and programs, stands a good chance of attaining its objectives. Not so the individual who persists in going it alone. Another important service of parties, not previously mentioned, is that of uniting persons and groups with diverse interests in support of some program, usually the result of compromise, which serves as a common ground upon which all or practically all are willing to stand. The announced program is the resultant of a process of negotiation among the various leaders and factions included within the party ranks. Persons with a sufficient number of interests in common are ordinarily able to reach agreement on candidates and issues to the extent necessary for cooperation in pursuit of the aim to gain control of the government.

Restrictions on freedom to form political parties are difficult to reconcile with the idea of democratic government. A defensible exception is the withholding of recognition of party status in the case of a group that is unwilling to compete for control of the government *only* in accordance with the rules of the democratic process, i.e., by confining its activities to peaceful and orderly participation in elections and by renunciation of forcible overthrow of the government as a means of attaining its objectives. Barring or outlawing a party because of dislike of its policy program is "bad business" in any community professing belief in democracy. Such a policy constitutes a long step in the direction of authoritarianism. It is based on the unwarranted assumption that democracy precludes the advocacy of certain types of governmental action, such as socialized medicine, public ownership of power plants, or subsidies to farmers. Once the door is opened to the drawing of a line of demarcation between permissible and non-permissible programs, the boundary line may be drawn anywhere by those in control of the government at a particular time. Free competition among freely organized parties that are free to advocate whatever policies they favor may, in this way, be brought to an end. Banning a party because of its avowed willingness to substitute force for appeals to the voting population is clearly a different matter. But even in this case abuses of power may occur because of the contention that a particular party, although not openly subscribing to the doctrine of force, nevertheless has resort to force in mind if and when the opportunity for success, by so doing, seems excellent.

Another exception to freedom to organize political parties, frequently defended by sincere believers in democracy, is that any party which intends to substitute authoritarianism for democracy, if it gains control of the government, may justly be outlawed. The logic of this position is that democracy does not require toleration of this particular way of committing suicide. If the people of a given country want to abandon democracy, that is their privilege, but the proper way of exercising it is through a constituent assembly, not by placing a party hostile to democracy in control of the government. The logical counter-argument to this contention is that if democracy means that the will of the people should prevail, then the people should be permitted to bring about the termination of democracy in whatever way they prefer. Logic aside, it probably makes little difference whether democracy is brought to an end in one way or another, assuming that the inhabitants of a country no longer desire it.

Subject to such controversial exceptions as the foregoing, it seems safe to assert that the greater the freedom to form parties, the greater the consistency with democratic doctrine. An *open* party system exists if this freedom is unrestricted, or nearly so. A system may be described as *closed*, if this freedom is severely restricted; clearly so if only one party or two parties are allowed to function, less clearly if a substantial number of parties are permitted to operate.

A party system may be of the open or closed type—assuming the acceptibility of the distinction drawn in the preceding paragraph. The resultant party *situation* is another matter. Under a closed system, the number of existent parties depends on the degree of restriction imposed on the formation of parties. If only one party is sanctioned, a one-party situation exists, if merely two, a two-party arrangement, and so on. Open party systems may result in one, two, or multiple party situations, not because of restriction on the allowable number of parties, but because of the degree of support which voters give to the various parties which have been organized.

A one-party situation arises if one party is so strongly supported as compared to its competitors that it dominates the political scene and almost invariably emerges as the victor in elections. It enjoys a virtual monopoly of controlling the government, not by fiat, but because opposition parties are unable to win significant support. Open systems of the two-party variety are characterized by the continual success of either of two major parties in the winning of elections. Control of the government is attained by one or the other of these two parties. One or more minor parties may compete in elections but usually without more success than gaining minority representation in the legislature or occasionally winning a particular office. A multiple-party situation exists if no party, among the three or more in competition, is strong enough to obtain control of the government. Government by a coalition of parties is the result. Occasionally, one of the major parties may be successful in its quest for control of the government, but not ordinarily.

An open party system, whatever the resultant party situation, is consistent with the requirements of democracy. As for closed systems, the fact of their conflict with democratic principles seems indisputable. Nevertheless, the degree and effect of the restrictions on freedom to form political parties should be taken into account before deciding whether or not a country with a closed system has a non-democratic type of government. The drawing of a sharp line of distinction may prove untenable, simply because a particular governmental system, although exhibiting shortcomings in some respects, may fully meet democratic requirements in others. Some governments may be less democratic than other governments but still fall short of being authoritarian. A twilight zone, rather than a rigid line, exists between unqualified authoritarianism on the one hand and clearcut democracy on the other.

Two-party situations prevail in some democracies; multiple party situations in others. Why? A thorough investigation of each case is essential to a defensible response. The reasons for existence of a two-party condition in one country may differ from those that account for the same situation in another. A few factors which may be causative will be mentioned.

One is the extent of consensus concerning matters to which vital importance is attached, such as the type of economy, the relations between church and state, or the proper province of government. Uncomprising attitudes are likely to develop in regard to fundamentals, and if opinion is sharply divided about a sufficiently large number of basic issues, a multiple party situation may develop. Another determining factor may be the conditions prevailing in a country at the time of origin of parties. Only two parties may at first be organized, for instance, and if no others appear for an extended period of time, support of one or the other may become habitual. Thus the timing and nature of historical events may account for the type of party situation currently existent in a particular place. The one party situation in the southern states of the United States seems attributable, primarily, to the slavery issue, the outcome of the Civil War, and subsequent events. A third cause of a particular situation, among others that might be influential, is the method of election used in connection with a particular pattern of government.

Survival of the two-party situation that prevails, at least nominally, in the United States is due in large measure to the fact that a party, to gain control of the Presidency and also of Congress, must be able to win in enough states and congressional districts to obtain a majority of the electoral college and a majority of seats in the Senate and House. Use of the single choice-plurality mode of election in combination with district elections makes it absolutely necessary that a party's voting strength be appropriately distributed throughout the country instead of being confined for the most part to one section. Majority election methods also would require proper geographical distribution of party support. This geographical factor would not be as important if either the list or single transferable vote systems of proportional representation were in use. In any event, the fact that territorial distribution of partisan strength is necessary to gain control of the national government causes people to compose their differences and work together under the banner of either the Democratic or the Republican party, if only on the occasion of a national election.

Both two- and multiple-party situations fulfill the requirements of democratic government. Each has its advantages and disadvantages.

If two parties dominate the political scene, one or the other will gain control of the government and be fully responsible for what takes place. The party out of control will furnish the opposition which experience has shown to be an effective means of decreasing the likelihood of misgovernment on the part of the in-party. The out-party, if properly led, is ever-ready to call the public's attention to what is going on, and, by offering criticism during the lawmaking process, to influence the formulation of policy. Being represented in the legislature, it participates as a minority group in the decision-making function of that body.

An asserted advantage of the two-party situation is that the voter finds it easier to inform himself about the candidates and programs of two major parties than to keep track of the activities of a multiplicity of parties. To be sure, minor parties exist even in a two-party situation, but ordinarily one of the two major parties will emerge as the winner in an election, and consequently, the voter, knowing this to be the case, can concentrate on the offerings of the two principal competitors. The task of choosing between candidates and programs is simplified.

The fact that the voter's choice, for all practical purposes, is confined to one of two parties is said to be a disadvantage of the two-party situation. He feels impelled to support one of the two, even though he dislikes both, because he feels that he will be wasting his vote if he casts it for a minor party that is clearly doomed to defeat.

The asserted advantage of a multiple-party situation is that voters are more likely to find a party, among the many in competition, which they can support, not as the lesser of two evils, but as a party of which they really approve. Since no party is likely to gain control of the government in a multiple-party situation, the voter does not consider his vote wasted in backing the party that best expresses his views concerning desirable public policies.

Another claimed merit of a multiplicity of parties is that the bargaining and compromising that ordinarily are involved in the formulation and adoption of policies take place openly in a legislature which is composed of the representatives of many parties.

Special-interest groups, functioning as political parties, are more readily identified by the public than if they engage in lobbying and other forms of pressure politics, as they commonly do if not directly represented in the legislature. Bargains and compromises are effected behind the scenes to a greater extent under a two-party than under a multiple-party situation.

The principal disadvantage of a multiple-party setup is that it necessitates coalition government. Since no party is in complete control of the government, responsibility for what is done or left undone is shared by a number of parties rather than borne by a single party. The result is said to be greater confusion on the part of the electorate and less vigorous and more vacillating government. Collective responsibility produces poorer results than single responsibility.

Divided opinion prevails concerning the relative merits of two-party and multiple-party situations. Rational argument is unlikely to have much, if any, effect on developments in a particular country. But one thing seems clear, neither situation conflicts with democratic doctrine. Conclusive evidence in support of a different conclusion is lacking.

Pressure Groups and Pressure Politics

Freedom of association gives rise to numerous organizations in addition to political parties. Individuals with one or more common interests form associations because of the realization that collective action is more likely to bring about desired results than individual effort. Furthermore, cooperative action is absolutely necessary for the attainment of many objectives. Examples of purposive associations are labor unions, organizations of professional men, e.g., doctors of medicine, farm bureaus, chambers of commerce, churches and consumers' cooperatives.

The primary objective of most associations is to promote the special interests of their members, perhaps their economic betterment, as in the case of labor unions and many other groups, or the practice of a preferred religion, or the advancement of scientific knowledge about various phenomena, natural or social. Associations of this type do not seek to gain control of the government by placing their members in office. But they have an interest in what the government does insofar as its policies may affect their interests favorably or adversely. This interest is usually secondary or incidental to the major purpose which led to their formation. Sometimes associations of the type under consideration are solely concerned with matters governmental. Examples are leagues of women voters and taxpayers associations. Each of these groups endeavors to influence governmental action without attempting to gain control of the government in the way that political parties do.

In a democracy purposive associations are free to exert such influence on the course of governmental action as they can, subject only to such restraints as to method as are designed to prevent what are considered to be abuses of the freedom which they commonly enjoy. The list of prohibited techniques is likely to include bribery, excessive contributions to the campaign funds of candidates and parties, intimidation through the use or threatened use of violence, disorderly demonstrations, picketing in specified places, and deliberate attempts to interfere with the enforcement of law.

One method of exerting influence that is hardly open to question is the dissemination of information designed to convince public officials and the general public of the desirability or undesirability of particular policies. The case for or against a policy under consideration may be presented in various ways, by testifying before legislative committees, through radio and television broadcasts, by speeches before audiences, by advertisements and articles in newspapers and periodicals, through the distribution of pamphlets, by house-to-house canvassing, and by sundry other means. The information that is provided may or may not be dependable. It may even be designed to mislead or deceive. But these are hazards necessarily associated with freedom of speech. As long as counter-arguments are presentable, it is altogether likely that unwarranted claims or fraudulent contentions will be exposed as such.

Various other means of exerting influence are commonly considered proper. The endorsement of candidates and parties, the conducting of campaigns to arouse support for or opposition to particular policies, the writing of letters or the sending of telegrams to legislators, efforts to persuade party leaders and parties to take a definite stand in support of whatever it is that an association desires, and the circulation of a petition for or against some measure—all of these are legitimate methods of influencing, directly or indirectly, the determination of governmental policy.

The effectiveness of sundry means of pressing for or against the adoption of policies varies with time, place, and circumstance. It seldom is predictable with accuracy. Well-organized and large-scale propaganda drives conducted by groups with adequate financial resources probably stand a better chance of success than sporadic attempts to influence the actions of public officials. But even the best-managed propaganda campaigns are likely to prove ineffective unless conditions are such that there is at least a fair chance of a favorable response by the general public. At times when uncertainty prevails concerning the appropriate way of solving a specific problem, e.g., unemployment, a cleverly conducted propaganda drive in behalf of a particular solution may produce the desired result. However, if a deep-seated conviction that something is evil, or good, exists in a community, the most intensive and skillful propagandizing is unlikely to prove fruitful. At the moment, for example, in spite of the bitter controversy about integration, it seems highly improbable that propaganda in behalf of a restoration of slavery would be successful in persuading the inhabitants of the United States to re-establish this institution.

Pressure groups may, and sometimes do, resort to tactics of questionable propriety. An example is the threat of a strike by laborers, or of a work stoppage by manufacturers, unless their *legislative demands* are met. "Hold-up" actions of this type, although not involving resort to violence, are certainly less defensible than reliance on persuasive argument. A tactic similar to the threat of a strike was the proposal of several leaders of the Civil Rights Movement that the refusal of Congress to enact a suitable law prohibiting discrimination be followed by a paralysis of traffic movement through the stratagem of having willing persons, white or black, lie down in streets, on railroad tracks, and on the landing and take-off strips of air fields. It is unlikely that this particular threat accounted for eventual passage of the Civil Rights Act of 1964. The worthiness of an objective does not justify any and all means of attaining it. As questionable as the strategies just mentioned, if not clearly reprehensible, are the casting of aspersions on the character of a candidate or an official, intentional withholding or distortion of the facts concerning a particular situation, and the boycotting of stores until merchants lend their support to the policies favored by a pressure group.

The ingenuity of men gives rise to techniques of pressure politics too numerous to mention. Many of them are in no sense a menace to the democratic process of government. In fact, the opportunity to resort to legitimate means of exerting pressure through collective action may offset organizational arrangements, such as the strictly equal representation of areas regardless of population, which fall short of measuring up entirely to asserted democratic standards. Some methods, obviously, are so reprehensible that their use deserves condemnation whether resorted to under authoritarian or democratic governmental systems. Examples are bribery and threat of assassination.

The chief menace of pressure politics in a democracy, even if culpable methods of exerting pressure are never used, is that some associations may become so powerful because of their wealth, size, and economic function that public officials become unduly subservient to them. A militant, well-organized, and resourceful minority may succeed in dominating the political scene. Such a situation is particularly bad if the leaders and members of such a minority show little concern for the general welfare. Lack of community-mindedness is often exhibited by pressure groups, by the weaker as well as the stronger ones. The propensity to identify a special interest with the general interest is common to individuals in general, but the unfortunate consequences of this inclination are most likely to be experienced when exhibited by particularly powerful groups. Presumably, the remedy for this situation is the development of greater concern for the common welfare. How to accomplish this is a difficult question to answer. A typical response is "through education."

The discussion so far has been confined to the activities of associations (organized groups) with respect to government. A few observations about unorganized interest-groups are in order. Examples of such groups are bus riders, consumers of tobacco, and the viewers of television programs. These groups may become organized. Until they do, their influence on the course of governmental action is ordinarily both indirect and problematical. Office-holders who make policy-decisions commonly give consideration to the interests of groups of this type, if only because a hostile reaction of their members to particular policies may complicate the task of law enforcement and possibly result in defeat, at the next election, of those in control of the government. Generally speaking, however, the interests of a passive and unorganized group carry less weight with politically-minded officials than those of an active and militant association that presses hard for such governmental action as it desires.

In a democracy, policy-decisions are eventually made by those leaders and parties placed in control of the government by popular vote, but this governmental process, to be thoroughly democratic, ought to be preceded and followed by the free discussion of issues within a community which guarantees adequate opportunity for *all* to influence the trend of political events. If this opportunity is denied, or severely restricted, organizational arrangements which include provision for election of key officials, seemingly adequate representation, liberal voting qualifications, and safeguards against election abuses lose much of their value.

Public Opinion

Some reference to public opinion invariably occurs in discussions about democracy. Supposedly, public opinion plays a major role in the formulation and adoption of policy by the officials of a democratic government. The "realism" of this supposition is a matter of controversy, largely, although not entirely, because of disagreement concerning what is meant by both "public" and "opinion" when these words are used in combination.

The following discussion is based on a broad meaning of "public opinion," viz., that it includes all opinions (beliefs, views, convictions, persuasions, or judgments) identifiable in a community, irrespective of their basis and of the number of persons by whom held. Unanimity of opinion is rare, general opinion less so. As a rule considerable diversity of opinion prevails, especially at initial stages of the discussion of some problem. More often than not, particular opinions merely have minority support. An opinion may be based on knowledge and deliberation concerning a specific problem, or it may be founded on superstition, prejudice, faith in the judgment of a leader or of one's closest associates, or on various considerations other than the thoughtful weighing of evidence in regard to the relative merits of different policies. Neither the quality of an opinion nor its basis is pertinent to its inclusion within the "public opinion" category. An individual's political behavior is affected by his "opinions," regardless of their foundation.[36]

Officials attach importance to opinions of the public, both in democracies and in countries with authoritarian regimes. Their efforts to win popular support for contemplated or adopted policies indicate that public opinion requires consideration in connection with the process of governing. Effective techniques for manipulating opinion have been developed and utilized by governmental agencies as well as by private associations. Thus the problem of determining the extent to which opinions of the public influence the behavior of officials is not the only one to which attention should be directed. Equally important is the question of opinion-creation by public officials. Governmental shaping of opinion may be accomplished in various ways, including resort to all the methods of thought control that have been developed by private interests. Factors contributing to successful manipulation are the prestige of many officials, such as the chief executive and experienced members of the legislature, and the advantageous position enjoyed by officials because of their possession of information which may not be available to outsiders. This situation exists in many areas of governmental activity, especially in the field of foreign affairs.

Inasmuch as freedom of speech, freedom of assembly, and freedom of association, as well as popular election of key officials, are features of democracy, the contention that public opinion materially influences the determination of governmental policy is understandable. A conclusion to this effect is certainly tenable if public opinion is defined so broadly as to include all opinions held by the various members of a politically organized community. Ordinarily, the shaping of policies is affected by the views of many persons and groups outside the government. Experts and spokesmen for interest-groups are frequently consulted by officials entrusted with the power to make final decisions on questions of policy. As previously observed, the representations of pressure groups influence policy-determination. So do the programs of political parties, and if a party manages to gain control of the government, its views on questions of policy largely prevail during the period of its dominance. The opinions of experts, pressure groups, and political parties are all part of the totality of opinion identifiable in a community. Consequently, the proposition that public opinion is a factor of major significance in the policy-determining process has a factual foundation.

But what about the relative importance of minority opinion and widely-supported or general opinion? In all probability, prevailing opinion in a democracy tends to be controlling with respect to the general direction in which the government proceeds, for example, toward a socialized economy in preference to the maintenance of an essentially private enterprise system. Whether a generally held opinion, if there be such, has a greater effect than minority opinion on the formulation of *particular* policies is another matter.

It is difficult to ascertain the extent of public support for an adopted policy. The democratic process of government is characterized by discussion and the interaction of competing opinions, but policy-decisions are ultimately made by public officials. Although these decisions represent resultants of the democratic process, that fact fails to warrant the conclusion that general opinion, assuming its existence, has prevailed over a minority point of view. Many factors have a bearing on the outcome of the governmental process in a democracy. Among them are the quality of competing opinions, the resources of advocates of specific policies, the type of party system, the procedural practices of the legislature,[37] and the organizational features of a particular democratic government, such as the plan of representation, the election methods in use, and the relations between the legislative and executive branches. For reasons pointed out in previous chapters, a majority vote in the legislature is by no means indicative of the views of either a majority of the electorate or a majority of the general public. Furthermore, it is doubtful that general opinion often exists concerning the proper solution of a particular problem. The apathy of numerous people, the complexity of many social situations, and the uncertainty of large numbers of persons as to what constitutes a satisfactory policy are factors which reduce the likelihood that a particular opinion is held by a sufficiently large proportion of the population to justify the conclusion that it is a general opinion. In all probability, most opinions merely have minority support.

Democracy involves "bargaining" among interest-groups inside as well as outside the government. The policies finally adopted are products of interacting opinions—the opinions of officials and the opinions of the public. Minority opinion may very well prevail over an opinion that receives widespread support. As long as the opportunity to influence the course of governmental action is assured through such guarantees as freedom of speech, freedom of assembly, and freedom of association for political as well as for other purposes, the requirements of democracy are met, *provided the "people" possess the right to determine from time to time "who shall do the governing."* Apart from the necessity of liberal voting qualifications in conjunction with the election of key officials, the existence of democracy is not dependent on any *single* feature of governmental organization, such as a certain mode of election, the type of executive, or the number of chambers comprising the legislature. Flexibility in matters of organization, as previously asserted, is consistent with the "democratic idea." Organizational details, objectionable as some of them may seem, such as equal representation of areas regardless of population, are not as determinative of the presence or absence of democracy as sometimes is claimed. What is really essential to democratic government is open competition for control of the government in combination with adequate opportunity for all individuals and groups to participate freely in the discussion and bargaining which culminate in the establishment of governmental policy. If this opportunity is guaranteed, the successful competitors for public office remain subject at all times to the many pressures which may be brought to bear upon them by the different interest-groups which ordinarily develop within a community.

STUDY QUESTIONS

1. Why is the majority rule conception of democracy largely mythical?
2. What are the distinguishing characteristics of political parties?
3. Discuss the functions of political parties in a democracy.

4. How do *open* differ from *closed* party systems?

5. Does the existence of a one-party situation signify that the party system is *closed* rather than *open*? Does such a situation mean that no other parties are functioning?

6. Why is an *open* party system more consistent with the requirements of democracy than a *closed* system?

7. Distinguish between two-party and multiple-party situations; what are the claimed advantages of each?

8. What appear to be some of the causes of different party situations in different countries?

9. Why is a properly-led and unified opposition party advantageous in a democracy?

10. What is a pressure group? What is meant by "pressure politics?"

11. What practices are resorted to by pressure groups in order to attain their objectives? Which of these practices are legitimate in a democracy? Which are reprehensible?

12. What is the chief menace of pressure politics in a democracy?

13. Discuss the nature and significance of unorganized interest-groups.

14. What is "public opinion?"

15. How important is public opinion in a democracy? Discuss the relative importance of minority opinion and general opinion.

16. What are the various factors which have a bearing on the outcome of the governmental process in a democracy?

CHAPTER 6

DEMOCRACY, LIBERTY, AND EQUALITY

Many persons assume that the establishment of a democratic system of government necessarily results in a large measure of individual liberty and also guarantees a substantial degree of equality among the members of a body politic. This assumption is warranted to only a limited extent.

As previously pointed out, certain liberties are indeed essential to democracy, and consequently its establishment accounts for their existence. These liberties include rights of direct or indirect participation in the process of government, freedom of speech and of the press, freedom of assembly, freedom of association, and freedom from arbitrary arrest and imprisonment. Other liberties may be highly prized by individuals or groups, but their indispensability to democracy is at least disputable if not clearly undemonstrable.

Some degree of equality is also an essential of democracy, viz., political equality and equal enjoyment of the basic freedoms just mentioned. Political equality requires that qualifications for voting and for holding office be the same for all persons, that every person's vote count as much as any other person's in determining the outcome of an election, that all individuals may organize and join political parties, and that all are equally entitled to participate in the nomination of candidates for public office through such methods and under such conditions as have been established by law. As for the basic freedoms,[38] their guarantee to *all* persons is a requisite of democracy. Inequality in the possession of these liberties is incompatible with democratic doctrine. However, legal equality in the matter of basic rights does not guarantee that all individuals will be equally able to take full advantage of the rights conferred. For example, some persons, by reason of superior education or greater wealth, may be in a better position to exercise these rights than the poorly educated or the many persons with severely limited economic resources. Recognition of this fact has led to the view that something more than legal equality is essential to "genuine" democracy. The soundness of this view is a subject of controversy.

Individual and group liberties of various kinds have been associated with both authoritarian and democratic types of government. Examples are religious freedom and freedom of private enterprise in the production of wealth. Both of these freedoms are or were at one time sanctioned in various countries with authoritarian regimes. In fact, both received recognition prior to the development of democracy in modern times. Equality in the possession of various rights also is provided for in many authoritarian as well as democratic countries. It is sometimes contended that more liberty and greater equality are attainable in democracies than in states in which authoritarianism prevails. The validity of a generalization to this effect is open to question.

So much depends on time, place, circumstance, tradition, and other determining factors.

Democracy and Liberty

The Nature of Liberty. Liberty is definable from two distinct points of view. One is objective; the other subjective.

From the objective standpoint, liberty consists of the totality of individual and group rights of self-determinable action which are recognized and sustained in a particular community. "Self-determinable" means that individuals and groups are free to follow their own judgment in the choice of objectives and the ways and means of attaining them—free as a matter of right in the sense of not being duty bound to abide by the directives of others. The autonomous individual may, of course, be subject to various external influences. Objectively considered, liberty exists to the extent that *some* rights of self-determinable behavior, whatever they may be, receive recognition.

Many persons equate liberty with certain favored and highly valued rights of discretionary action. Denial of these rights is said to indicate lack of liberty. This point of view, which involves an evaluation of rights, is clearly subjective. To people who identify liberty with specific rights which are considered fundamental, the mere fact that individuals possess *some* rights of self-determinable action is insufficient to warrant the conclusion that liberty exists. Inasmuch as opinions differ concerning the comparative value of different rights, controversy as to the presence or absence of liberty in particular countries seems inevitable if liberty is associated with selected rights of discretionary action.

Limited Liberty Prevails. No matter how liberty is defined, whether objectively or subjectively, absolute freedom is an unattainable ideal. As long as individuals live in association with one another, limited liberty is the best to be had. Externally imposed restraints of some sort, restraints which are considered rightful, always circumscribe individual freedom of action in some respects.

A condition requisite to the enjoyment of liberty by *all* members of a community is the imposition of restraints on the free behavior of each. The recognition and protection of rights of self-determinable action necessarily involves the duty of all to refrain from infringing upon the rights of free action which each individual possesses. A right which no one need respect is meaningless. To the extent that everyone is duty-bound to refrain from interfering with the behavior of others, liberty is limited rather than absolute.

The very conception of absolute freedom of action *in general* is fanciful. If all persons were absolutely free to do as they pleased, the extent of an individual's actual liberty would be measured by his power to do what he wanted and by his ability to resist invasive action by others. Might would replace right. For example, the right to own property would be valueless in a community wherein *every individual* possessed the absolute right of acquiring property *in any way he saw fit*. Anyone could rightfully take and keep possession of anything he desired, provided he were powerful enough to do so. Theft would not be considered a crime. Absolute freedom to do anything in whatever way a person chooses would prevent attainment of a peaceful and orderly social life. Without restraints of any kind, liberty might be a blessing for the powerful and unscrupulous; it would be a menace for the weak or the conscientious members of a community.

What has been said so far is generally true, but in regard to some types of individual activity, absolute freedom of action is compatible with effective exercise of the same freedom by all persons. The nature of the action is such that its performance cannot prevent like action on the part of other members of a particular community. A case in point is freedom of speech. Absolute freedom of speech is conceivable and also conferable. Its possession and exercise by all persons would not have the same consequence as absolute freedoms of the type that render a right valueless by making personal power the measure of a man's liberty. A person may say anything he pleases without, by so doing, curtailing the free expression of opinion by anyone else. Even so, freedom of speech, like all freedoms except one, is subject to limitation, and various restrictions on free speech are commonly imposed in all countries, either by law or by community opinion, usually by both.

Freedom of thought is the only freedom that cannot be limited through the establishment of binding restrictions of the type that prove effective as a means of controlling individual behavior. As long as an individual fails to reveal his thoughts, he may think what he pleases without experiencing the unpleasant consequences to which actions may give rise. Thought followed by speech or other action may result in the imposition of penalties. Freedom of thought has never meant that a man's ideas are solely the product of his own deliberation, free from external influences of any kind. Everyone's thinking is conditioned by his social and physical environment. Moreover, "thought manipulation" takes place through education, propaganda, and other techniques. An individual who believes himself to be a free thinker may be so subservient to unperceived restraints that few of his thoughts are really his own. However, the fact that external influences affect thinking does not mean that dictatorial control of the thoughts of some men by other men occurs. Attempts to impose or to prohibit designated thoughts or beliefs *through law* are doomed to failure. Thinking as one pleases qualifies as a freedom which is absolute in the sense of not being subject to effective restraint by command.

The Extent of Liberty. In bodies politic the nature and extent of individual liberty is largely determined by the body of law which governmental officials undertake to enforce. Lawmaking is a function in which various governmental agencies participate, including the judicial as well as the legislative and executive organs of government. Whatever the character of the lawmaking process or the sources of the content of particular laws, the law of the land establishes rights of self-determinable action which individuals in general are duty-bound to respect. Remedies are customarily provided for persons whose rights have been infringed either by public officials or by private persons. Since rights are ordinarily limited in scope, the law that confers freedoms also serves as an important source of restraint. Negatively, liberty is definable as freedom from restraint. From this point of view, the fewer the restraints imposed by law the greater the sphere of self-determinable action.

Law is by no means the only determinant of the degree of individual liberty. Social restraints of an extra-legal character are also operative in all communities. Most persons are aware of the restrictive effects of custom, tradition, and public opinion. An individual may refrain from doing something he has a legal right to do because he realizes that his contemplated action runs counter to prevailing opinion or established custom. He fears adverse comment, social ostracism, or other types of social pressure which are likely to be directed against non-conformists. A person who says what he thinks or aligns himself with unpopular movements may, as a consequence, be fired by his employer or suffer from discriminatory tactics of various sorts. In short, the full enjoyment of legal liberty requires a tolerant society unreservedly committed to the idea of freedom within the limits established by law.

Although the content of law in general is largely the resultant of current conditions of social life and the social heritage of a given community, particular laws may conflict with traditional behavior patterns and consequently fail to achieve their objectives. For this reason the enactment of a suitable Civil Rights Act may not prove sufficient to insure the liberty to which Negroes would seem to be entitled as a matter of principle, fairness, and decency in a country that claims devotion to democracy, freedom, and equality of opportunity for all. The law may require a restaurant owner to serve Negroes as well as white persons, but the Negro customer may be treated in such a way that his return is unlikely. Again, as a matter of law, Negroes may have the right to purchase homes in any residential area. Nevertheless, the reaction of the inhabitants of a neighborhood may be so bitter and violent that the value of the legal right is largely, if not entirely, nullified. Obviously, too, the integration of public schools in the United States has proceeded very slowly because of persistent disapproval in many communities.

Individual liberty also may be restricted as a consequence of the functioning of various voluntary associations. Joining an association usually involves restraints on freedom of action because of the conditions attached to membership. Furthermore, the internal organization of an association is often of such a character that the rank and file of its members are denied an effective voice in the determination of its policies. If, as a matter of law, belonging to an association is optional rather than compulsory, the obligations of members, even though highly restrictive, are properly describable as self-assumed rather than externally imposed. Under some circumstances, however, an individual opposed to joining an association may do so to avoid the consequences of refusal. The policies of associations frequently affect the freedom of non-members. If, for example, various manufacturing firms and labor unions agree on a closed shop, an individual's liberty to seek employment at a place of his own choosing is seriously curtailed. Getting a job may be contingent on becoming a union member. The restrictive effects of collective action on individual liberty are increased if the right of associations to engage in specified activities is made exclusive by law, but even in the absence of exclusive legal rights, the existence and functioning of associations often results in restraints which directly or indirectly have an effect on the scope of individual liberty.

In all communities both legal and extra-legal factors determine the extent of individual and group freedom. This observation holds true for both democratic and authoritarian countries. The legal factor is the law of the land as prescribed and enforced by governmental agencies. Custom, tradition, and prevailing community attitudes are examples of social factors of the extra-legal variety.

Insofar as governmental policies have a bearing on the extent of individual liberty, the question arises as to whether greater liberty is enjoyed under democratic than under authoritarian regimes. Up to a certain point an affirmative answer to this query is defensible. The basic freedoms essential to democracy can hardly be withdrawn or substantially restricted without putting an end to democratic government. Beyond that point, the appropriate response is "not necessarily so."

A democratic government may discriminate against minority groups and seriously curtail their liberties. That has certainly been the case in bodies politic with democratic political institutions which have adopted policies of segregation based on racial considerations. Democracy has not prevented the enactment of various laws based on prejudices of one sort or another.

Quite apart from motivations leading to arbitrary discrimination against minority groups, the inhabitants of a democracy may seek objectives which are attainable only at the price of serious curtailment of the sphere of self-determinable action. Economic security, for instance, may be valued more highly than individual liberty. Presumably, the people eventually get what they want in a democracy, and if their desire for liberty is subordinated to other considerations, limitations on liberty ensue. Democracy provides the opportunity to obtain freedoms of various kinds but it does not guarantee the conferment and protection of liberties other than those that are absolutely essential to its survival.

The current policies of many democracies afford ample evidence of the fact that democratic governments, for the asserted purpose of promoting the general welfare, impose numerous restraints on individual liberty. Among such policies are compulsory military service, compulsory education, compulsory health insurance, Sunday blue laws, and prohibition of the manufacture and sale of intoxicating beverages. Many other compulsions restrictive of freedom could be added to this list, including the ever-increasing curtailment of economic liberty. Contrary to the impression of many persons, freedom of religion, desirable as it may be, is not assured simply because of the existence of democratic political institutions. If the people of a democracy favor a ban on religious freedom, there is nothing to prevent them from having their way. What the inhabitants of a democracy want, they are able to get through the democratic process of government, even though what they want is not what some persons believe they ought to want.

Constitutional Guarantees of Liberty. The basic freedoms essential to democracy, as well as others to which great importance is attached, are commonly guaranteed by constitutional provisions. This practice is explainable by the desire to prevent their withdrawal, modification, or infringement by the persons momentarily in control of the government. Rights against invasive or restrictive action by a democratically constituted government are believed to be as necessary to liberty as protection against the violation of rights by private individuals. The prevalence of this belief in countries with democratic institutions indicates lack of complete confidence in the dependability of the democratic process as a safeguard against serious inroads upon liberty. Turnover in the personnel of legislative bodies and other policy-determining agencies occurs frequently and legislative majorities of the moment may be disposed to adopt policies that deprive individuals and groups of liberties deemed to be fundamental. Fear that this may happen is allayed by the inclusion of a bill of rights in the constitution of the body politic. These constitutional guarantees apply to administrators of the law as well as to lawmakers.

One of the rarities of the twentieth century, exemplified by Great Britain, is a country without a documentary constitution. In Britain, no limitation on governmental action through the medium of a constitution of this type is provided. Highly regarded individual liberties, including those requisite to democracy, are established and safeguarded by the body of ordinary law, by respect for historic agreements and understandings, by the weight of tradition, by the restraining effect of public opinion, and by reliance on the ballot box. Liberty in Great Britain seems to be as secure as in any other country.

Constitutional guarantees of various freedoms never operate automatically. Apart from the need for some means of enforcement, determination of their meaning and their applicability to particular situations is necessary. It seems impossible to word a specific guarantee so clearly and precisely as to preclude difference of opinion as to what is meant. Even if no disputes concerning meaning develop, controversy ordinarily arises as to whether or not particular governmental actions are violative of certain guarantees.

All organs of government operating under a documentary constitution engage in the process of construing its provisions. Interpretation normally precedes the taking of action. Constitution-makers are confronted with the problem of deciding on the organ, if any, which is to be the final interpreter, i.e., to possess the authority of the last word. A constitution ought to be explicit on this point but the framers of some constitutions, notably that of the United States, have failed to indicate clearly with whom final interpretation rests. Reliance then must be placed on the drawing of inferences.

In most democracies the principle of legislative supremacy prevails. Final interpretation of the constitution rests with the legislature, and its conclusions are binding on the courts as well as on other governmental agencies. In the United States, final interpretation of the national constitution has become a recognized right and responsibility of the judiciary, more specifically, the Supreme Court. The Court asserted and exercised the right of judicial review in the *Marbury v. Madison* case. Its contention that judicial supremacy was established by implication, although occasionally challenged, has been acquiesced in ever since 1803. Some constitutions create a special constitutional tribunal or committee for discharge of the all-important function of settling constitutional disputes, but usually this body possesses a more restricted right of review than the courts of the United States.[39]

The organ possessing the right of final interpretation ultimately determines the extent of constitutionally guaranteed rights. If it concludes that a particular right falls short of being absolute, the door is open to restrictive governmental action. Restrictive measures are subject to eventual endorsement by the organ which speaks the authoritative last word, provided that the issue of constitutionality is raised in accordance with the procedure established for this purpose.

An interesting question concerns the compatibility, with democratic government, of particular arrangements for final interpretation. If the principle of legislative supremacy prevails and the legislature meets the requirements of democracy, the charge of "undemocratic" is not likely to be advanced. Although the "representative" legislature becomes the final judge of its own authority, even to the extent of placing limitations on the exercise of constitutionally guaranteed rights, the voting public is able to hold it accountable for its interpretation of the supreme law of the land, viz., the constitution, which is commonly looked upon as an expression of the will of the people in regard to the fundamental features of the body politic's governmental system.

If the final settlement of constitutional disputes is vested in a court, objection on the ground that this arrangement violates democratic principles is improbable if the court is composed of judges chosen by the electorate for limited terms or if provision is made for either popular recall of the court's members or a popular veto of its decisions. The appropriateness of judicial review in a democracy is apt to be questioned if the judges hold office for life, regardless of the method of selecting them, and if their removal may be accomplished only through a difficult process resulting in conviction on charges of criminal misconduct. This situation exists in the United States in the case of national courts organized under Article III of the Constitution.[40]

Members of the Supreme Court are appointed by the President with the advice and consent of the Senate, and, as stated in the Constitution, "shall hold office during good behavior." [41] These words concerning tenure have been construed to mean "for life." Judges of the Supreme Court are removable from office only if impeached by the House of Representatives for treason, bribery, or other high crimes and misdemeanors and subsequently convicted by the Senate by a two-thirds vote of those present and voting, provided a quorum has been assembled. The Court is free from accountability to the President, the Congress, or the voters for the way in which it interprets the Constitution. Presumably the judges have a sense of responsibility for proper discharge of their all-important function of final interpretation. Although that has been the case, the fact remains that the Court has a wide choice among possible interpretations, especially so in connection with such constitutional guarantees as "due process of law" and "equal protection of the laws." There is truth in the observation that the Court functions as a continuous constitutional convention.

How can an arrangement of this type be reconciled with democratic government? Several answers of an affirmative type may be given.

In the first place, the Constitution may be amended [42] to take away this power of the courts or to set aside or overrule particular judicial interpretations. This "amendment" argument is criticized on a number of grounds. One is that no opportunity for a nation-wide direct popular vote is provided and another that the ratifying procedure permits minority domination, since each state, regardless of its size, is entitled to but one vote. A combination of thirty-eight states having less than half of the total population can ratify a proposed amendment and thirteen of the least populous states containing a very small percentage of the country's inhabitants are able to prevent ratification. In both cases the desires of a minority would prevail over the wishes of a majority. Furthermore, a minority in either the House or the Senate may block the proposal of amendments and a minority of the state legislatures may prevent the calling of a national constitutional convention. This indictment of the amending procedure as undemocratic is less serious than it seems. Even though combinations of the type mentioned may occur, freedom of speech, the functioning of political parties, and the periodic election of members of Congress and state legislatures permit sufficient indirect popular participation in the amending process to overcome the delaying tactics, even if temporarily successful, of obstructive minorities. The desires of the many eventually prevail over the views of the few.

Another response to the question posed above is that judges of the Supreme Court are sensitive to popular and professional criticism. The Court functions in a democratic environment, a fact of which its members are certainly aware, and the freedom of speech exercisable in a democracy provides opportunity to influence the trend of its constitutional interpretations. That the Court has responded to "public opinion" in the course of time is an observation to which various persons who have studied its behavior subscribe.[43] Whatever the cause, the Supreme Court's interpretation of the Constitution has on the whole met the changing needs of a dynamic society.

Finally, even though final interpretation may rest with a "politically irresponsible" court, this feature of a governmental system is not the sole determinant of its general character. The judicial role in the governmental process is passive, and as long as the active branches of government, such as the legislative and the executive, are organized in line with democratic requirements, the governmental system as a whole is scarcely rateable as undemocratic.

Some proponents of democracy, referred to as "majoritarian democrats," contend that any institutional or procedural obstacles that prevent a majority from having its way are incompatible with democracy. An example of such an impediment is constitutionally guaranteed rights in combination with judicial review by an "irresponsible" court. Another is the requirement of an extraordinary majority, such as two-thirds or three-fourths, for the passage of a bill or the adoption of a constitutional amendment.

Persons who disagree with this contention point out that the people of a country may prefer a constitution which prohibits transitory majorities in the legislature from taking action or pursuing policies that conflict with matters generally considered so fundamental, e.g., religious freedom and freedom of speech, that disregard of them should never be permitted. The constitution establishes the basic rules in accordance with which the democratic process of government is to be conducted from day to day, week to week, and year to year. Changes in these rules may be made by amending the constitution whenever the desire for alterations arises. Presumably, the amending process permits reasonably effective popular participation, directly or indirectly, in the proposing and ratifying stages.

Concluding Observations. Freedom in general is limited rather than absolute. In all communities restraints on individual freedom of action are imposed by law. The law of the land confers rights of self-determinable action and at the same time places limitations upon them. Apart from constitutionally guaranteed freedoms, if there be such, legal liberties are derived from the body of ordinary law which is the resultant of an exercise of law-making powers by legislative, executive, administrative, and judicial agencies of government. Theoretically, courts merely decide what the law is and apply it in the settlement of particular controversies. Actually, courts participate in the creation of law.[44] The limits of constitutionally guaranteed freedoms are ultimately established by the governmental agency which possesses the authority of final interpretation. This agency may be the legislature, a court, or some other governmental organ.

Social as well as legal restraints curtail individual freedom of action. Customs, traditions, and prevailing feeling and opinion in the community often prevent individuals from doing what they have a legal right to do. In addition, various conditions are essential to the effective enjoyment of legal liberties. Lack of wealth or education, for example, are obstacles or hindrances to the advantageous exercise of many of the freedoms conferred by law. A legal right of self-determinable action loses much of its value in the absence of adequate opportunity to take advantage of the freedom which, as a matter of law, an individual possesses.

This phase of the general problem of liberty will be given further consideration in the ensuing discussion of democracy and equality.

The foregoing observations about liberty are pertinent to both democracies and countries with authoritarian regimes. In either case the scope of individual freedom depends to a considerable extent on the policies which governmental agencies pursue. The democratic process of government may result in numerous restraints on individual and group behavior. In the long run, restrictions on individual and group freedom represent a response to prevailing social conditions and to the goals which a body politic seeks to attain, e.g., security against unemployment or a more equitable distribution of wealth. Anyone who believes that democracy, in itself, is a guarantee of liberties other than those requisite to a democratic system of government is in need of enlightenment. The basic freedoms indispensable to democracy are relatively secure, but only because their withdrawal or substantial impairment would bring democratic government to an end. If the people of a democracy desire additional liberties, they will have to take full advantage of every opportunity which the democratic process provides to gain and retain freedoms to which great value is attached.

Democracy and Equality

The only equality clearly essential to democracy is equal possession of the political rights and basic freedoms heretofore identified. Equality in other respects, if attainable at all, depends on the objectives sought by a democratic government and on the means requisite to their achievement.

Some kinds of equality, it seems safe to assume, are unattainable. Differences among individuals in intelligence, in talents, in temperament, and in physical characteristics, so far as we know, are inherent in mankind. Other diversities, probably ineradicable, include personal qualities like wisdom, prudence, resourcefulness, and courage. Insofar as such characteristics are acquirable, equalization is theoretically possible. For all practical purposes, however, it may be assumed that differences in these and other personality traits will always exist among individuals.

Various kinds of equality are attainable. Among them are equality before the law, equality of opportunity, equality of wealth, and equality of treatment. Some equalities may be established by law, but legal stipulations make headway slowly if popular opposition is widespread, intense, and persistent. Furthermore, the enactment of laws aimed at promoting or insuring equality is unlikely in the absence of strong pressure for the kind of equality that is sought by the sponsors of specific policies. Generally speaking, the attainment of realizable equalities depends on the convictions that prevail in particular communities.

Equality before the law means that persons in general possess the same legal rights and responsibilities. It signifies the absence of a policy of conferring special rights and privileges on some social classes or castes and denying them to others. Legal inequality exists if a line is drawn, for example, between the nobility and the common people and the rights and duties of the former class differ materially from those of the latter. However, the general principle of equality before the law does not require that *all* members of a body politic be legally equal *in every respect*. Absolute legal equality regardless of sex, age, or other considerations may prove disadvantageous from the standpoint of the general welfare or of the well-being of particular categories of individuals.[45] A body politic is free to decide on the circumstances under which differences in legal rights and duties are desirable and justifiable. Democracy requires equality in the enjoyment of such fundamental freedoms as freedom of speech and freedom of association and also in the matter of political rights for persons able to meet prescribed standards of competence, such as qualifications for voting and for holding office. Legal inequalities in other respects are compatible with democratic government. The demand for a substantial degree of legal equality is usually great in democratic countries, but the establishment of absolute legal equality in disregard of the social consequences of such a policy is neither requisite to democracy nor a necessary outcome of the democratic governmental process.

Equality of opportunity is commonly advocated on two principal grounds. One is the desirability of enabling each individual to develop his capacities to the greatest possible extent. The other is to permit individuals in general to take full advantage of their legal rights. For both purposes, an adequate education and appropriate economic resources are necessary. Without education an individual is unlikely to realize his potentialities or to be aware of his legal rights and the remedies available in the event of their infringement. Without sufficient funds he is unable to do many of the things that he is free to do as a matter of law, such as attending a university, traveling, or resorting to the courts for the redress of grievances.

Various factors other than wealth and education have a bearing on equality of opportunity. Among them are good health, leisure time, and adequate governmental protection against the invasive actions of individuals and groups that have no respect for the rights of others. Another factor of major importance to the equalization of opportunity is the availability of facilities for the effective exercise of certain rights, such as freedom of speech, freedom of assembly, and freedom of learning.

A legal grant of freedom of speech, to be of maximum significance, requires equality of opportunity to obtain a widespread hearing for one's views. Generally speaking, some individuals are in a far better position than others to get speaking time on radio or television programs, to have articles and books published, or to conduct propaganda campaigns. Both wealth and education are important assets in this connection. Unless most people have ready access to proper facilities for publicizing ideas and disseminating information, a guarantee of freedom of speech proves more beneficial to the powerful and influential few than to the many with limited resources. To be effective, freedom of speech requires easy accessibility to adequate means of communication between the individual and the general public. Freedom of assembly, too, is dependent on the availability of places for holding meetings and on the ease of obtaining permission to use them. As for freedom of learning, its value is greatly diminished in a community which fails to provide satisfactory educational facilities for the rank and file of its inhabitants. Many other instances of the relationship between rights and opportunities may occur to the reader.

Substantial equality of opportunity is probably more likely to be provided for in democracies than in authoritarian countries, but it may not be. To the extent that it is, individuals are in a position to better themselves in many ways. However, equalizing opportunities is by no means a guarantee of equal results. Differences among individuals usually lead to various inequalities. To prevent this from occurring would require the imposition of many restraints on individuals and tend to nullify the benefits derivable from the establishment of equality of opportunity.

The contention that democracy requires an equal or relatively equal distribution of wealth is often advanced. Economic systems, such as capitalism, which result in a marked inequality of economic resources are said to render formal arrangements of a democratic type meaningless. Wealth is a source of power. Democracy for the rich, but not for the poor or the limited income groups, is asserted to be the inevitable result of great disparities in economic resources. This claim is commonly advanced by proponents of a socialized economy. Of various counter-contentions, only one will be mentioned at this point because the matter will be given further consideration in the following chapter. It is argued that in a democracy numbers count for as much as wealth both in elections and in the bringing of pressure to bear on public officials. Organized groups of individuals with limited personal wealth may possess considerable economic power—power in terms of funds and power attributable to the part played in the process of production. Labor unions, for example, have adequate financial resources and in addition, by resorting to strikes, are in a position to paralyze the economy. The threat of a strike may be sufficient to obtain desired legislation. For reasons such as this, the point is made that the wealthy have been placed on the defensive in various democracies and that a capitalistic economy has not prevented this from occurring.

Whatever the merits of arguments pro and con concerning the compatibility of democracy and inequality in the distribution of wealth, the fact is that equality in economic resources has not been achieved in countries commonly classified as democracies. Nor have democratic governments endeavored to do more than eliminate the most objectionable economic inequities. Their policies have been designed, primarily, to offset various disadvantages attributable to limited individual wealth and to establish minimum standards of economic security.

The notion that democracy requires equality of treatment is entertained by some people. This belief often leads to demands for equality that are difficult to justify from the standpoint of both individual and group welfare. Examples are opposition to different educational programs for fast learners and slow learners in the elementary and secondary schools, to deferments from military service for married men, for university students, or for specialists of various types, and to the establishment of office-holding qualifications which many citizens are unable to meet. If a democratic government succumbs to pressure for "equality of treatment" regardless of the social consequences, the policies it adopts are likely to prove harmful rather than beneficial to the members of a community. Blind and irrational insistence on equality of treatment under any and all circumstances may lead to the discrediting of democracy and to advocacy of some type of authoritarianism. Persons who, in the name of democracy, demand that all individuals should be treated alike in all situations are laboring under a misconception of the nature of democratic government. They also fail to realize that no society can afford to disregard individual differences, conflicts of interest, and diversity of needs in devising satisfactory solutions of the many problems that arise in all communities. In some matters equality of treatment is desirable and advantageous; in others the contrary is true. To treat all people the same under all circumstances involves disregard of considerations of both fairness and expediency.[46]

Greater equality often requires a curtailment of liberty. Whether it does depends on the kind of equality which is sought. For example, no substantial sacrifice of liberty is necessary for the purpose of establishing equality before the law. However, the attainment of equality or approximate equality in wealth would require a multiplicity of restrictions on the economic freedom of individuals and groups. At the very least, equalization in wealth would involve redistribution through progressive taxation in combination with governmental services for the special benefit of the economically handicapped.

If uniformity in many phases of life is demanded in the name of equality, individual liberty must be restricted to whatever extent the goal of uniformity requires. A community has to decide which is the more important, liberty or equality. A significant degree of freedom is likely to result in inequalities of one type or another, whereas a large measure of equality is usually attainable only by limitation of the scope of individual liberty. The price to be paid for various equalities is the establishment of restraints which may prevent individuals from developing their personal capacities to the greatest possible extent. Individuality is sacrificed for the sake of equality.

Democracy, as a process of government, merely guarantees the liberties essential to its existence. It requires equality only in regard to political rights, safeguards against arbitrary arrest and imprisonment, and the possession of, and opportunity to exercise, such basic freedoms as freedom of speech, assembly, and association. The attainment of additional freedoms and equalities depends on the policies which a democratically organized community decides to pursue.

STUDY QUESTIONS

1. From what different points of view is liberty definable? Explain each of them.

2. Why does limited rather than absolute liberty prevail in all countries?

3. In what sense is freedom of thought absolute?

4. Discuss the various sources of restraint on individual and group liberty.

5. What are the reasons for questioning the validity of the assertion that greater liberty is necessarily enjoyed in a democracy than in a country with an authoritarian regime?

6. Why resort to constitutional guarantees of rights in a democracy?

7. Which is preferable and why: final interpretation of constitutional guarantees of rights by the legislature or by the judiciary, i.e., the courts?

8. What kinds of equality are attainable? What kinds unattainable?

9. What kinds of equality are essential to democracy?

10. What is meant by equality under the law? Is absolute equality in this sense desirable or undesirable? Give reasons.

11. Why is equality of opportunity desirable? What are the ways and means of achieving it?

12. Why does equality of opportunity fail to guarantee equal results?

13. Discuss the relation between democracy and equality in wealth.

14. Why is the notion that democracy requires equality of treatment a hindrance to effective democratic government?

15. Why does the attainment of equality in many matters necessarily require the curtailment of liberty?

CHAPTER 7

DEMOCRACY, SOCIALISM, AND COMMUNISM

The assertion that democracy's survival depends on the retention of a "capitalistic" economy is frequently made, particularly in the United States. Historically, capitalism has existed in combination with both authoritarian and democratic governments. This fact is not denied, but the conviction prevails in various circles that the replacement of capitalism by some kind of socialized economic order, such as socialism or communism, will eventually lead to authoritarianism in fact even though the form of democratic government may be preserved. In short, without capitalism, democracy is doomed. Some persons concede the combinability of democracy and a socialized economy but contend that certain hazards are involved and express fear that democracy is likely to perish if complete socialization occurs. Still others reject these pessimistic views and maintain that the risk of a downfall of democracy is no greater with one political-economic combination than with another. There are those, too, who insist that "real" democracy is unattainable without economic socialization. Formal democracy is the best to be had in communities characterized by a markedly uneven distribution of wealth.

Proof of the truth or falsity of the foregoing contentions is unlikely. For the present, at least, the available evidence is inconclusive. An understanding of the primary features of different economic systems is obviously requisite to a meaningful appraisal of claims and counter-claims. Since the principal rivals of capitalism are socialism and communism, the distinctive characteristics of only these three types of economy will be summarized.

Capitalism

Capitalism is the commonly used label for a "private enterprise" system. The production of wealth in its various forms is undertaken for the most part by private individuals or groups who decide what to produce and how much, assemble the needed instruments of production, and assume the responsibilities and risks involved in ventures of this type. Most enterprises are privately owned and operated. Their products, either commodities or services, are sold in a market that is competitive in some degree, frequently highly so but sometimes considerably restricted because of the development of monopolistic practices. Public or governmental enterprises commonly exist, but the proportion of wealth produced by them is relatively small. The production and marketing of products by private producers is usually subjected to governmental regulation, which varies in nature and extent from time to time and from place to place. However, this regulation by government falls short of making a myth of private enterprise, provided that private persons retain a wide range of discretion in deciding whether or not to produce and sell particular goods and services.

Various types of income are obtainable by individuals under a private enterprise system. Owners of land receive income in the form of rent; owners of capital are paid interest; and entrepreneurs, those who undertake the responsibilities and risks of starting a business, obtain income in the form of profits, provided their ventures prove successful. The most important other type of income is compensation for the rendition of personal services. Most individuals rely primarily on this source of income which is paid as a salary, wage, or piece-work reward for work that is done.

The distribution of wealth is largely accomplished through the pricing process involved in the marketing of goods and services. Considerations of supply and demand are important determinants of the share of annually produced wealth obtained by the individual members of a community in which a private enterprise economy functions. Initially, at least, the distribution of wealth is effected in this way. Thereafter, if a demand therefore prevails, redistribution may be achieved through various devices, including taxation.

Socialism

Socialism is a term that has acquired various meanings. It refers primarily to a type of economy that differs fundamentally in certain respects from capitalism. Private enterprise in the production of wealth is either entirely prohibited or confined to comparatively minor and small-scale undertakings, e.g., light industry and the handicrafts, as distinguished from the major and basic enterprises that constitute the most essential and vital part of an economy.[47]

Socialism has been defined as "that organization of society in which the means of production are controlled, and the decisions on how and what to produce and on who is to get what, are made by public authority instead of by privately-owned and privately-managed firms." The march into socialism means "the migration of people's economic affairs from the private into the public sphere."[48] By "public authority" and "public sphere" are meant the body politic and its governmental agencies. At what point in "the march" an economy is properly describable as socialistic, rather than capitalistic, is difficult to say.

A completely socialized economy is no longer advocated by many, if not by most socialists,[49] but a description of the principal features of such a system affords a convenient means of conveying understanding of the essential nature of socialism. Reference will be made later to what are commonly spoken of as "mixed economies."

In an economy that is entirely socialized, the entrepreneurial function is discharged solely by appropriate agencies of government.[50] Private ownership of land and capital for productive purposes is prohibited. The state owns these instruments of production.[51] As for the management and operation of particular enterprises, that also is a responsibility of the state acting through whatever agencies are deemed suitable for this purpose.[52]

All of the features mentioned are determinative of the income available to individuals. As a consequence of public ownership of land and capital and of public discharge of the entrepreneurial function, income in the form of rent, interest, and profit accrues only to the state. The income of individuals, subject to possible minor exceptions, is confined to compensation for personal services. Each individual is employed by the state in some capacity and receives a salary, wage, or piece-work remuneration for the part he plays in the productive process. The possible exceptions occur if the government pays interest on savings accounts or government bonds or permits private ownership of land for personal residential purposes.

Control over the distribution of wealth rests with the government. It fixes prices, decides on the compensation to be paid individuals, and also determines the nature and amount of other permissible individual income. Generally speaking, socialists believe that an individual's share of the wealth should depend on the services he renders in the process of production. Strict equality of compensation has been advocated by some socialists.

Private property is not entirely eliminated under complete socialism. Private ownership of producer's goods—yes; private possession and use of consumer's goods—no. An individual may purchase consumer's goods at the centers of distribution maintained by the state, such as state-owned and operated department stores, hardware stores, or liquor stores. What he buys is his for the purpose of personal consumption, just as under a private enterprise economy. What he is able to buy depends on his income and on what is available for purchase. In this respect, socialism and capitalism are alike. But under capitalism, private individuals or associations decide what to produce and offer for sale; under socialism, the government decides. Under both systems the needs and desires of consumers undoubtedly influence the decisions which are made.

What has been said above holds true in every respect only in the event of complete socialization. If small-scale private enterprise is permitted, as advocated by many socialists, e.g., Norman Thomas, private productive undertakings and individual ownership of land and capital survive as a minor feature of the economy. Consequently, some individuals, as enterpreneurs or as owners of land or capital, will obtain income in the form of profit, rent, or interest.

As observed in the discussion of capitalism, a private enterprise system is not characterized by the complete absence of public enterprise. Provision is commonly made for government ownership and operation of water supply and sewerage systems, highways, parks, transportation and communication systems, and various other wealth-producing ventures. To the extent that it is, the economy involves a combination of public and private enterprise. If this combination develops to the point where neither public nor private production of wealth predominates, the economy is best described as "mixed," indicating that the economic order falls short of being either clearly socialistic or obviously capitalistic. A steady increase in the substitution of public for private enterprise is indicative of a march toward socialism.

So far, practically all that has been said pertains to the economic aspects of socialism. It is important to note that contemporary socialists believe in democracy and favor evolutionary rather than revolutionary methods of attaining their objectives. They dislike authoritarianism and usually concede that individuals will be worse off under a combination of socialism and authoritarianism than under a private enterprise economy combined with democratic government. The former combination is sometimes referred to as "state capitalism."

Socialists are sincerely concerned about the welfare of all individuals, not merely that of a select few. So are most of the advocates of other types of economy. The fact of agreement on this point is often overlooked because of disagreement concerning the best means of attaining the desired end.

Communism

Communism as a way of life is distinguishable from the communist movement. The latter consists of the ways and means pursued by communists for the purpose of attaining the former. Marxists contend that the downfall of capitalism is inevitable as a consequence of the operation of laws of social evolution revealed to Marx through study of the history of mankind. His investigations unearthed conclusive evidence, so it is claimed, that the entire social superstructure at any period of history is attributable to economic causes, particularly to the forces and techniques which have been developed for the production of wealth.

Marxian economic determinists maintain that the relations of production, i.e., property relations, correspond to the modes of production. When the latter undergo change, chiefly because of technological developments, and property relations remain unaltered, revolution is inevitable. The dominant economic class is overthrown by the oppressed and exploited class or classes and a new economic order comes into being. Due to the operation of laws of social development, history has been marked by a succession of economic orders. Slave economies were replaced by feudalism and it in turn by capitalism. The passing of capitalism is imminent and the ultimate and unavoidable outcome of the developmental process will be a classless, communistic society emerging from a transitional stage, socialism, which is marked by a dictatorship of the proletariat. This stage now exists in the U.S.S.R.

Lenin, rather than Marx, developed and used the technique of revolution. He provided the leadership necessary to establishment of an effective dictatorship of the proletariat. His teachings and experiences were endorsed by his successors, first Stalin and then Khrushchev. Each of the latter is credited with important contributions to the communist movement and its doctrines. The movement, to state the case briefly, is characterized by leadership of the Communist Party and by resort to any and all means, including violence, deception, infiltration, and temporary collaboration with non-communistic parties, that will hasten the inevitable disappearance of capitalism. Ruthlessness in the choice of means has resulted in many practices that conflict with approved standards of democratic behavior.

Communism, as a type of economy, involves the complete abolition of private enterprise in the production and distribution of wealth. All economic activity is undertaken by the community through whatever agencies are considered suitable for the production of goods and services. The community is the sole entrepreneur, the only owner of land and capital, and the only manager of productive enterprises. It alone controls the distribution of wealth in conformity with the communistic principle of distribution according to need. The sharing of wealth in accordance with need, instead of on the basis of services rendered, is the primary *economic* difference between communism and socialism. Private ownership of consumer's goods probably will

survive under communism. The following significant pronouncement concerning consumer's goods is included in the 1961 *Programme of the Communist Party of the Soviet Union,* viz.,
"Articles of personal use will be in the full ownership of each
member of society and will be at his disposal." [53]

So far, no mention has been made of the state or government
in describing communism. The reason is that the Marxists assert
that the state will wither away once a classless, communistic
society becomes a reality. If this proves to be the case, such a
society will be anarchistic as well as communistic. Anarchism
is characterized by the absence of government and by full reliance on voluntary cooperation. The question arises as to whether
"the withering away of the state" really means the disappearance
of government as a type of social control of individual behavior.

Marx and Engels conceived of the state as an instrument of
violence, oppression, and exploitation in the hands of a dominant
economic class. Logically, if the state is defined in terms of class
and as a weapon used in the course of class warfare, the need
for it will cease upon attainment of a classless society. However,
political scientists subscribe to a different view of the nature of
the state. A community qualifies as a state if it is absolutely
autonomous or independent and if social control of the governmental type is exercised over its members. This type of control
is organized, applied on a community-wide or territorial basis,
and made effective, if necessary, through resort to compulsion by
force. Should control of this kind survive in a communistic
society, the state, as defined by political scientists, would continue to exist despite the disappearance of classes.

Only the event of a classless communistic society will provide
a definite answer concerning the fate of government. The 1961
Programme of the Communist Party includes statements bearing
on this question, but the assertions which are made seem inconclusive. A few quotations will indicate why.

It is stated that "communist production demands high standards of organization, precision, and discipline, which are ensured, not by compulsion, but through an understanding of

public duty, and are determined by the whole pattern of life in a communist society." [54] Again, "communism is a highly organized society of free, socially conscious working people in which public self-government will be established." [55] One more pronouncement, among others which might be quoted, is pertinent to the matter under consideration, viz., "Public functions similar to those performed by the state today in the sphere of economic and cultural management will be preserved under communism and will be modified and perfected as society develops. But the character of the functions and the ways in which they are carried out will be different from those under socialism. The bodies in charge of planning, accounting, economic management, and cultural advancement, now government bodies, will lose their political character and will become organs of public self-government. . . . Universally recognized rules of the communist way of life will be established whose observance will become an organic need and habit with everyone." [56]

Such phrases as "not by compulsion" and "observance will become an organic need and habit" are suggestive of anarchism, i.e., a society based solely on voluntary cooperation. What is meant by loss of "political character" and becoming "organs of public self-government" is not clear. These expressions may be intended to signify voluntary cooperation, but no specific statement of that effect is made, although the inference may be drawn from the other phrases quoted above. The issue is important in a discussion of democracy only because of its bearing on the question of the compatibility of democracy in the political sense with a communistic economy. If a communistic society is anarchistic, government in the usual sense of the term no longer exists.

About one point there is no room for doubt. The state that "withers away" is the dictatorship of the proletariat which the Marxists refer to as democracy for the workers, i.e., for the majority, and not merely for the minority, viz., the capitalists, as in a private enterprise economy. During the socialistic stage which marks the transition from capitalism to communism, the dictatorship of the proletariat is essential. The need for it disappears upon development of the classless communistic society, provided that capitalist encirclement of the communistic countries no longer presents a threat.

It is difficult to envisage a society without government. Provision for compulsory controls seems unavoidable in a highly organized and complicated society. Individuals and groups are likely to disagree concerning the objectives to be sought through collective action and also about the proper ways of attaining them. The obligations of individuals in particular situations may be uncertain and give rise to dispute. It is doubtful that problems of this type can be solved satisfactorily and expeditiously unless some arrangement is made for the making of final and authoritative decisions to which dissenting individuals and groups may be compelled to conform, if unwilling to do so. Conceivably, of course, the social consciousness or community-mindedness of people in general may be developed to so high a degree that resort to compulsion may never be necessary. Even so, recognition of the obligation to abide by authoritative decisions is a minimum requisite.

The authoritative agency of final decision in a classless communistic society may prove to be the Communist Party which is looked upon as the vanguard of the proletariat. During the socialist stage in the transition from capitalism to communism, the party plays a dominant role. Furthermore, as stated in the 1961 *Programme of the Communist Party of the Soviet Union,* "the period of full-scale communist construction is characterized by a further *enhancement of the role and importance of the Communist Party* as the leading and guiding force of Soviet society." [57] There is no indication that it will cease to function in this capacity after the period of full-scale construction has come to an end.

Socialized Economies and Democracy

Democracy, as the term is used in this text, denotes a political system or process of government. Socialism and communism are the two kinds of socialized economy that have been described and compared with capitalism in the sense of a private enterprise system for the production and distribution of wealth. The question to be discussed is the compatibility of democracy with either socialism or communism. Various proponents of capitalism insist that economic socialization necessarily results in the passing of democracy, in substance if not from a strictly formal standpoint. Among those who disagree with this contention are foes as well as friends of socialization.

Before undertaking a consideration of arguments pro and con, it is essential to remind the reader that the relative merits of different types of economy are not pertinent to the point at issue. One may be convinced that a private enterprise system is the most efficient and effective means of producing wealth, but that fact, if it be a fact, does not prove that capitalism is requisite to democracy. Nor does a claim of superiority for either socialism or communism justify the conclusion that democracy in the governmental sense is unattainable without them.

A socialized economy undoubtedly entails far greater restraints on economic liberty than does capitalism. This assertion seems unassailable on any grounds. But the drastic curtailment of economic liberties need not involve sacrifice of the political and other basic freedoms indispensable to democracy. As previously pointed out, a substantial degree of public enterprise exists in various democratic countries that have a private enterprise economy. Presumably, the substitution of public for private enterprise in certain areas of economic activity has been the result of decisions reached through the democratic process of government. That being the case, it would seem that complete or nearly complete socialization may be achieved either gradually or rapidly through the same process, if the people of a democracy so desire. What the consequences of such action will be with respect to the survival of political democracy is actually the point at issue.

Economic planning and the adoption of a binding plan appear essential to both socialistic and communistic economies. The plan may, of course, be altered from time to time in accordance with the judgment of the authoritative policy-determining and planning agencies of the community. But the fact that an obligatory plan is necessary accounts for the contention by some persons that democracy will perish.

Friedrich A. Hayek, for example, maintains that a democratic government and a planned economy are incompatible.[58] He is convinced that the eventual outcome of long-range economic planning is a dictatorship by economic experts. Representative assemblies are incapable of reaching agreement on the provisions of a comprehensive, systematic, and unified plan.

To quote Hayek: "The welfare of a people, like the happiness of a man, depends on a great many things that can be provided in an infinite variety of combinations. It cannot be adequately expressed as a single end, but only as a hierarchy of ends, a comprehensive scale of values in which every need of every person is given its place. To direct all our activities according to a single plan presupposes that every one of our needs is given its rank in an order of value which must be complete enough to make it possible to decide among all the different courses which the planner has to choose. It presupposes, in short, the existence of a complete ethical code in which all the different human values are allotted their due place."[59]

Hayek asserts that if a unitary plan is to be established, a social view about what ought to be done must guide all decisions. The people of a democracy may favor adoption of a system of directed economy because of the belief that it will produce great prosperity, but agreement on the desirability of planning is unlikely to be supported by agreement on the ends to be attained. Inability of the people and their representatives to agree on any particular plan will result in a demand that planning be taken out of politics and placed in the hands of experts—permanent officials or independent autonomous bodies. Planning leads to dictatorship.[60] "It is the price of democracy that the possibilities of conscious control are restricted to the fields where true agreement exists and that in some fields things must be left to chance. But in a society which for its functioning depends on central planning this control cannot be made dependent on a majority's being able to agree; it will often be necessary that the will of a small minority be imposed upon the people, because this minority will be the largest group able to agree among themselves on the question at issue." [61]

One line of response to Hayek's position is that most, if not all, policies adopted by a democratic government are the result of competition among conflicting interests and different scales of values. There are few, if any, "fields where true agreement exists." This fact has not prevented the reaching of final decisions through the democratic process of government. That process commonly involves delays and compromises, as it undoubtedly would in so important a matter as the formulation and adoption of a single economic plan. But the attainment of majority agreement on the ends to be sought through planning seems probable, especially because of the knowledge that an adopted plan always remains subject to revision through the usual policy-determining procedures of a democratic government. As long as the door to change remains open, uncomprimising attitudes are less likely to be maintained.

If it be true, as Hayek contends, that it will frequently be necessary, in connection with central planning, to impose the will of a small minority on the people, the appropriate response is that the same thing often occurs in democracies functioning in a capitalistic environment. Evidence that all of the policies adopted in a democracy conform to the will of a popular majority is lacking. For reasons stated in earlier chapters, a majority vote in the legislature is by no means a certain criterion of majority popular support. In a democracy the active and informed few make most of the decisions; the passive many experience the results of whatever policies are adopted. However, the voters through periodic elections are able to change the key governing personnel and the freedoms associated with democracy provide individuals and groups with the opportunity to influence the outcome of the decision-making process and to bring about desired changes in policy. As for the experts, they are likely to be influential in shaping the policies of all countries, regardless of the type of economy. Some critics of democracy contend that experts invariably run the show, whatever the form of government. If this be the case, neither a private enterprise nor a socialized economy will prevent domination by the experts.

Fear that the liberties essential to democracy may be lost in the event of complete socialization of the economy accounts for another line of argument to the effect that socialism and communism constitute threats to the survival of democracy. R. M. MacIver, an eminent sociologist and political theorist, summarizes this point of view in the following quotation: "Under complete collectivization the administrative and executive powers of government must be vastly increased. The administrative determinations of the central planning body would be decisive for the well-being of the whole community. Invested with such powers the executive would tend to dominate the legislative, a situation inimical to democracy. Collectivism does not reform man's lust for power, which grows more exacting as power grows. In the mixed economy there is not the monopoly of power that the socialist economy inevitably entails—monopoly in the sense that now there are no foci of power outside the political order. In the mixed economy every man's livelihood and his economic position is not in the last resort dependent on the action of government. There are resistance points at which in the relative independence of their economic position men and groups can take a stand against the encroachments of political power. In the socialist economy only the effectiveness of public opinion can curb the excesses of government. This control is indeed the most salutary of all controls, as it is the only truly democratic one. If it can be made fully effective under collectivism then the problem is solved. But in politics the ideal easily becomes the enemy of the attainable. When government owns such direct sovereignty over the fortunes of men in every rank of life the tendency to make its favor or disfavor the criterion of merit and the basis of selection to positions of responsibility will have far greater range than it already has in the non-socialistic state. Men aspiring to leadership, and indeed all men, will feel that their life chances hang on their positive attitude' toward the establishment. It will consequently be harder to hold the cultural liberties that are the mainstay of democracy and the last safeguard against tyranny. The corrupting influence of the possession of power will not dissolve because the profit motive is ruled out. When that avenue to power is closed the traffic of ambition will be the more ruthlessly concentrated along the political avenue." [62]

The concentration of economic and traditional political power in the same hands, so the argument runs, will greatly influence the behavior of men in voting, in seeking authoritative positions, and in their relations with public officials. Fear of punitive repercussions will lead to a serious curtailment of criticism and of opposition to those in control of the government. Legal guarantees of freedom of speech, freedom of association, and various political privileges tend to become meaningless if people are afraid to exercise them. The measure of success in life will be the gaining and retaining of power over the lives of men and unscrupulous behavior for the sake of "getting ahead" will become the order of the day.

Complete socialization would involve government ownership and control of all publications, including newspapers and periodicals, and such modes of disseminating information as the radio and television. Consequently, the meaningful exercise of freedom of speech would depend on the policy which those in control of the government saw fit to pursue with respect to the use of these facilities by individuals and groups desirous of presenting their views to the general public. The government would be in control of all of the principal sources of information—a situation not conducive to effective popular control of those who hold public office. Even now, in capitalistic democracies, the secrecy policies of governments, usually defended on grounds of national security, constitute a menace to democracy.

Since so many socialists no longer advocate complete socialization, private enterprise in the publication and information fields may survive in particular countries despite substantial expansion of the public sector in the production of wealth. But whether the requirements of democracy in regard to adequate sources of information are better met by private rather than by public instrumentalities is a debatable question. Private agencies for the procurement and dissemination of information often pursue policies of questionable merit from the standpoint of consistency with the democratic process of government. The problem of furnishing the general public with needed information is not so simple that it can be solved merely by a choice between public and private enterprise in the discharge of this important function.

Partial socialization in some form in various countries, e.g., Sweden, has failed to undermine their democratic political institutions. Nor has democracy been endangered by such extension of the area of public enterprise as has occurred in Great Britain. Extended experience with a large-scale and almost completely socialized economy has been confined to the U.S.S.R., a country in which an authoritarian tradition has prevailed for centuries. The Russian Communists claim that their present system of government is democratic in character, but this contention is rejected as untenable by the democracies of the Western World whose concept of democracy differs from that of the Russians. Whatever the merits of the claims of both sides concerning the criteria of democracy, it seems clear that the communist *movement* is characterized by practices of a non-democratic type. Resort to revolution, to any and all means of attaining a desired end, to the instigation of uprisings in other countries, to the ruthless suppression of opposition, and to dictatorial techniques of various kinds—these are phases of the movement which are irreconcilable with the precepts of democracy. Not only that, but the leaders and supporters of any movement, communistic or otherwise, who believe that any tactics are justifiable for the purpose of gaining their objectives are likely to become victims of the means they employ and discard their democratic ideas, if they had any in the first place. Democratic pretensions may, of course, be maintained for propaganda purposes. In the course of time, after attainment of the ends sought through any and all means, democratic practices may gain a foothold and eventually prevail, but not as readily as might have been the case if the movement had been conducted at all times in conformity with the requirements of the democratic governmental process.

The essential difference between socialistic and communistic economic systems is the approved principle determining the distribution of wealth. Communism involves distribution according to need; socialism, according to the value of services rendered in the productive process. If social control of the governmental variety survives in a communistic society, as it may despite talk of the withering away of the state, this *economic* difference between socialism and communism is unlikely to be determinative of the presence or absence of democratic political institutions. The principle controlling the distribution of wealth has little or no bearing on the combinability of democratic government with a socialized economy.

Speculation concerning the compatibility of democracy and a completely socialized economy will continue as long as absolute proof of either compatibility or incompatibility is lacking. In all likelihood the experience of one country will differ from that of another. Practical obstacles to the functioning of democracy in combination with economic socialization may have to be overcome, as they need to be in countries with a private enterprise system, but impediments of this type are not necessarily insurmountable. Future developments throughout the world should be awaited before drawing final conclusions about the combinability of various types of economy with different kinds of political institutions. The survival of democracy in a particular country with a firmly established democratic tradition may reasonably be anticipated even if complete socialization takes place, especially if the transition from a capitalistic to a socialized economy occurs gradually. In other countries the political consequences of entire collectivization may well be different.

This discussion will be brought to a close by making two assertions. First, the existence of democratic political institutions is an inadequate guarantee of the survival of capitalism. Second, in all probability democracy in the political sense is likely to be established or survive, regardless of the nature of the economic order, in any country in which the demand for democratic government is sufficiently widespread, strong, and persistent.

STUDY QUESTIONS

1. What are the distinctive characteristics of each of the following types of economy, viz., capitalism; socialism; communism?

2. What is the present-day attitude of most socialists toward complete socialization?

3. What use is or has been made of the principle of distribution according to need in the United States?

4. Why is the downfall of capitalism considered inevitable by orthodox Marxists?

5. What do Marxists mean by "the withering away of the State?" When will this "withering away" occur?

6. Present the arguments for and against the combinability of democracy in the political sense with (a) a socialistic economy and (b) a communistic economy.

7. What are Hayek's reasons for maintaining that a democratic government and a planned economy are incompatible?

8. Why does MacIver fear that the liberties essential to democracy may be lost in the event of complete socialization of the economy?

9. Compare the views of Dahl and Ebenstein in regard to the combinability of democracy and socialism (see Appendix).

10. What are the thoughts of Schumpeter about the consequences of economic socialization for democratic government? (see Appendix)

11. What will be the effect of economic socialization on individual liberty?

12. What type of government is favored by most socialists? Why?

CHAPTER 8

THE ATTACK

ON DEMOCRACY

In ancient as well as later times the merits and defects of different systems of government were a subject of controversy. Proof of the superiority of one system as compared to others has often been attempted but never achieved. Justification is another matter and those favoring a particular form of government have succeeded in justifying it to their own satisfaction, if not to that of others. One reason for the continuance of controversy is disagreement concerning the standards to be applied in an appraisal of governments. Another reason is that even those who agree upon some standard or standards disagree as to whether or not a particular system of government meets these standards either in principle or in practice.

The position taken in this book is that the desirability of a form of government depends on time, place, and circumstance. To contend that democracy is preferable under any and all conditions involves disregard of many factors that should be taken into account in organizing the government of a particular country. The same observation applies to those who insist that authoritarianism is always superior to democracy. Among the factors that ought to be considered are the cultural development of a body politic's population, the economic status of the bulk of its inhabitants, established customs and traditions, and the type of government which the people in general prefer. Democracy is unlikely to prove a success, whatever its potential advantages may be, in a country in which most of the people are illiterate and extremely poor, if not poverty-stricken, or if the desire for democracy is either absent or confined to a small minority. Similarly, an authoritarian regime is neither likely to function satisfactorily nor survive indefinitely if the demand for democracy is widespread, persistent, and militant.

In the preceding paragraph the phrases "prove a success" and "function satisfactorily" were used. What are the criteria of success and satisfactory functioning? The criteria suggested here are 1] generally effective and economical government, 2] reasonably prompt solution of the most pressing problems arising in the community, 3] actual operation in conformity with the basic principles upon which the governmental system is founded, and 4] the prevalence of social stability in the sense of no evidence of serious discontent on the part of the governed population. These suggestions may be criticized as inadequate by many persons. Criticism is inevitable because the matter under consideration involves value judgments.

Although the choice between authoritarianism and democracy ought to be made for particular countries, rather than for countries in general, an examination of the claimed advantages and disadvantages of both systems seems worthwhile inasmuch as the establishment of one rather than the other may sometimes be determined by consideration of asserted merits and shortcomings. Of course, the existence of either type of government in a particular country may have been the result of an unpremeditated response to the pressure of circumstances. Nevertheless, the drafters of a documentary constitution usually have some range of choice, and continued support for an established system may depend, to some extent at least, on the claims made in behalf of different patterns of government. Whether arguments pro and con have much, if any, bearing on institutional developments is a debatable question. In any event competition among ideologies occurs, and political philosophers have devoted considerable time and thought to an appraisal of different forms of government. A review of the arguments advanced for both authoritarianism and democracy should prove interesting, even if rational argument has little or nothing to do with what has happened or will happen in particular countries.

Many of the claims advanced in behalf of different systems of government are unsupported by impressive evidence. The same observation applies to asserted shortcomings. It is easy to make a seemingly plausible claim but difficult to demonstrate that actual experience justifies it. The multiplication of arguments pro and con is a common practice of parties to a controversy, perhaps because of the conviction that the more numerous the claims for or against something, the stronger the case. However, a single contention based on credible evidence is probably worth much more than a half dozen that are essentially speculative in character.

Democracy is attacked from two different points of view. One is that the attainment of democracy is impossible. Its apparent existence is a myth. According to the other, democracy, although possible, is undesirable. Those who concede that democracy is attainable, but condemn it on various grounds, not only stress its asserted defects but also direct attention to what they believe to be the advantages of some authoritarian type of government. Persons who insist that democracy is mythical obviously are convinced that authoritarianism prevails and that people have never had, nor will have, any choice in the matter.

The Impossibility of Democracy

The few always rule, regardless of particular forms of government. This statement summarizes the position of those persons who deny the possibility of democracy. The belief that government by the many exists or has existed anywhere is an illusion. In so-called democracies, what really takes place is quite different from what seems to occur. Such devices as representative assemblies, elections, limited terms of office, and competition among political parties merely conceal what inevitably happens in bodies politic, viz., oligarchical government.

Periodic elections fail to accomplish their asserted purpose, which is to enable those who are governed to hold public officials accountable for their actions and thereby to bring about the adoption of policies which the people favor. The outcome of an election determines which individuals are to hold elective positions for a designated period of time, but the mere fact of election does not warrant the conclusion that the many rather than the few run the political show. In fact, the results of an election are ascribable to successful manipulation, by the few, of the voting public, and such competition as occurs is among individuals and groups belonging to the ruling class which inevitably arises in all societies. Furthermore, the basic freedoms associated with democracy, such as freedom of speech and of the press, freedom of assembly, and freedom of association, fail to have the effect on government which the proponents of democracy claim. Opinions of the public are not decisive in the making of policy-decisions by the few. Besides, public opinion is itself primarily, if not exclusively, the product of skillful propagandizing on the part of a small number of individuals. Allegations of the foregoing type are among the reasons commonly advanced in support of the contention that democracy is impossible.

In addition, oligarchical government is said to be an organizational necessity, or the inevitable consequence of the need for leadership, or the unavoidable result of dependence on the knowledge of experts, or the inescapable outcome of ever-occurring conspiracies of power. One or more of these contentions is offered in support of the view that minority government always occurs despite resort to devices which are supposed to bring about democratic government.

Subscribers to the "organizational necessity" thesis maintain that management of the affairs of any organization or association is essential to the attainment of its objectives and that the managerial function is necessarily confined to the few. Management by all the members of an association or by a majority is out of the question. The managing minority makes all the important decisions on questions of policy and its nominal responsibility to the entire association is of negligible significance. Even though changes in the managing personnel may occur, the fact remains that the few rather than the many do the all-important managing. If it be pointed out that an association may provide for the over-ruling of a managerial decision by a majority vote of the association members, the usual response is that the leaders of the successful opposition also constitute a minority of the association membership. Associations of the governmental type, i.e., bodies politic, are no different in this respect than associations of a non-governmental character, including business enterprises, religious sects, educational associations, and political parties. Minority control is inescapable as a matter of necessity.[63]

A need for leadership is said to be necessary for any undertaking on the part of a group of individuals. Without it, effective action is unlikely. Even if not indispensable, leadership occurs in fact because some persons are more disposed than others to take the initiative in urging action of one type or another. Leaders are few in number, followers many. Whatever the character of the final action that is taken, it is the result of proposals advanced and negotiations conducted by those who provide leadership. One leader may be more successful than others in winning support for his policy proposals, but the fact remains that the course of action eventually pursued originated with leaders and finally emerged as a result of competition among the various suggestions emanating from leaders. The influence of passive participants in the decision-making process is insignificant.[64]

Dependence on the recommendations of "experts" is a common occurrence in the process of government, especially in regard to the solution of complicated problems with which most persons are unable to cope because of limited knowledge of the kind called for in many situations. Expert personnel is found in the administrative branch of government, and many competent observers have pointed out that presidents, cabinets, and assemblies in countries with nominally democratic political institutions tend to follow the recommendations of experts, more or less as a matter of course. The existence of this tendency is insufficient to warrant the conclusion that an apparently democratic government is really an oligarchy composed of experts. But persons who attribute the impossibility of democracy to the need for experts contend that far more than a tendency is evident. As they see it, the experts dominate the scene and constitute a ruling oligarchy—not always the same experts but a minority group nevertheless despite a changing personnel.

The conspiracy-of-power explanation of the inevitability of oligarchy is based on the belief that the drive for power is a characteristic of men in general. This thirst for power results in domination by the successful power-seekers who are necessarily few in number. Power is the capacity to get what you want by whatever means prove effective. These means may range anywhere from the persuasiveness of a magnetic personality to the ruthless employment of physical force. In one way or another the power-hungry gain control of the government, and authoritarianism prevails even in countries with governmental systems that outwardly appear to be democratic in character.

An elite of some kind, constituting a minority group, does the governing in all bodies politic, both actually and formally in some cases, in reality although not formally in others. The ruling elite may consist of the managerial element, or the experts, or the successful leaders, or the victorious power conspirators, or of some other identifiable group, such as the wealthy or the experienced politicians. With respect to the type of government, the result is the same—authoritarianism. Democracy is simply unattainable.

This point of view is based on a particular conception of democracy. Democracy is identified as government by the people or a government under which the will of a popular majority rules.

Presumably, the actions of a representative assembly reflect, accurately, the desires of the general public. In the first chapter, Bryce's quoted definition of democracy, for example, includes the phrases "where the will of the whole people prevails in all important matters" and "government in which the will of the majority of qualified citizens rules, taking the qualified citizens to constitute the great bulk of the inhabitants."

A different conception of democracy was also presented. For instance, Schumpeter was quoted as follows: "The democratic method is that institutional arrangement for arriving at political decisions in which individuals acquire the power to decide by means of a competitive struggle for the people's vote." And other commentators on democracy have asserted that the people do not and cannot govern, but merely control the government through elections and by manifestations of public sentiment. This conclusion concerning the nature of democracy is consistent with the view that policy-decisions are made by the few rather than by the many, but it includes the important point that the qualified voters decide, from time to time, which few shall do the governing. Since the electorate possesses the right to shift control of the government from one group to another, the responsibility of those who govern to those who are governed is clearly established. This conception of democracy also stresses existence of the opportunity to influence the course of governmental action through exercise of such basic freedoms as freedom of speech, freedom of assembly, and freedom of association.

The "impossibility of democracy" contention is plausible if democratic government is defined as a system under which policy-decisions constitute expressions of the will of the people or of a popular majority. Its credibility is certainly questionable from the standpoint of those who conceive of democracy as an arrangement under which the primary role of the people is to decide who shall do the governing, in the sense of formulating, adopting, and enforcing governmental policies, for a designated number of years.

The Undesirability of Democracy

Many persons who concede the attainability of democracy oppose it because of its asserted defects and their conviction that an authoritarian system of government is demonstrably superior. Various grounds in support of the claim that democracy is undesirable have been advanced.

Emphasis is placed on the natural inequality of men. Differences among individuals in intelligence, judgment, skill, temperament and the like are too obvious to admit of dispute. Democracy involves the conferment of equal political rights on individuals of greatly different capabilities. The result is that quantity rather than quality prevails in the general governmental process. As long as each man's vote counts the same as that of other men in determining the outcome of an election, numbers alone have significance in the political field. Any candidate or party able to attract the most voting support wins office or gains control of the government, even though the voters providing the votes needed for victory consist for the most part, if not entirely, of the inferior members of the body politic.

The people in general are poorly informed, easily deceived, and readily swayed by appeals to emotion, especially because the vast majority are decidedly mediocre in ability and lack a genuine interest in the attainment of good government. Demagogues are more likely to be elected than candidates who are really well-qualified to hold public office.

Politicians of the unsavory type rise to the top. Their interest in government is self-aggrandizement in one form or another. They show little or no concern for the public welfare, being more interested in the spoils of office than in anything else. Graft and corruption in government are the inevitable consequence. Exploitation of the public is the order of the day. It continues unabated because the voters in general are too gullible to realize what is taking place or too anxious to share the spoils of office. Reformers in the field of government usually meet with a cool reception on the part of the vast majority of voters.

Legislative bodies become the battle ground of selfish interest-groups. Deals are negotiated among the many scramblers for favors at public expense and concern for the general welfare counts for little, even though lip service is commonly paid to it in order to cover up the exploitation of the people that always occurs. Members of the legislature are supposed to represent the public, but more often than not they are merely the agents of various seekers of special privilege. The typical representative is usually a mediocrity who is as easily misled, even if genuinely concerned about the interests of the public, as the gullible voters who have placed him in office.

Democratic governments are claimed to be extremely inefficient and ineffective, if not thoroughly corrupt. Continuous turnover in top personnel, and also in personnel at the lower levels, is an obstacle to the efficient and effective performance of governmental functions. Even more serious is the inevitable concern about re-election. Policy-decisions that may alienate large segments of the voting population are usually avoided, no matter how meritorious or how essential to the public welfare a proposed policy may be. To get into office and remain there is a consideration that ordinarily overrides concern for the best interests of the people. Ineffective government also is attributable to the fear that rigorous law enforcement may have unfortunate and disastrous political consequences. The desire to avoid offense to groups of voters whose support is essential to an electoral victory frequently accounts for laxity in the administration of particular laws. Seekers of special privilege are present in all societies, but their political potency is greater in a democracy than in countries with authoritarian governments, so the opponents of democracy claim.

Another line of attack on the desirability of democracy is that the granting of political equality leads to many demands for equalization that are detrimental to the best interests of both the community as a whole and its individual members. The pressure for equalizing wealth becomes great and results in undesirable restraints on personal liberty. Insistence on equality in various other matters frequently leads to the adoption of unwise policies and to the rejection of sound proposals. In some democracies, for example, there is considerable opposition to an educational policy which classifies pupils on the basis of intelligence and provides different programs of instruction for children with differing aptitudes. Democracy, it is asserted, requires that all be treated alike. Again, the equality idea is a cause of opposition to office-holding qualifications which many, perhaps most, persons are unable to meet. It also gives rise to the contention that all members of an association, regardless of its character or purpose, should be guaranteed an effective voice in the *management* of its affairs. Serious inroads on liberty are often condoned because of the belief that democracy requires the elimination of as many inequalities as possible. As a rule persons who condemn democracy do so partly because of the conviction that democratic government inevitably results in unreasonable and inequitable demands for various kinds of equality in addition to equality of opportunity and equality in the possession of political and civil rights.

A criticism of democracy related to the "irrational clamor for equality" is that it leads to a dislike of non-conformity. The mass of people resent manifestations of superiority or difference and the weight of their opinion produces conformity. Although the freedoms associated with democracy are supposed to promote individuality, the results of democratic government are clearly in conflict with this doctrinal expectation.

Democracy is an obstacle to progress and to the prompt solution of many social problems. The general public is suspicious of change and opposes departure from customary ways of doing things. Governmental officials are reluctant to take action which may result in defeat at the next election. They prefer to await the development of a favorable public opinion before adopting known solutions of troublesome problems. Educating the public is a difficult task largely because of the ignorance and prejudices of the people in general. Needed reforms are frequently postponed indefinitely because of the weight of uninformed opinion. In the United States, for example, it has been extremely difficult to overcome opposition to zoning, to redevelopment plans, to the reorganization of state and local governments, and to compulsory immunization against various diseases. The situation is aggravated because vested interests are quick to take advantage of the ignorance and gullibility of the public. Moreover, the democratic lawmaking process offers excellent opportunity for delaying and obstructive tactics.

H. L. Mencken, in his day a severe critic of democracy, expressed opinions rather typical of the views of persons who consider democracy undesirable. He was convinced that the great mass of men lack the competence to govern themselves. Mencken spoke of the complex of prejudices which is known as public opinion, of the bitterness of the masses when anything describable as actual superiority is sensed, and of the tendency of democratic countries "to pass over statesmen of genuine imagination and sound ability in favor of colorless mediocrities." Democratic man is unable to conceive of a good that is not his own and rarely opens "his mouth for fairness, for justice, for decency between man and man." Liberty, in any true sense, is a concept beyond the reach of the inferior man's mind. Mencken further contended that progress is always opposed by the masses and that public policies, in a democracy, are determined "by small minorities playing on the fears and imbecilities of the mob— sometimes minorities of intelligent and honest men, but usually minorities of rogues." [65] Democracy, where it exists, amounts to no more than the rule of the incompetent, prejudiced, and easily deceived mob.

Many persons who consider democracy undesirable, like those who believe it impossible, apparently conceive of democratic government as a system under which the people actually govern in the sense of deciding on the policies of government, either directly or indirectly through their chosen agents who hold public office. Seemingly, the mandate theory of a representative's duty is taken for granted as an essential feature of democracy.

Moreover, these critics apparently think of a population as consisting of two clearly distinguishable parts, the elite on the one hand and the masses on the other. When they speak of democracy as government by the masses, they imply that the elite are excluded from effective participation in the governmental process, whereas the elite may and do participate and probably provide much of the leadership that characterizes collective action of any type, including the political. In any event, the democratic process enables the elite to exert influence over the rest of the population and consequently to play a significant role in policy-determination.

The asserted shortcomings of democracy are supplemented by claims concerning the advantages of authoritarianism. Authoritarian governments are pictured as far superior, for various reasons, to governmental systems of the democratic type.

Authoritarianism, whether of the autocratic or oligarchic variety, greatly increases the likelihood, if it does not insure, that the best and most able members of the body politic will exercise the powers of government. The influence of the mediocre and generally incompetent masses will be reduced to a minimum. Quality rather than quantity will prevail in the governmental process. The fact that men are inherently unequal is sufficient justification for denying significant political privileges to the masses and vesting a monopoly of political authority and power in the able few. It is assumed that the ruling few will consist of the best or most qualified members of a community, not of the mediocre or worst elements.

If control of the government be confined to a privileged class, presumably an elite, members of this class may be trained for the proper discharge of their political responsibilities. In the case of hereditary monarchy, heirs to the throne undergo preparation at an early age for their eventual role in the governmental process. The ruling class will be free to concentrate on civic affairs and thus be well-qualified by training, as well as by reason of superior ability, to decide questions of policy and to insure efficient and effective administration. Not being dependent on popular election to office, those who rule are not likely to appoint incompetent persons to governmental positions in order to gain and retain the support of various interest-groups within the population of the body politic.

The rulers under an authoritarian type of government stand above the self-seeking parties and factions that develop within countries having democratic governments. If the latter appear, the ruling class need not bow to such of their demands as may be detrimental to the best interests of the body politic. As long as control of the government does not depend on elections, pressures brought to bear by different interest-groups may be ignored, especially because those who govern need not be, and seldom are, associated with such groups as members or sponsors.

Inasmuch as the governing elite under an authoritarian system is not identified with any group striving for special favors within the power of government to grant or deny, and also because continuance in control of the government does not require the winning of elections, public officials are more likely to be concerned with promotion of the welfare of the body politic as a whole than with the adoption of policies designed to satisfy the seekers of special privilege. Promotion of the interests of the general public supersedes other considerations in the formulation and adoption of governmental policies.

Democracies experience frequent turnover in the personnel of the highest public offices, since control of the government commonly shifts from one political party to another. Not so in the case of authoritarianism. The governing elite is assured of political dominance for a long period of time. Consequently, it may develop long range plans and be able to carry them out as circumstances warrant. Stability and continuity of policy are most likely to be attained under authoritarian regimes. The uncertainties so evident in connection with democratic government are reduced to a minimum.

Another claimed merit of authoritarian government is its capability for vigorous, effective, and efficient action. Democracies are plagued by endless debate, procrastination, and hesitation about taking action for fear of alienating voters whose support may make the difference between victory and defeat at scheduled elections. A ruling elite, secure in its command of the government, can act quickly and decisively whenever occasion demands. Placating dissenters and obstructionists is unnecessary. The effective and efficient administration of adopted policies is also highly probable, partly because of superior personnel and better procedures and partly because popular interference in the process of administration is less likely to occur than in a democracy.

A related contention is that authoritarian governments need not await the development of favorable public opinion before embarking on policies that are known to promote attainment of a better life. Possible reactions of the public may be taken into account but not to the extent of failing to do what needs to be done in order to make progress toward improved living conditions and the gaining of worthwhile objectives. The masses are always suspicious of innovation and seldom realize that departure from traditional ways of doing things may be of genuine benefit to all.

For the various reasons stated above, authoritarian governments are stronger and more effective than governments of the democratic variety. A weak government results in disrespect for law and order, fails to protect individuals in the enjoyment of their legal liberties, and invites movements designed to weaken, if not overthrow, it.

Individual and minority rights are more secure under authoritarian regimes. One asserted reason has already been mentioned, viz., the greater strength and effectiveness of authoritarian government. But it is also contended that the pressure for conformity so characteristic of democracies is lacking. The ruling elite is more favorably disposed toward diversity and individuality than are the masses of a democracy obsessed with the desire for equality in all things.

Finally, authoritarians aver that ruling elites are rarely guilty of acting hastily in response to the waves of emotion and prejudice that frequently engulf the masses. Officials of a democratic government may take action contrary to the dictates of sound judgment simply because of the thoughtless demands of the people. Their political future is at stake. Authoritarian rulers proceed cautiously. They are not likely to be swayed by momentary impulses of the masses.

The foregoing review of the claims in behalf of authoritarianism has involved constant reference to the ruling elite. Who are the elite? What distinguishes them from the rank and file of the population of a body politic? Presumably, the elite are the ablest members of a community, always comparatively few in number. Depending on the particular protagonist of authoritarianism, the elite may be the wealthy, the property owners, the captains of industry, the members of a particular race, the few who possess qualities of leadership, the members and descendants of blue-blooded families, the extremely well-educated, the persons who are successful in the competition for power, the strong as distinguished from the weak, and perhaps the experts who have achieved preeminence in various branches of knowledge. The criterion of the able as distinguished from the unable seems to be a controversial matter; unavoidably so, it would seem.

Some of the claims in behalf of authoritarianism may seem incredible in view of what has happened in various dictatorships of the twentieth century. It must be remembered, however, that many of the asserted merits of authoritarian government were advanced long before such recent occurrences as Fascism in Italy, National Socialism in Germany, and the Communist dictatorship in the U.S.S.R. Authoritarianism assumes different forms, and many of its proponents disapprove of the kind of authoritarian government that has appeared recently in various countries. The non-democratic governments of Great Britain from 1689 to 1832, of the German Empire, 1871-1918, and of Japan until the end of the second world war differed greatly from the regimes of Mussolini and Hitler.[66] Furthermore, the present tendency to identify authoritarianism with totalitarianism is unwarranted in the light of historical evidence. Numerous authoritarian governments of the past never endeavored to wield the extensive and all-pervasive control that totalitarianism involves.

Totalitarianism is a policy—a policy of extreme statism which is characterized by the absolute subordination of individual and group interests to those of the state and by the attempt to direct and control all social activity and both the thinking and behavior of individuals to whatever extent is believed necessary for achievement of a way of life that is considered superior to all alternatives. Difficult as it may be for many people to realize, it is possible, though perhaps improbable, for a democracy to pursue a totalitarian policy. Many authoritarians insist that the menace of majority tyranny is more to be feared than tyrannical action on the part of a ruling elite. Whether they are right or wrong continues to be a subject of controversy.

As for the claimed advantages and the asserted defects of any system of government, it is essential to remember that claims are not proof of the validity of whatever assertions are made. Another point to keep in mind is that different systems may give different results in particular cases. What happens in one place or at one time may not occur in another place or at a different time.

The line of attack on democracy has been presented. Some persons are convinced that democracy is impossible; others concede its possibility but seriously question its desirability. In the following chapter, the case for democracy will be reviewed. Proponents of democracy not only advance various positive arguments in its support but attempt to refute the different claims made by the advocates of authoritarianism.

STUDY QUESTIONS

1. Discuss the contention that the preferability of either democracy or authoritarianism depends on time, place, and circumstance.

2. What are the criteria of successful and satisfactory government?

3. What reasons are advanced in support of the claim that democracy is impossible?

4. Why is democracy considered undesirable by those of its opponents who concede its possibility?

5. Why is it evidently impossible to *prove* that democracy is superior to authoritarianism, and vice versa?

6. What are the positive claims in behalf of the superiority of authoritarianism to democracy?

7. Discuss the contention that authoritarian governments are more effective and efficient than governments of the democratic variety.

8. What are the criteria of the elite as distinguished from the masses?

9. Explain the statement that totalitarianism is a policy rather than a form of government.

10. Why is it unlikely, even if not impossible, that a democratic government will pursue a totalitarian policy?

CHAPTER 9

THE CASE FOR
DEMOCRACY

In presenting the case for democracy, attention will be directed first to the defense of democratic political institutions against the hostile criticisms advanced by the proponents of authoritarianism. Thereafter, the positive contentions in behalf of democratic government will be presented. Neither the arguments for democracy nor those in support of authoritarianism *prove* that either system is the superior of the other. Both friends and foes may believe that their contentions constitute proof, but the fact that the controversy continues indicates that conclusive evidence is lacking. The subjective factor looms large in evaluations, and a comparison of governmental systems involves value judgments as well as questions of fact. To demonstrate conclusively that *something ought to be* is an undertaking that differs considerably from that of gathering and presenting convincing evidence of *what is*.

Response of the Friends of Democracy to the Claims of Its Opponents

In answer to the contention that democracy is impossible, its defenders point out that a misconception of the nature of democratic government accounts for this claim. The initiation and eventual adoption of policies by the few rather than by the many undoubtedly occurs, but democracy merely requires that the active few be chosen from time to time by the passive many and that the people in general have ample opportunity to influence the course of decision-making. This opportunity is provided by the basic freedoms associated with democracy—freedoms in addition to the political rights which enable the electorate to determine who shall govern. The freedoms referred to are freedom of speech and of the press, freedom of assembly, freedom of association, and freedom from arbitrary arrest and imprisonment. If it be claimed, as it often is, that the ruling few consist of individuals and groups whose identity is unknown to the general public, the fact remains that these invisible persons must act through the public officials, accountable to the voters, who possess authority to legislate and to administer legally established policies. Moreover, the invisible few are by no means insusceptible to the influences and pressures resulting from popular exercise of the basic freedoms mentioned above. The democratic process of government enables the many as well as the few to participate, directly or indirectly, in determination of the part to be played by government in the social life of a community.

Persons who are convinced that democracy is impossible reject this line of defense. They consider it another example of self-delusion by the advocates of democracy. As they see it, rulership by the few is an inescapable phenomenon which occurs in spite of legal provision for various kinds of freedom. Nominal freedoms mean little in view of the realities of social life. The response of those who favor democratic government and believe in its possibility is that democracy, at least, provides the people with a choice between competing oligarchies, simply because periodic elections are held, and that such a choice is far better than no choice at all. The latter situation exists in countries which maintain governmental systems marked by an absence of meaningful elections and by denial of freedom of association for political purposes. Formal arrangements in conformity with the requirements of democracy are far superior to constitutional provisions which clearly vest the exercise of governmental authority in a privileged and closed minority of some type.

Generally speaking, the defense of democracy against critics who concede its possibility but insist on its undesirability is that the claimed shortcomings of democracy as compared to authoritarianism are unsupported by conclusive evidence. In short, the charges are for the most part untrue. The fact that certain malpractices have occurred in various democracies at particular times does not warrant the conclusion that the evils to which attention is called are inherent in the democratic process of government. Effective remedies are available, and the standard of government in any country, whether authoritarian or democratic, is largely a consequence of public service traditions and the prevailing code of community ethics. No form of government is in itself a guarantee of operational excellence.

Historical study reveals that fraud, corruption, inefficiency, and ineffectiveness have been exhibited at least as often in authoritarian countries as in democracies. The public officials of democratic governments compare favorably in competence and integrity with those that have held or hold office under authoritarian regimes. If authoritarianism had resulted in as high a quality of government as its proponents claim, the movement toward democracy and away from authoritarian government probably would not have occurred.

The charge that democracy opens the door to majority tyranny is met by the counter-contention that the historical record reveals innumerable cases of arbitrary, capricious, and oppressive government by ruling minorities. Enlightened or benevolent autocrats and oligarchies have been few in number. The only ultimate remedy for arbitrary and oppressive authoritarianism is revolutionary action. In a democracy popular elections offer an orderly means of terminating arbitrariness in government, even in cases of majority tyranny. Successive majorities are not always composed of the same individuals, inasmuch as the democratic process is conducive to freedom of movement from one group to another. A particular majority today may lose enough of its members to become a minority tomorrow. The population of a democratically organized country is not rigidly divided into a permanent majority and a permanent minority in the way that the ruling minority under an authoritarian system is separated from the governed masses to whom significant political rights are denied.

The charge that democracy results in government by the ignorant and generally incompetent masses is met in several ways. In the first place, persons of outstanding ability may participate as freely in the democratic process as individuals of more limited capability. The more able element in the population may and does furnish leadership and guidance in the formulation and adoption of governmental policies. There is little evidence to support the assertion that special knowledge and expert service are unappreciated in democracies. Secondly, the defenders of democratic government claim that it has solved social problems as successfully as have the rulers of authoritarian bodies politic. A comparison of policies does not warrant the conclusion that those of the democracies are the product of ignorance and incompetence and those of authoritarian regimes the outcome of a process in which intelligent deliberation predominates. Finally, people of average intelligence, knowledge, and skill are as likely to possess sound judgment and common sense as persons with high intelligence ratings, superior education, and outstanding competence in a particular speciality, such as medicine or nuclear physics. The average man may not know how to solve various problems, but he is an adequate judge of the results of particular governmental policies.

Fear that the conferment of political equality will lead to the demand for many other equalities of an undesirable type is said to be largely unwarranted. In the short run, such demands may occur and result in concessions to the groups insisting upon them, but in the long run the survival of policies designed to produce greater equality is unlikely if it becomes apparent that the results of such policies are detrimental to the interests of the general public. Misconceptions concerning the relationship between democracy and equality are exposable through the process of education and also by means of the lessons of experience.

The proponents of democracy are unimpressed by the talk about elites and the desirability of confining political rights to them. Who are the elite? What are the distinguishing criteria? The wealthy, the captains of industry, the owners of land, the members of blue-blooded families, the possessors of a university degree, the aged, or some other identifiable minority? Those who suggest one or more criteria of the foregoing type are confronted with the necessity of showing that the selected criteria are reliable indicators of an unusual aptitude for government and that failure to confer political privileges exclusively on them endangers the general welfare. The burden of proof rests with the authoritarians.

The claim that democracy is an obstacle to progress receives the response that historical evidence in support of this charge is lacking. At least as much, if not more, progress toward improved living conditions, the conquest of nature, and a better life in general has been made in countries with democratic governments as in those having authoritarian regimes. The achievements of the democracies in science, in engineering, in the arts, in literature, and in the production of wealth have not been surpassed by non-democratic bodies politic.

Arguments to the effect that democracy results in standardization, conformity to mass opinion, and the discouragement of individuality have little merit in the opinion of the proponents of democracy. They contend that the liberties essential to democracy encourage diversity and that genuine equality of opportunity for individuals-in-general to make the most of themselves is more likely to be provided for in the democracies than elsewhere. Authoritarians are by no means dedicated to the cause of liberty and non-conformity. Their past performances justify a contrary conclusion.

The contention that elites act more rationally and less emotionally than most people meets with the usual denial that this is actually the case. Again, an appeal is made to historical experience. Levelheadedness is largely a matter of individual temperament and many of the most intelligent and talented persons the world has known have been guilty of extremely irrational behavior. Allegations to the effect that average human beings who constitute the vast majority of a population tend to be more prejudiced and more irrational than the members of an elite, in their judgments and reactions to the issues that arise in a community, remain to be proved as true.

The discussion so far has amounted to a review of claims and counterclaims. It might be continued to the point of considering every conceivable indictment of democracy and every response to the effect that the charges presented are either untrue or just as applicable to authoritarianism as to democracy. Neither the foes nor the friends of democracy seem open to persuasion by the force of argument. In some cases, the cause of controversy is due to disagreement concerning the nature of democracy or to difference of opinion in regard to the correct interpretation of events. Usually, however, the chief explanation of insistence on the superiority of one type of government to its alternative is that conflicting values are involved. Proving that one value judgment is absolutely right and another unquestionably wrong is a difficult, if not impossible, task. Another factor contributing to persistent controversy is probably the contention that democracy is always preferable to authoritarianism under any and all conditions, or authoritarianism to democracy. If it were conceded that neither is necessarily the better at all times and in all places, agreement might be reached in particular cases that one system is preferable to the other. Under certain conditions, each type of government is advantageous in some respects and disadvantageous in others.

Positive Arguments in Support
of Democracy

A centuries-old contention in favor of democracy, far more widely advanced in the past than today, is that democratic government is a matter of natural right. Various political philosophers have pictured life in a state of nature (as distinguished from civil society), claimed that all persons are equally free under natural law, and asserted that certain disadvantages of living in a state of nature led men, by a contract to which every individual was party, to establish a civil society characterized by governmental institutions. The social contract theories of Locke (17th century) and Rousseau (18th century) were advanced in support of popular government. Not so, for example, that of Hobbes (17th century). Hobbes, who preferred monarchy to either aristocracy or democracy, maintained that the sole reason for the creation of government was the attainment of personal security. His social contract provided for absolute rather than limited government, regardless of the form of government established.

A brief summation of Locke's views will serve the purpose of illustrating the natural rights justification of popular government. Locke asserted that men living in a state of nature under natural law possessed perfect freedom and equality. Unfortunately, their equal freedom was marked by uncertainty because each individual functioned as interpreter, judge, and administrator of the law of nature. To escape from the inconveniences, uncertainties, and dangers to life attributable to this situation, men contracted to join and unite into a community for the preservation of their natural right to life, liberty, and property and for the attainment of a peaceful and secure existence. The contract established a body politic within which "the majority have the right to act and conclude the minority." It was supplemented by a subsequent agreement between the body politic and the persons who were to exercise governmental powers.

Locke stressed consent of the people as the foundation of government and favored a limited government of a representative type. He wrote in support of the Glorious Revolution of 1688 which marked the establishment of limited monarchy and parliamentary supremacy in England. His justification of popular government as a matter of natural right was logically deducible from two propositions, viz., that all men are born free and equal and that the purpose of government is the safeguarding of natural rights. Individuals living in a state of nature would not have agreed to the substitution of civil for natural society if doing so had involved complete subordination to a government in no way subject to popular control.

The "natural right" justification of democracy was incorporated in the Declaration of Independence of 1776. In the words of Thomas Jefferson:

"We hold these truths to be self-evident; that all men are created equal; that they are endowed by their Creator with inherent and unalienable rights; that among these are life, liberty, and the pursuit of happiness; that to secure these rights governments are instituted among men, deriving their just powers from the consent of the governed; that whenever any form of government becomes destructive of these ends, it is the right of the people to alter or to abolish it, and to institute a new government, laying its foundation on such principles and organizing its powers in such form as to them shall seem most likely to effect their safety and happiness."

Although Jefferson was a firm believer in democracy, the quoted words of the Declaration of Independence, if strictly construed, merely assert that the people have the right to choose whatever form of government they prefer and to alter it whenever it no longer safeguards basic inalienable and inherent rights. It may be inferred in the light of conditions then prevailing that a government subject to effective popular control was obviously preferable to an authoritarian governmental system. Whether or not this inference is warranted, the Declaration explicitly states that governments derive their just powers from the consent of the governed.

The contention that individuals have a natural right to the political and other basic freedoms that characterize democracy is a line of argument that many persons today consider unconvincing. Dispute prevails concerning the existence of natural law and natural rights. If the term "natural" simply signifies something that ought to be, the claim that democracy is a natural right amounts to an assertion that democracy is more desirable than authoritarianism, without indicating why. By "natural," some persons mean consistent with or following from the intrinsic nature of men as biological specimens or from the realities of social life at some designated period of time. Or they may have in mind laws which are not man-made—laws which are an expression of divine will, or the dictate of a universal and right reason, or laws of social life which are the inevitable product or resultant of a social process that operates independently of the willing of men. Those who conceive of "natural" in any of these senses are commonly called upon to prove that what they claim is really true. So far, they have been unable to produce absolute proof, at least not to the satisfaction of their principal critics.

The case for democracy need not be based on a natural rights or natural law philosophy. Many of the proponents of democracy present arguments in justification which are unaffected by the controversy about natural law and natural rights.

John Stuart Mill, for example, favored democracy of the representative type for several principal reasons. In discussing the question of the ideally best polity, he asserted, in the first place, that "the rights and interests of every or any persons are only secure from being disregarded when the person interested is himself able, and habitually disposed, to stand up for them," and secondly, "that the general prosperity attains a greater height, and is more widely diffused, in proportion to the amount and variety of the personal energies enlisted in promoting it." "We need not suppose that when power resides in an exclusive class, that class will knowingly and deliberately sacrifice the other classes to themselves; it suffices that, in the absence of its natural defenders, the interest of the excluded is always in danger of being overlooked; and, when looked at, is seen with very different eyes from those of the persons whom it directly concerns." In proportion as any persons are excluded from participation in the process of government, "the interests of the excluded are left without the guarantee accorded to the rest, and they themselves have less scope and encouragement than they might otherwise have to that exertion of their energies for the good of themselves and of the community, to which the general prosperity is always proportioned." [67]

Many other proponents of democratic government have argued that self-government through the devices of democracy is the most effective way of promoting the general welfare. Government of any type involves both the imposition of restraints on human behavior and the determination in some degree of the conditions under which people live. All persons feel the effects of public policies and bear the brunt of the costs incurred. Politically irresponsible rulers should never be entrusted with the establishment of policies which affect the lives, the liberty, and the property of all persons to an extent that is never negligible and, more often than not, extremely great.

Mill also maintained that forms of government have an influence on personal character. He believed that popular government was far superior to any other type in the development of desirable character traits. After distinguishing two types of character, the active and the passive, he asserted that the passive type is favored by the government of one or a few and the active self-helping variety by government of the many. Representative government promotes the development of individual self-help and self-reliance, provides an incentive to self-improvement through self-discipline and education in order to qualify for participation in the governmental process, and tends to develop concern for the public welfare rather than preoccupation solely with selfish, personal interests. Thus democracy does more than enable individuals to protect themselves against misgovernment and free them from dependence on others for promotion of their well-being. It increases the likelihood that individuals in general will become community-minded and more disposed to take the initiative in bringing about the solution of social problems. Active citizenship will replace the passive submission to constituted authority so characteristic of populations in countries with authoritarian governments.[68]

Although Mill considered representative government the ideally best polity, he did not take the position that it was suitable for all communities. He asserted that it could not permanently exist unless a people were willing to receive it, willing and able to do what is necessary for its preservation, and willing and able to fulfill the duties and discharge the functions which it imposes on them. He also stated that there are cases in which some other form of government is preferable, principally when the people, in order to advance in civilization, have some lesson to learn, some habit not yet acquired, to the acquisition of which representative government is likely to be an impediment.[69]

Democracy is also considered preferable to authoritarianism because the freedoms on which it is based are in harmony with the process of social thought. This process, in the words of Ernest Barker, "is a process in which all members of Society can freely share, and to which they can all contribute freely." Barker contends that the state should be true to the society from which it comes and consequently "the process of the activity of the State should also be a process in which all its members can freely share and to which they can all freely contribute." "We may argue," he continues, "that this demand is satisfied, and satisfied only, by the democratic State." Social thought develops "by the way of a plurality of ideas, by the way of debate and discussion between the different ideas" as they come into contact with one another. The democratic process of government corresponds closely to the way in which social thought evolves, i.e., by full and free discussion and the interchange of ideas.[70]

A second main justification of democracy in Barker's opinion is that it contributes to development of the capacities of personality. Like Mill, he emphasizes the value of a process of government that, to some extent, serves a character-building purpose. The justification of a particular system of government is not solely a matter of effective and efficient operation. Due weight should be attached to its effect on the personalities of the individuals comprising the body politic.[71]

Many friends of democracy have argued that it enhances the dignity of the individual because of the basic freedoms conferred upon all persons regardless of differences among them and also because democracy is associated with the conviction that the intrinsic worth of all persons is the same, inasmuch as all are human beings and, as such, equally entitled to make the most of themselves. Democracy rejects the view that some men, by nature, are destined to be slaves or serfs and that only the members of an elite are deserving of freedom and the opportunity to develop their personal capacities to the greatest possible extent. The obvious inequalities among men in intelligence and aptitudes do not alter the fact that human beings equally possess the fundamental characteristics which distinguish man from other living organisms. Proponents of democracy attach great value to the uplifting and stimulating psychological effect, upon individuals in general, of equality in the possession of the basic freedoms that democratic government involves. Each individual is looked upon as an end in himself rather than as a means of serving the interests of a chosen few. Participation in the democratic process of government accomplishes more than the development of mind and character. It frees individuals in general from the feeling that their lives count for little or nothing except as contributors to the welfare of a privileged minority.

Democratic governments are more likely than those of an authoritarian type to pursue policies which create substantial equality of opportunity and promote the general welfare. This probability is due to recognition of the equal worth of all individuals, simply because they are human beings, and to the fact that the democratic process of government provides the opportunity for all individuals, acting singly or collectively, to influence the course of governmental action. Fair consideration of the interests of all individuals and groups is likely to occur in the formulation and adoption of policies by officials who are politically responsible to the voting public.

Democracy in the political sense is asserted to be the best way of securing unity in diversity. Diversity among individuals and groups is a social fact. A democratic system of government is based on recognition of this fact and takes advantage of it in the decision-making process.[72] Lawmaking by representative assemblies, the opportunity to organize political parties and compete for control of the government, the holding of periodic elections, and freedom to criticize and oppose—these features of democracy, as well as others to which attention has been called, indicate both acceptance and utilization of the fact that social life is characterized by many diversities of interest. At the same time, democracy constitutes an effective means of giving expression to the sense of unity which a people possesses. Unity is manifested by acknowledgment of common interests and values, by cooperation for the achievement of desired ends, by participation in the governmental process, and by the general willingness to conform to decisions resulting from the interaction of competing interests and opinions. Democratic government opens the door to eventual agreement on some policy, frequently by way of compromises, which competing interest-groups consider satisfactory on the whole, if not in every respect. Unity is preserved in spite of conflicting interests because of the knowledge that the democratic process provides ample opportunity to bring about changes in policy and also because of the realization that a democratic government functions as the agency of the whole people as distinguished from a privileged class and that its purpose is to promote the interests of all of the groups included within the body politic.

Its accomplishments may fall short of expectations, but intentional exploitation or mistreatment of individuals and groups is less likely to occur than under authoritarian regimes.

The proponents of democracy consider it the best known and most practicable safeguard against arbitrary and capricious government. Public officials who are responsible to the people are not likely to abuse their powers. If they do, their replacement is readily accomplished through the elective process. Furthermore, officials who are subject at all times to public criticism in a community in which freedom of speech prevails seldom prove insensitive to charges of arbitrary action. The risk of tyrannical action by occasional majorities is slight because the democratic political process is characterized by checks and balances that sooner or later result in fair treatment for minority groups. As expressed by Commager with special reference to the United States: "Anyone who has followed the slow and tortuous course of a major public issue—through the arena of public opinion, into the party conventions and caucuses, into the halls of Congress and the rooms of appropriate committees, knows how much of delay, of balance, of compromise, is implicit in our political machinery. A good part of our politics, indeed, seems to be concerned with reconciling majority and minority will, class hostilities, sectional differences, the divergent interests of producer and consumer, of agriculture and labor, of creditor and debtor, of city and country, of tax-payer and tax-beneficiary, of the military and the civilian. In small issues as in great, the result is generally a compromise. Democracy, in short, whether from instinct or from necessity, furnishes its own checks and balances—quite aside from such as may be provided in written constitutions." [73] Whatever the hazards of majority tyranny may be, the proponents of democracy consider them negligible in comparison with the menace of arbitrary and capricious government associated with rulership by the one or the few.

The case for democracy has been summarized by Carl Becker, historian, to be its acceptance, as ends, of the fundamental rational and humane values men have commonly employed in measuring the advance or decline of civilization and also its reliance on a maximum of voluntary assent and a minimum of coercion in order to realize them. These values have been identified as "faith in the dignity and worth of the individual man as an end in himself," the belief that "it is better to be governed by persuasion than by coercion," the belief that "fraternal good will is more worthy than a selfish and contentious spirit," the belief that "in the long run all values are inseparable from the love of truth and the disinterested search for it," and the belief that "knowledge and the power it confers should be used to promote the welfare and happiness of all men rather than to serve the interests of those individuals and classes whom fortune and intelligence endow with temporary advantage." The values just mentioned are older and more universal than democracy and "have a life of their own apart from any particular social system or type of civilization." [74] But democracy accepts these values in theory and realizes them in practice better than other forms of government and is "to that extent in harmony with the age-long impulse to know that which is true and to follow that which is good—. . . ." [75]

Democracy is also looked upon with favor on the ground that it is the only system that permits the people in general to bring about a change in government in a peaceful and orderly manner if and when a change seems advisable. Ballots rather than bullets serve this purpose. If misgovernment occurs in a democracy, the people have the opportunity to rectify the situation at election time in the event that the pressure of public opinion and the criticism of opposition parties fail to bring about an improvement. Under authoritarian regimes, since the popular election of key officials is not available as a remedy, all that the people can do, if persistent criticism fails, assuming that it is permitted, is to resort to tyrannicide or revolution. Steps of this kind may be taken if government is poor in quality or arbitrary and oppressive in character, but the risks are great and the social results may be disastrous, even worse than the conditions that cause recourse to these measures of desperation. Effective, non-violent remedies are denied the people in bodies politic that are organized along authoritarian lines.

It sometimes is claimed that democracy is a preventive of excessive intervention in the affairs of individuals. A democratic government is less likely than an authoritarian type to become over-powerful and to attempt domination of all aspects of community life. In a democracy, the people are able to put a stop to the undue expansion of governmental activities and controls. In the long run, restraints on individual freedom will be tolerated only if the need therefor is clearly essential to promotion of the common welfare.

Still another justification of democracy is that the democratic decision-making procedure is the only one that does not block the possibility of change with respect to social goals. One of the "musts" of science is that the door to inquiry be kept open at all times and never blocked in any way. Men are fallible and consequently are never justified in refusing to consider the possibility that they may be wrong. What appears to be a demonstrated truth may later be shown to be untrue. For example, a given substance may be classified by chemists as an element rather than a compound, but subsequent research may show that it is a compound, not an element. Chemists in general, of course, although they do not always say so, really mean that "so far as we now know" certain substances are elements. The qualifying phrase indicates support for the recommendation that the way of inquiry should never be blocked if individuals desire to know the truth about things. In the social as well as the physical world, search for the truth requires that all obstacles to the way of inquiry be removed.

The foregoing line of reasoning in justfication of democratic government is presented by T. L. Thorson.[76] "Man's situation in politics is but an aspect of his situation in the world generally. The over-riding characteristic of this situation is one of ignorance, of limited intellectual capacity. Socrates was right when he suggested that the essence of wisdom was the recognition of our intellectual limitations. The recognition of these limitations *is* the foundation of sound philosophizing. The human problem with respect to politics is not unlike the human problem with respect to science. Both arise against a background of ignorance and incapacity, and both are to be solved by recognizing these limitations." [77]

As Thorson sees it, "if there is no way of predicting with certitude the consequences of political decisions or of establishing the ultimate "rightness" of any social goals, then any governmental system premised on the realization of such possibilities is not and cannot be justified by such premises." [78] Inasmuch as the rightness of particular political decisions cannot be proved, the establishment of a decision-making procedure that leaves the way open for new ideas and social change is clearly justifiable. The democratic process of government "leaves the way open"; authoritarian systems do not. Democracy's principles of popular sovereignty, political equality, individual political rights, and majority rule, asserts Thorson, constitute a combination that spells out the recommendation: "Do not block the possibility of change with respect to social goals."

The case for democracy, as usually presented, includes a combination of affirmations concerning the merits of democratic government and denials of the various claims made in behalf of authoritarianism. Positive arguments in support of democracy are often attacked on the ground that they are based on premises which are untrue. For example, the natural rights line of reasoning in justification or proof of the claim that democratic government is essential meets with the contention that the natural rights philosophy is merely a myth. Or again, the contention that democracy is the ideal polity because individuals are the best judges and guardians of their own interests is rejected as untenable because it is based on a false major premise.

It is unlikely that rational arguments, pro and con, of one type or another will ever convince all persons that democracy is preferable to authoritarianism, or vice versa, especially not if it be contended that one system is superior to the other under any and all conditions. Particular persons and groups of persons may, of course, attach greater value to some claims than to others and conclude that the weight of argument favors one of the two competing systems. If, in a particular country, the bulk of the population is convinced of the superiority of one of these systems, its demand therefor, if persistent, may result in establishment of the political institutions that are desired.

However, the demand for a particular system is not necessarily due to a rational consideration of arguments pro and con. Rationalization of what is wanted for the sake of satisfying special interests is a common phenomenon. And whether the demands of special interest-groups receive recognition in the structure of government probably depends on their power, on their capacity to get what they want because of their size, their effective organization, their wealth, the importance of their role in the prevailing type of economy, and their possession of various other sources of power. A struggle for power among different interest-groups occurs in all communities. Its outcome depends on the way in which power is distributed. Some power situations are probably more favorable to the establishment and survival of democracy than others.

The sources of power are many. Among them may be ideas. If it were not for belief in the power of ideas, individuals probably would seldom bother to argue for and against some way of life. The disputants about the relative merits of democracy and authoritarianism apparently believe that ideas have an effect on events. They may be right. In view of the fallibility of man, insistence that they are wrong seems inadvisable. Consequently, consideration of the claims for and against both democracy and authoritarianism ought not to be dismissed as a futile pastime.

STUDY QUESTIONS

1. What is the response of the advocates of democracy to the sundry claims of the proponents of authoritarianism?

2. What is the reaction of the friends of democracy to the contention that democratic government results in government by the ignorant and generally incompetent masses?

3. Discuss the question of whether or not democracy has proved an obstacle to progress.

4. What are the various positive arguments in support of democracy? Which of these do you consider most convincing?

5. What are the weaknesses of the "natural rights" justification of democracy?

6. What were John Stuart Mill's principal reasons for favoring democracy of the representative type?

7. Why does Ernest Barker consider democracy preferable to authoritarianism?

8. What are claimed to be the psychological advantages of democracy?

9. What is meant by "unity in diversity?" Why is democracy the best way of achieving unity despite the fact of diversity among individuals?

10. What are the fundamental rational and humane values of men which democracy accepts in theory and realizes in practice better than other forms of government?

11. Discuss the question of whether democracy is an effective guarantee against excessive intervention in the affairs of individuals.

12. How is democratic government justified by T. L. Thorson?

13. To what extent is the future of democracy dependent on rational argument in its favor?

14. If it be true that the few always rule, why consider democracy preferable to authoritarianism?

CHAPTER 10

THE FUTURE

OF DEMOCRACY

A discussion of the future of democracy obviously involves rejection of the contention that democracy is impossible. If democracy is an illusion, as maintained by Michels, Mosca, and Pareto, this monograph represents a waste of time and effort, unless a benefit of some sort is derived from consideration of the fanciful. To those who concede the possibility of democracy and also assert that it exists or has existed in various countries, an inquiry into the prospects for its survival is likely to seem worthwhile, despite the hazards of prognostication.

Any observations about democracy, including predictions concerning its future, depend on what is meant by "democratic government." Many persons think of democracy as a political system under which the will of the majority of the people or of the electorate prevails on questions of policy. Others subscribe to the view that democracy exists in any community in which the people choose those who do the governing and possess adequate

171

opportunity to influence the course of governmental action during the intervals between elections. Conclusions with respect to the existence of democracy in the past, the present, and the future are largely dependent on which of these concepts of democratic government is considered sound. In this chapter, as in those preceding, discussion is based on the opinion that the second definition is superior to the first. The majority-rule conception of democracy is unrealistic.

Modern democracy is a phenomenon of the nineteenth and twentieth centuries. It is the resultant of an evolutionary process which had its beginnings in the distant past. Among the various factors which contributed to its growth were technological developments that changed the character of economic and social life, religious movements, and abuses of power by authoritarian rulers.

Technological innovations brought about the industrial revolution of the eighteenth and nineteenth centuries. Introduction of the factory system stimulated the production of wealth on a much larger scale than had previously been possible and contributed to the trend towards urbanization. The growth of manufacturing, together with a continuation of the expansion of commerce which had begun prior to the industrial revolution, gave rise to the accumulation of wealth in forms other than land and created a wealthy middle class which was able to exact political concessions from ruling autocrats and oligarchies. Economic power ceased to be a monopoly or near-monopoly of landowning aristocrats, as it had been in times past. Laborers, although at first the victims of exploitation by manufacturers, gained economic strength because of their important role in a productive process characterized by the division of labor and mass production. The organization of labor, a comparatively recent development, greatly increased labor's economic and political potency.

Invention of the printing press in the fifteenth century was a technological achievement of great importance. It made possible the extensive diffusion of knowledge which occurred in succeeding centuries. The industrial revolution produced a far greater diversity of interests among individuals and groups than had existed in countries with agricultural economies, but the gradual improvement of methods of communication and transportation brought local communities and different interest-groups into closer contact with one another and resulted in an increasing awareness of common interests.

The diffusion of knowledge and economic power, along with the growing sense of a community of interests, set the stage for broadening the base of the governmental pyramid. Substantial elements of the population in particular countries were in a more favorable position than formerly to combat abuses of governmental authority on the part of politically privileged minorities. Economic and social pressures generated by technological developments contributed greatly to the growth of democratic political institutions in various countries.

Religious movements played a part in the democratizing process. Emphasis on the equal worth of all human beings in the eyes of the Creator and on the inherent dignity of all men furnished doctrinal support for claims to greater political equality. The battle for religious freedom following the Reformation showed that defiance of the powers-that-be could meet with success and also resulted in that toleration of dissent which is one of the requirements of democracy.

Abuses of power and incompetence on the part of authoritarian rulers were largely responsible for movements aimed at limiting the powers of government and providing for more widespread participation in the governmental process. The malfunctioning of autocrats and oligarchies created suffering and discontent sufficiently great to produce demands for reform which led in the direction of a more democratic government and eventually to popular control of public officials in particular communities. James Bryce asserts that "the earlier steps towards democracy came not from any doctrine that the people have a right to rule, but from the feeling that an end must be put to lawless oppression by a privileged class." [79] "When a rising occurred it was because men desired good government, not self-government." [80]

Bryce attributes the progress of popular government in the

modern world to the following four causes: the influence of religious ideas; discontent with royal or oligarchic misgovernment and consequent efforts at reform; social and political conditions favoring equality; and abstract theory.[81] The last of these was a contributing factor of comparatively minor significance.

Bryce's summation of the evolution of democracy in Great Britain shows how slowly the transference of power from the few to the many occurred in that country. "Throughout this long march from feudal monarchy to extreme democracy which occupied three centuries, the masses of the people, whether peasants in the country or artisans in the towns never (except in 1832) clamoured for political power. The ancient system was gradually broken down by the action of a part of the upper class aided by the bulk of the middle classes. The really active forces were, in the earlier stages of the march, the pressure of religious and civil tyranny which could be removed only by setting Parliament above the Crown, while in the later stages the operative causes were: First, the upward economic progress of the middle and humbler classes, which made it seem unfair to keep them in tutelage; secondly, the wish to root out the abuses incident to old-fashioned oligarchies and create a more efficient administration; and thirdly, the tendency of the two political parties to make political capital for themselves by proposals likely to attract both the unenfranchised masses and those who, sympathizing with the masses, thought they would be better cared for if they received full civic rights. Abstract principles, theories of political equality as prescribed by natural justice, played some part only at four epochs: during the Civil War; at the Revolution of 1688; during the years when the contagion of the French Revolutionary spirit of 1789 was active; and lastly, during the Chartist period, when there was much suffering and consequent discontent among the working class." [82]

In the case of the United States, most of the persons settling in the English colonies came from the middle and lower classes. They sought economic betterment and escape from oppression at home. The vast and undeveloped resources of the North

American continent, the availability of land for settlement west of the Atlantic coastal area, the equalizing conditions of frontier life, the absence of a long-established aristocratic tradition, and the remoteness of America from Western Europe were among the special factors which helped produce democratic government in the United States. By the middle of the nineteenth century universal manhood suffrage had been established in most parts of the country. The natural rights ideology was generally accepted as valid inasmuch as it harmonized with the environmental conditions which prevailed in the newly settled land.[83]

Of the principal factors contributing to the evolution of modern democracy, exploitation and oppression of the many by the ruling few and economic and social changes attributable to the industrial revolution were probably the most important. Various other causes, such as the conditions of living in new and undeveloped lands, were operative in particular cases.[84] However, political democracy has failed to materialize in many instances in which the conditions for its development seemed favorable. Neither cultural nor economic advancement, or both in combination, necessarily give rise to democratic government. Nor does misgovernment always lead to the substitution of democracy for authoritarianism. Miscellaneous factors, among them war, a firmly established authoritarian tradition, the absence of serious grievances, and social inertia, may counteract the social forces conducive to democracy. Separate historical investigation is necessary to ascertain the reasons for the presence or absence of democratic political institutions in particular countries.

The Future of Democracy

Predictions about the future of governmental systems are subject to error at any time and especially so during periods of rapid social transformation. Many economic and social changes are presently occurring as a result of the scientific conquest of nature, the mechanization of industry, rising standards of living, and a steadily growing population. Governmental services and regulations are multiplying and the march towards socialization proceeds apace. Private enterprise survives in many countries, but the system is markedly different from that which predominated during the nineteenth century. Large-scale productive operations, even though privately owned and managed, are really collective undertakings. The threat of war is ever-present, and if the great powers should resort to nuclear warfare, mankind may be exterminated. Under these circumstances any pronouncements concerning the outlook for democracy in the decades ahead are necessarily speculative. Reasons for anticipating that it will survive are offset by factors which appear unfavorable to its continued existence.

The fact that an ever-increasing number of people are receiving an adequate education is a condition favoring democracy's survival. Industry's need for scientists, engineers, managerial experts, and skilled workers serves as a stimulus to the establishment of more and better educational institutions and programs. Ignorance is on the wane, not only because of greater emphasis on the social importance of widespread formal education, but also because of the excellent means of disseminating information which are now available and undoubtedly will be improved upon in the years to come. It is doubtful that informed populations will be satisfied for any extended period of time with a political system that denies them an effective voice in government, particularly under conditions which result in an increase in governmental controls and services. However, experience in some countries, e.g., Germany, indicates that an educated public may sometimes prefer authoritarianism to democracy.

The growing importance of government in the lives of individuals should strengthen the desire for democratic political institutions. An expansion of governmental functions seems inevitable in highly complex societies. That being the case, it is improbable that people will favor rulership by a politically irresponsible minority in preference to an arrangement which enables the general public to decide, from time to time, who shall do the governing and also permits individuals and groups to influence the shaping of policy through exercise of the freedoms associated with democracy.

Scientific and technological progress has promoted economic well-being in many countries. It also has resulted in a high degree of functional specialization in modern society. In some respects these developments brighten the outlook for democracy. Greater economic security places people in a better position to demand meaningful political rights. Political power is not easily acquired by poverty-stricken populations. The economic position of most men is also strengthened by the division of labor in the production of wealth and by the resultant interdependence of the numerous participants in the productive process. Groups which render indispensable services are able to bargain effectively for political as well as economic privileges, provided such groups become organized and take full advantage of their opportunities. Strikes and other obstructionist practices afford means of paralyzing or slowing down wealth production to so great an extent that the political and other grievances of interest-groups cannot long be ignored. Economic power, one of the sources of political power, no longer depends primarily on the ownership of property.

The prospects for democracy are darkened by some of the social consequences of technological innovations. Its future may be endangered by the complexity of social life and by the increasingly vast operations of government attributable to this fact and to the unprecedented growth of population made possible by the solution of major health and economic problems. Conditions such as these tend to elevate the position of experts and bureaucrats in the social structure. The ultimate result may be irresponsible rulership by the specialist and managerial classes.

The replacement of men by machines is by no means a new development, but when this phenomenon occurs at a rapid rate it creates problems which, if unsolved, probably constitute more of a threat to democracy than to authoritarianism. As the ranks of the unemployed and discontented grow in size, the chances that some form of authoritarianism will replace democracy increase. Loss of economic power by a substantial proportion of the population may result in the loss of significant political privileges. Many persons, becoming convinced that economic security is more important than political liberty, may lend support to opponents of democracy who promise a prompt solution of the unemployment and other economic problems.

A consequence of large-scale industry and the increasingly great degree of social interdependence has been the collectivization of productive enterprises, including those which continue to be privately owned and managed. Public enterprises have grown in number and governmental regulation of private interests has been expanding steadily. Various countries have substituted a socialized or largely socialized economy for an essentially private enterprise system. An era of creeping socialization has begun. The effect of these developments on democracy's future is a matter of controversy.

The contentions on both sides of this question have been reviewed in a preceding chapter. Many persons concede that the co-existence of democracy with a socialized economy is possible. Others go so far as to maintain that economic socialization is essential to the attainment of democracy in fact as well as in form. Those who disagree either assert that a private enterprise economy is indispensable to the survival of democracy or contend that the maintenance of democracy in fact, even if formally established, will become extremely difficult if economic and political power are concentrated in the same hands. The latter point of view is based on the fear that people whose employment opportunities and economic resources are completely under the control of public officials will become too subservient to the latter to exercise their political privileges as freely as genuine democracy requires. Apprehension concerning democracy's survival is also attributable to the anticipated dangerous consequences of government ownership and control of all sources of information, including newspapers, radio, and television. It will be easy for officials to mislead the public and difficult to preserve the freedom of speech which is so essential to the democratic process.

Socialization may prove fatal to democracy, as many of the proponents of capitalism contend, or it may be a necessary condition to fulfillment of the democratic idea, as its most enthusiastic advocates maintain. Experience in one country will probably differ from that in another and perhaps the determining factor will be non-economic in character, such as the strength of the democratic tradition at a particular time and place or the degree of cultural advancement of a particular people.

Two menaces to democracy are international warfare and bitter internal dissension concerning the proper way of eliminating deep-seated social maladjustments. War involves resort to authoritarian practices, breeds intolerance, and endangers the survival of basic freedoms, especially freedom of speech. Peace is more conducive to the development and successful functioning of democratic political institutions. It is difficult to believe that a continuation of international crises resulting in war or serious threats of war can have anything other than an adverse effect on the future of democracy. As for bitter internal dissension, a frequent consequence is the breeding of irreconcilable attitudes and demands which hinder, if they do not prevent, the settlement of controversies through discussion and negotiation. Bullets may be substituted for ballots, as they were on the occasion of the Civil War in the United States, and as they have been in other countries. Various scholars have concluded that consensus in regard to the fundamental features of social life is requisite to the existence and proper working of democracy. If consensus disappears, the disappearance of democracy is probable. This conclusion, like so many others concerning democratic government, has been criticized on the ground of lack of conclusive evidence.[85]

More than forty years ago, James Bryce asserted that popular government has usually been sought, won, and valued, not as a good thing in itself, but as a means of getting rid of tangible grievances or of securing tangible benefits. When these objectives have been attained, the interest in democracy has tended to decline. He also said: "Popular government has not yet been proved to guarantee, always and everywhere, good government.

If it be improbable, yet it is not unthinkable that as in many countries impatience with tangible evils substituted democracy for monarchy or oligarchy, a like impatience might some day reverse the process."[86] This statement was made shortly after the conclusion of World War I at the height of optimism concerning the spreading of democracy throughout the world. Subsequent events have furnished ample evidence in substantiation of Bryce's cautiously worded observation.

Although neither the establishment nor the disappearance of democratic government is predictable with any high degree of certainty, it is likely that the survival of democracy in particular judisdictions will depend in large measure on the quality of its performance and on the extent and intensity of devotion to its principles. Loss of faith is apt to occur if the democratic process proves unequal to the task of solving the problems confronting a specific country. Growing discontent may very well lead to its replacement by some type of authoritarianism. But the life expectancy of an authoritarian government is also probably dependent on its utility in meeting the needs of a politically organized community. If it fails to do so, a democratic system may take its place, as has happened in the past.

Improvement in the operational effectiveness of democratic governments should increase their chances of survival. A weakness which has become evident in some democracies is the endeavor of the legislature to assume the role of leadership in policy-determination instead of confining its activities to exercising various controls over the executive, to approval or disapproval of the executive's policy recommendations, and to functioning as an organ for the expression of public opinion. The complexity of government in modern society is so great that the executive is better qualified than a large and unwieldy legislative assembly for discharge of the function of leadership in the solution of numerous extremely complicated problems.

In discussing the malady of democratic government in the twentieth century, Walter Lippmann distinguishes between 1] *governing* which he defines as the administration of the laws and the initiative in legislating and 2] *representing* the living persons who are governed. He attributes the weakness of democratic government to a derangement of these primary functions. The "governing" function which should be discharged by the executive has been taken over in large measure by the "representative" legislature. "The power of the executive has become enfeebled, often to the verge of impotence, by the pressures of the representative assembly and of mass opinions. This derangement of the governing power has forced the democratic states to commit disastrous and, it could be, fatal mistakes. It has also transformed the assemblies in most, perhaps not in all, democratic states from the defenders of local and personal rights into boss-ridden oligarchies, threatening the security, the solvency, and the liberties of the state." [87] Devitalization of the governing power (as defined by Lippmann) is said to be the malady of democratic states. "As the malady grows the executives become highly susceptible to encroachment and usurpation by elected assemblies; they are pressed and harassed by the higgling of parties, by the agents of organized interests, and by the spokesmen of sectarians and ideologues. The malady can be fatal." [88]

Lippmann's view that the modern democratic state suffers from a radical deficiency and his diagnosis of the nature of this deficiency is disputable, but his observation that serious shortcomings in a governmental system can be fatal is sound. Weak governments, be they democratic or authoritarian in character, are likely to be short-lived.

In the years to come, as at present, both democratic and authoritarian governments will probably co-exist in the world community. Democracy's future in particular countries depends on the outcome of a continuous reaction between social forces that tend to produce authoritarianism and those which are conducive to the origin and survival of democratic political institutions. At one time the resultant of this reaction may be a democratic system; at another time an authoritarian regime. No one can foretell accurately which of these competing and conflicting forces will predominate in particular countries and for how long, but the survival chances of democracy seem fairly good in places where it has gained a firm foothold and proved reasonably successful in discharging the heavy responsibilities of government in modern society.

STUDY QUESTIONS

1. What factors contributed to the emergence and growth of democratic government?

2. What was the significance of technological innovation in bringing about the substitution of democracy for authoritarianism?

3. What contributions to the development of democracy were associated with religious movements?

4. What is Bryce's explanation of the earlier steps toward democracy? What are the causes to which Bryce attributes the progress of popular government in the modern world?

5. Why are predictions about the future of governmental systems, including democracy, hazardous?

6. What are some of the reasons for anticipating the survival of democracy?

7. What social consequences of technological innovations darken the prospects for democracy's survival?

8. Why is international warfare a menace to democracy?

9. Why is bitter internal dissension a threat to the continuance of democratic government in a given country?

10. Discuss the importance of the quality of democratic government as a determinant of its prospects for survival.

11. Explain Lippmann's view concerning the malady of democratic government in the twentieth century.

12. What are your views in regard to the future of democracy?

END NOTES

CHAPTER 1

1. Aristotle, in discussing aristocracy, stated that the rulers are the best men or have at heart the best interests of the state and its citizens.

2. *The Federalist Papers*, No. 10.

3. In some "representative" democracies, direct action by the qualified voters on questions of policy sometimes occurs through such devices for direct legislation as the initiative and the referendum. Submission of constitutions and constitutional amendments to the voters for approval also is provided for in some bodies politic.

4. J. W. Garner, *Political Science and Government* (New York, American Book Co., 1928), p. 317.

5. J. Bryce, *Modern Democracies* (New York, The Macmillan Co., 1921), Vol. I, p. 22. With permission of The Macmillan Company.

6. J. A. Schumpeter, *Capitalism, Socialism, and Democracy*, 3rd ed. (New York, Harper & Brothers, 1950), p. 269.

7. *Ibid.*, p. 273.

8. E. E. Schattschneider, *The Semi-Sovereign People* (New York, Holt, Rinehart and Winston, 1960), p. 141.

9. R. M. MacIver, *The Ramparts We Guard* (New York, The Macmillan Co., 1952), pp. 27, 28. With permission of The Macmillan Company.

10. F. A. Hermens, *The Representative Republic* (Notre Dame, University of Notre Dame Press, 1958), p. 31.

CHAPTER 2

11. The term "election" is used in this text to signify either direct choice by the body of qualified voters or choice by the vote of

persons whom the qualified voters have selected for the sole purpose of choosing designated officials. In the latter case indirect election occurs. In most democracies "direct election" is preferred to the "indirect" type. Direct election may be indicated at times by such phrases as "popular election" or "choice by the electorate."

The term "appointment" signifies selection by such organs of government as the chief executive, department heads, the legislative body, or the courts. In the case of a plural body like a legislature, its members may vote to determine who shall be appointed to a particular position, but this mode of choice is not included within the meaning of the term "election" as herein used. It may be argued that legislative selection is a mode of indirect election if the electorate has chosen the members of the legislature. However, it seems more appropriate to speak of "legislative appointment" inasmuch as members of a legislature are chosen primarily for purposes other than the selection of certain officials.

Modes of selection other than either election or appointment are sometimes resorted to in "democracies." Examples are choice by lot (selection of jurors) and the inheritance of office, e.g., the British House of Lords. The compatibility of inheritance of office with democratic government depends on the powers assigned to and actually exercised by a body composed of hereditary members.

12. The question of administrative feasibility should be considered during the process of policy formulation in the broader sense, i.e., the determination of objectives and the general ways of attaining them. But after a general policy decision has been made, officials responsible for its execution still need to settle matters of administrative policy.

13. Policy in the sense of ends sought and general ways of achieving them; not issues of administrative policy.

14. In the United States, judges of the national (federal) judiciary are appointed by the President with the advice and consent of the Senate. A minority of the states provide for appointment.

15. The recall is characterized by the filing of a petition demanding removal which is followed by an election at which the voters decide the issue. Qualified voters are eligible to sign the petition and

a prescribed minimum number of signatures is required. The details of recall procedure vary considerably among the bodies politic providing for this mode of removal.

16. The abuses of power referred to are those believed likely to develop if the officials who enact laws also administer them and decide controversies arising under the law. In the words of Madison (Federalist Papers, No. 47); "The accumulation of all powers, legislative, executive, and judiciary, in the same hands, whether of one, a few, or many, and whether hereditary, self-appointed, or elective, may justly be pronounced the very definition of tyranny."

17. Some countries, e.g., Great Britain, require membership in the legislature, either the upper or the lower chamber, if there be two; some permit outsiders as well as members to serve in the cabinet; occasionally, membership in the legislature is prohibited.

18. "Dissolution" means termination of the existence or "life" of the legislative body.

19. "Judicial independence" may also be associated with other forms of government, e.g., the cabinet-parliamentary plan. The phrase means that the courts are free to decide cases without interference on the part of other branches of government or by private persons or groups. Under a separation of powers type of government, judicial independence is based on constitutional guarantees against invasive action by the other branches of government. Statutory provisions are relied on to prevent intervention by private interests. In the case of a governmental system organized in accordance with the doctrine of integration, judicial independence depends on the policy pursued by the dominant branch of government. This branch must voluntarily provide by law for an independent judiciary.

20. A suspensive differs from an absolute veto in that the former may be overridden by the legislative body.

21. No President may be selected for two successive terms.

22. Other controls over administration are available to the council. Examples are control of the purse strings and the adoption of ordinances dealing with matters of administrative organization and procedure.

23. Other forms of government may be equally satisfactory in this respect.

CHAPTER 3

24. *Supra.*, Chapter I.

25. The Supreme Court of the United States subscribes to a much broader and questionable conception of weighted voting in taking the position that legislative districting schemes which give the same number of representatives to unequal numbers of constituents have the effect of debasing or diluting the weight of a citizen's vote (*Wesberry v. Sanders*, 376 U. S. 1; *Reynolds v. Sims*, 377 U. S. 533).

Plural voting, sometimes equated with weighted voting, assumes different forms. One type involves the casting of a ballot in more than one constituency. For example, a person may be permitted to vote in one constituency because he resides there and in another because he owns real property or conducts a business within its territorial limits. In the case of functional representation, an individual would be entitled to vote in as many functional constituencies as his membership in different associations warranted. Various factors require consideration in passing judgment on the compatibility of this type of plural voting and democracy. For instance, permitting a person to participate in the selection of officials of two different municipalities is an arrangement that differs from one under which an individual is allowed to vote in two or more constituencies for the purpose of selecting members of a national legislature. The latter situation is a feature of functional representation—a scheme of representation which many persons would hesitate to condemn as "undemocratic."

26. *National Civic Review*, Vol. LII, No. 6, June 1963, p. 328.

27. Congressional districts: *Wesberry v. Sanders*, 376 U. S. 1; state legislatures and the equal protection clause: *Reynolds v. Sims*, 377 U. S. 533; *WMCA, Inc. v. Lomenzo*, 377 U. S. 633: *Lucas v. Forty-Fourth General Assembly of the State of Colorado*, 377 U. S. 713; *Maryland Committee for Fair Representation v. J. Millard Tawes*, 377 U. S. 656; *Davis v. Mann*, 377 U. S. 678; *Roman v. Sincock*, 377 U. S. 695.

The Equal Protection Clause reads as follows: "No State shall . . . deny to any person within its jurisdiction the equal protection of the laws." Equal protection has been construed to prohibit arbitrary, capricious, and unreasonable discrimination or classification.

CHAPTER 4

28. "Colonizing" means moving individuals into an electoral district temporarily, prior to an election, for the purpose of gaining a victory. "Repeating" signifies voting more than once at a particular polling place or traveling from precinct to precinct and casting a vote in each.

29. For an explanation of the Hallett and Nanson systems, see Hoag and Hallett, *Proportional Representation* (New York, The Macmillan Co., 1926) Appendix X, pp. 480-508.

30. In some jurisdictions using the Bucklin system, a third choice may be expressed for more than one candidate. But no candidate under either arrangement may be given a first, second, and third choice rating by the same voter.

31. The degree of correspondence depends on the number of seats to be filled. The larger this number, the closer the relationship between the percentage of votes polled by a group and the number of seats it obtains.

32. An available preference is a candidate who has neither been elected nor defeated. The random selection of surplus ballots involves a negligible chance of error.

CHAPTER 5

33. In some democracies provision is made for either the initiative or the referendum or both. Popular ratification of proposed constitutions or constitutional amendments also is provided for in some jurisdictions.

34. Majority votes commonly determine the action taken by collective bodies included in an authoritarian system of government.

35. James K. Pollock, *Making Michigan's New Constitution, 1961-1962*, (Ann Arbor, Wahr Publishing Co., 1962), p. 17.

36. A definition of public opinion, among others in circulation, which differs from the one presented above, is that only widely-held opinion deserves description as "public" and that a judgment qualifies as an "opinion" only if it has been reached, by the persons proclaiming it, after the careful consideration of evidence pertinent to the matter at issue. This definition is obviously narrower than one which comprehends the totality of opinions ascribable to the individuals and groups comprising the population of a body politic.

37. Rules of procedure of a legislature may be of such a character that the views of the few rather than of the many prevail on questions of policy. A case in point is the power of standing committees in the Congress of the United States. Ordinarily, only bills reported on favorably by a standing committee receive consideration. A committee chairman is able to pigeonhole introduced bills to which he is opposed. His chairmanship, obtainable only if his party holds a majority of the seats in the chamber of which he is a member, is due to his seniority as measured by consecutive terms of service. Although he represents only a small fraction of the entire electorate of the United States, he is able to delay, if not prevent, the passage of legislation which he dislikes, no matter how widely supported a particular policy may be. His powerful position enables him to force compromises which otherwise would be rejected by the sponsors of a proposed law.

CHAPTER 6

38. Freedom of speech, freedom of assembly, freedom of association, and freedom from arbitrary arrest and imprisonment.

39. In some cases, as in the Fourth and Fifth French Republics, the constitutional committee or council is essentially a political body rather than a court in the strict sense of the latter term.

All courts in the United States may rule on constitutional issues if involved in cases brought before them. Final interpretation rests with the courts of last resort—the Supreme Court with respect to the Constitution of the United States and the court of last resort of each state in regard to the state's constitution.

40. In approximately three-fourths of the states of the United States, most judges are chosen by popular vote for limited terms of service—all judges in twenty-one of these states. The removal process is usually difficult. In eight states judges may be recalled by popular vote. No provision is made for a popular veto of judicial rulings.

41. This stipulation does not apply to the judges of courts created by Congress in the exercise of legislative powers based on constitutional provisions other than those included in Article III. Examples of "legislative" as distinguished from "constitutional" courts are courts established in the territorial possessions of the United States. Under Article IV, Congress is authorized to dispose of and make all needful rules and regulations respecting the territory belonging to the United States.

42. Proposal of an amendment requires a two-thirds vote in each house of Congress and the calling of a constitutional convention depends on a petition to that effect by the legislatures of two-thirds of the states. Ratification of a proposed amendment requires an affirmative vote of three-fourths of the states acting through their legislatures or specially chosen conventions, as specified by Congress.

43. "Perhaps in the end the problem of judicial review comes to this: is the accommodation of modern needs to ancient traditions (whether or not embodied in formal, written documents), is reconciliation of stability and change, essentially a judicial or a political function? Of course, we do not cling exclusively to one or the other. It is a matter of shifting tendency or degree on which the great democratic peoples—the British and the American—lean in opposite directions. That they are committed to legislative, and we to judicial, supremacy may rest in part on differing political party structures. The British have responsible parties; we do not. In any case, as a matter of history under both systems the pressure of public opinion in the long run seems finally to prevail. Provided the long run is not too long, surely this is as it should be in democratic countries." This quotation is from W. Mendelson, *The Constitution and the Supreme Court* (New York, Dodd, Mead, & Co., Inc., 1959), pp. 5-6.

44. Examples of judge-made law are the common law and judicial interpretations of statutes and constitutional provisions.

45. Child labor legislation limits the right of children to work and imposes obligations on employers. Limitations on the length of the working day and week for women may differ from those applying to men, as may legal stipulations concerning minimum wages. In these instances, the resultant legal inequalities are justifiable on the ground that age in one case and sex in the others, if disregarded, might adversely affect the health and/or morals of children and women. But equality before the law requires that all women and all children be subject to the same policy, whatever it may be.

46. "To treat men equitably we must often treat them differently, according to their situation and need," R. M. MacIver, *The Ramparts We Guard* (New York, The Macmillan Co., 1950), p. 126. With permission of The Macmillan Company.

CHAPTER 7

47. Among the basic enterprises are the steel industry, automobile manufacturing, power and light production, coal mining, transportation and communication services, and banking. Examples of minor undertakings are dry-cleaning establishments, laundries, automobile repair shops, and the servicing of radio and television sets.

48. Both quotations are from J. A. Schumpeter, *Capitalism, Socialism, and Democracy*, 3rd ed. (New York, Harper and Brothers Publishers, 1950), p. 415.

49. "In the light of the recent platforms and performances of the socialist parties comprising the Socialist International it [socialism] cannot be fairly defined merely as collective ownership of all the principal means of production and distribution by a democratic state. With varying degrees of explicitness socialist parties in office or on the road to office have accepted, at least for an indefinite present, a mixed economy with a large degree of ownership and control not only by voluntary cooperatives of producers and consumers but by private individuals," Norman Thomas, "Rethinking Socialism," *The Virginia Quarterly Review*, Vol. XXXIV (Winter 1958), p. 45.

50. The entrepreneurial function includes deciding what to produce and what mode of production to use. It involves provision of the needed instruments of production and assumption of both the responsibilities and risks associated with planning and the effectuation of plans.

51. "State ownership," as the phrase is used herein, comprehends instances in which the central government of the state is the owner of enterprises and also cases of ownership by local governments, e.g., municipally-owned transportation systems or power and light plants.

The ownership of instruments of production by a group such as a producers' or consumers' cooperative is not the equivalent of public or state ownership, even though socialists look with favor on the co-operative movement and sometimes refer to ownership by a cooperative as a form of public ownership. Cooperatives are no more "public" in character than an incorporated manufacturing enterprise having stockholders numbered by the hundreds or thousands. Customarily, the term "public" has meant the entire population of a territorially demarcated community, i.e., the people, indefinitely.

52. The management and operation of a publicly or state-owned enterprise may be entrusted to a governmental department, to a state-appointed board, to a governmental or public corporation, or to a producers' or consumers' cooperative. Cooperatives, if selected for the purpose of management and operation, function as agencies of the state or public in the production of particular commodities or services. In such instances, the cooperatives, although in charge of production, are not the owners of the enterprises which they manage.

53. Part Two, ninth paragraph.

54. *Programme of the Communist Party of the Soviet Union*, Part Two, paragraph 11.

55. *Ibid.*, paragraph 3.

56. *Ibid.*, Part Two, III, 2, paragraph 8.

57. Section VII, 2nd paragraph.

58. *The Road to Serfdom* (Chicago, University of Chicago Press, copyright 1944 by the University of Chicago).

59. *Ibid.*, p. 57.

60. *Ibid.*, pp. 61-62, 70.

61. *Ibid.*, p. 69.

62. *The Web of Government* (New York, The Macmillan Co., 1947), pp. 357-358. With permission of The Macmillan Company.

CHAPTER 8

63. As asserted by G. Mosca, *The Ruling Class* (New York, McGraw-Hill Book Co., 1939. Used by permission.) pp. 50, 51, 61: "In all societies . . . two classes of people appear—a class that rules and a class that is ruled. The first class, always the less numerous, performs all political functions, monopolizes power and enjoys the advantages that power brings, ... granting that the discontent of the masses might succeed in deposing a ruling class, inevitably . . . there would have to be another organized minority within the masses themselves to discharge the functions of a ruling class. Otherwise all organization, and the whole social structure, would be destroyed . . . all ruling classes tend to become hereditary in fact if not in law."

64. "Leadership is a necessary phenomenon in every form of social life. . . . there is a great scientific value in the demonstration that every system of leadership is incompatible with the most essential postulates of democracy. We are now aware that the law of the historic necessity of oligarchy is primarily based upon a series of facts of experience." . . .
"Every party organization represents an oligarchical power grounded upon a democratic basis. We find everywhere electors and elected. Also we find everywhere that the power of the elected leaders over the electing masses is almost unlimited. The oligarchical structure of the building suffocates the basic democratic principle." See Robert Michels, *Political Parties* (New York, Dover Publications, Inc., 1959), pp. 400, 401.

65. *Notes on Democracy* (New York, A. A. Knopf, 1926), pp. 16-55.

66. Neither Mussolini nor Hitler were hereditary rulers belonging to a royal family. Both were sons of middle-class parents. They were leaders of movements which involved the organization of a party, in one case the Fascist Party and in the other the National Socialist Party. These parties served as devices for gaining power, for maintaining the dictatorships against any opposition that might develop, and for cultivating widespread public support through use of propaganda or, if necessary, ruthless strong-arm techniques. In Britain during the eighteenth century and the early part of the nineteenth, political power was concentrated in the nobility, the higher clergy, and the propertied classes, especially the landowners. The government of the German Empire was an hereditary autocracy supported by a powerful landed aristocracy. Japan's government was autocratic for an extended period of time but during the decade or so immediately preceding the second world war of the twentieth century ultimate control over governmental policy was wielded by an administrative bureaucracy within which the military element predominated. The Emperor remained as an important ruler but the government was more of an oligarchy than an autocracy.

CHAPTER 9

67. The quotations in this paragraph are from J. S. Mill, *Utilitarianism, Liberty, and Representative Government* (New York, E. P. Dutton & Co., 1948, No. 482 of Everyman's Library), pp. 208, 209, 211. With permission of E. P. Dutton & Co., and J. M. Dent & Sons, Ltd.

68. *Ibid.*, pp. 211-216.

69. *Ibid.*, pp. 218-227.

70. The quoted phrases are those of E. Barker, *Principles of Social and Political Theory* (New York, Oxford University Press, 1951) pp. 204, 206.

71. *Ibid.*, pp. 208-209

72. R. M. MacIver, *The Ramparts We Guard* (New York, The Macmillan Co., 1950), Chapter 13; *The Web of Government* (New York, The Macmillan Co., 1947) pp. 403-446.

73. Henry Commager, *Majority Rule and Minority Rights* (New York, Oxford University Press, 1943), pp. 58-59.

74. The quoted phrases are from Carl Becker, "Some Generalities That Still Glitter," *New Liberties for Old* (New Haven, Yale University Press, 1941), pp. 124-151.

75. Carl Becker, *Freedom and Responsibility in the American Way of Life* (New York, A. A. Knopf, 1947), p. 64.

76. *The Logic of Democracy* (New York, Holt, Rinehart and Winston, 1962).

77. *Ibid.*, pp. 133-134.

78. *Ibid.*, p. 137.

CHAPTER 10

79. *Modern Democracies* (New York, The Macmillan Co., 1921), Vol. I, p. 26. With permission of The Macmillan Company.

80. *Ibid.*, p. 27.

81. *Ibid.*

82. *Ibid.*, pp. 31-32. The Chartists demanded political and social reforms. A People's Charter, drafted in 1838, included six points, viz., universal manhood suffrage, a secret ballot, abolition of property qualifications for members of Parliament, salaries for members of Parliament, annual elections, and equal electoral districts. Bryce's chapter on "The Historical Evolution of Democracy" contains brief observations about developments in various countries, including, in addition to Great Britain, the United States, Australia, Canada, France, and Switzerland. He also mentions causes which retarded or arrested the growth of democracy in certain countries, e.g., Germany.

83. For a brief but excellent discussion of the American political tradition see C. L. Becker, *Freedom and Responsibility in the American Way of Life* (New York, Alfred A. Knopf, 1947), Chapter I.

84. After pointing out that industrialization resulted in the formation of economic centers of power quite apart from the political centers and that economic power never was separable from the political prior to the industrial age, R. M. MacIver asserts that the state "thus moved towards democracy, not through the temporary insurrection of a subject class but through the operation of economic forces which reconstituted the basis of society," *The Modern State* (London, Oxford University Press, 1926), pp. 138, 140. The same author discusses the coming of democracy in *The Web of Government* (New York, The Macmillan Co., 1947), pp. 175-192.

According to C. L. Becker, historian, "In modern times democratic institutions have, generally speaking, been most successful in new countries, such as the United States, Canada, and Australia, where the conditions of life have been easy for the people; and in European countries more or less in proportion to their industrial prosperity. In European countries, indeed, there has been a close correlation between the development of the industrial revolution and the emergence of democratic institutions," *Modern Democracy* (New Haven, Yale University Press, 1941), p. 13.

85. See C. J. Friedrich, *Man and His Government* (New York, McGraw-Hill Book Co., 1963), pp. 344-345.

86. *Modern Democracies* (New York, The Macmillan Co., 1921), Vol. I, p. 42. With permission of The Macmillan Company.

87. *Essays in the Public Philosophy* (Boston, Little, Brown, & Co., 1955), pp. 54-55.

88. *Ibid.*, p. 27.

SELECTED READINGS

GROUP I

1. This is the phrase of A. D. Lindsay in *The Modern Democratic State* (Oxford University Press, 1943), Chap. 1.

SELECTED BIBLIOGRAPHY

Abernethy, G. L. ed., *The Idea of Equality* (Richmond, John Knox Press, 1959)

Agard, W. R., *What Democracy Meant to the Greeks* (Chapel Hill, University of North Carolina Press, 1942)

Babbitt, I., *Democracy and Leadership* (Boston, Houghton Mifflin Co., 1924)

Barbu, Z., *Democracy and Dictatorship* (New York, Grove Press, 1956)

Barker, E., *The Citizen's Choice* (Cambridge, Eng., The University Press, 1938)

Barker, E., *Reflections on Government* (New York, Oxford University Press, 1942)

Becker, C. L., *Modern Democracy* (New Haven, Yale University Press, 1941)

Becker, C. L., *New Liberties for Old* (New Haven, Yale University Press, 1941)

Boyd, W. J. D., *Patterns of Apportionment* (New York, National Municipal League, 1962)

Brogan, D. W. & Verney, D. V., *Political Patterns in Today's World* (New York, Harcourt, Brace & World, Inc., 1963)

Brogan, D. W., *The Free State* (London, H. Hamilton, 1945)

Bryce, J., *Modern Democracies*, Vols. I and II (New York, The Macmillan Co., 1921)

Cahn, E., *The Predicament of Democratic Man* (New York, The Macmillan Co., 1961)

Carr, E. H., *The New Society* (New York, St. Martin's Press, Inc., 1957)

Cary, J., *Power In Men* (Seattle, University of Washington Press, 1963)

Chambers, W. N. & Salisbury, R. H., eds., *Democracy in the Mid-Twentieth Century* (St. Louis, Washington University Press, 1960)

Chandler, A. R., *The Clash of Political Ideals*, 3rd ed. (New York, Appleton-Century-Crofts, 1957)

Chase, H. W. & Dolan, P., *The Case for Democratic Capitalism* (New York, Thomas Y. Crowell Co., 1964)

Coker, F. W., *Recent Political Thought* (New York, D. Appleton-Century Co., 1934), Chapters X-XIII.

Cram, R. A., *The Nemesis of Mediocrity* (Boston, Marshall Jones Co., 1921)

Dahl, R. A., *A Preface to Democratic Theory* (Chicago, University of Chicago Press, 1956)

Dickinson, J., "Democratic Realities and Democratic Dogma," *Am. Pol. Sci. Rev.*, XXIV, May, 1930, pp. 283-309

Ebenstein, W., *Today's Isms*, 3rd ed. (Englewood Cliffs, N. J., Prentice-Hall, Inc., 1961)

Fosdick, D., *What is Liberty?* (New York, Harper & Brothers, 1939)

Friedrich, C. J., *The New Belief in the Common Man* (Boston, Little, Brown & Co., 1942)

Gardner, J. W., *Excellence* (New York, Harper and Brothers, 1961)

Glover, T. R., *Democracy in the Ancient World* (Cambridge, Eng., The University Press, 1927)

Golob, E. O., *The "Isms"* (New York, Harper and Bros., 1954)

Hale, R. L., *Freedom Through Law* (New York, Columbia University Press, 1952)

Hallowell, J. H., *The Moral Foundations of Democracy* (Chicago, University of Chicago Press, 1954)

Hartz, L., "Democracy: Image and Reality," Cooperman, D. & Walter, E. V., *Power and Civilization* (New York, Thomas Y. Crowell Co., 1962) pp. 374-387

Hermens, F. A., *The Representative Republic* (Notre Dame, University of Notre Dame Press, 1958)

Hook, S., *Political Power and Personal Freedom* (New York, Criterion Books, 1959)

Hudson, J. W., *Why Democracy?* (New York, D. Appleton-Century Co., 1936)

Kitson Clark, G. S. R., *The Kingdom of Free Men* (Cambridge, Eng., The University Press, 1957)

Kornhauser, W., *The Politics of Mass Society* (Glencoe, Ill., The Free Press, 1959)

Labin, S., *The Secret of Democracy* (New York, The Vanguard Press, 1955)

Laird, J., *The Device of Government* (Cambridge, Eng., The University Press, 1944)

Lane, R. E., *Political Ideology* (New York, Free Press of Glencoe, 1962)

Larsen, J. A. O., *Representative Government in Greek and Roman History* (Berkeley, University of California Press, 1955)

Laski, H. J., *Liberty in the Modern State* (New York, Harper and Bros., 1930)

Lauterbach, A. T., *Economic Security and Individual Freedom* (Ithaca, Cornell University Press, 1948)

Lippmann, W., *Essays in the Public Philosophy* (Boston, Little, Brown & Co., 1955)

Lipson, L., *The Democratic Civilization* (New York, Oxford University Press, 1964)

Livingston, J. C. and Thompson, R. G., *The Consent of the Governed* (New York, The Macmillan Co., 1963)

MacIver, R. M., *Leviathan and the People* (University, Louisiana State University Press, 1939)

MacIver, R. M., *The Ramparts We Guard* (New York, The Macmillan Co., 1952)

Mayo, H. B., *An Introduction to Democratic Theory* (New York, Oxford University Press, 1960)

Mayo, H. B., *Democracy and Marxism* (New York, Oxford University Press, 1955)

McKeon, R., ed., *Democracy in a World of Tensions* (Chicago, University of Chicago Press, 1951)

Myers, H. A., *Are Men Equal?* (Ithaca, New York, Great Seal Books, 1955)

Neumann, F., *The Democratic and the Authoritarian State* (Glencoe, Ill., The Free Press, 1957)

Ortega y Gasset, J., *The Revolt of the Masses* (New York, W. W. Norton & Co., 1932)

Pennock, J. R., *Liberal Democracy* (New York, Rinehart & Co., 1950)

Perry, C. M., ed., *The Philosophy of American Democracy* (Chicago, University of Chicago Press, 1943)

Riemer, N., *The Revival of Democratic Theory* (New York, Appleton-Century-Crofts, 1962)

Roche, J. P. & Stedman, M. S., *The Dynamics of Democratic Government* (New York, McGraw-Hill Book Co., 1954)

Rockefeller Brothers Foundation, *The Power of the Democratic Idea* (Garden City, N. Y., Doubleday and Company, 1960)

Ross, A., *Why Democracy?* (Cambridge, Harvard University Press, 1952)

Russell, W. F., *Liberty versus Equality* (New York, The Macmillan Co., 1936)

Sait, E. M., *Democracy* (New York, The Century Company, 1929)

Sait, E. M., *Political Institutions* (New York, D. Appleton-Century Co., 1938), Chapters XVIII-XX.

Schattschneider, E. E., *The Semi-Sovereign People* (New York, Holt, Rinehart and Winston, 1960)

Simon, Y., *Philosophy of Democratic Government* (Chicago, University of Chicago Press, 1951)

Smith, T. V., *The American Philosophy of Equality* (Chicago, University of Chicago Press, 1927)

Spearman, D., *Modern Dictatorship* (New York, Columbia University Press, 1939)

Spitz, D., *Democracy and the Challenge of Power* (New York, Columbia University Press, 1958)

Spitz, D., *Patterns of Anti-Democratic Thought* (New York, The Macmillan Co., 1949)

Stamps, N., *Why Democracies Fail* (Notre Dame, University of Notre Dame Press, 1957)

Stapleton, L., *The Design of Democracy* (New York, Oxford University Press, 1949)

Swabey, M. C., *Theory of the Democratic State* (Cambridge, Harvard University Press, 1939)

Thomas, N., *Socialism Re-Examined* (New York, W. W. Norton & Co., 1963)

Thorson, T. L., *The Logic of Democracy* (New York, Holt, Rinehart and Winston, 1962)

de Tocqueville, A. C., *Democracy in America*, 2 vols (New York, A. A. Knopf, 1945)

Verney, D. V., *The Analysis of Political Systems* (London, Routledge & Paul, 1959)

SELECTED READINGS

Group I.

Excerpts from writings dealing with the nature of democracy.

Excerpts by L. Lipson; Carl L. Becker; W. M. McGovern; John Laird; H. B. Mayo; R. M. MacIver; W. Lippmann; E. E. Schattschneider; R. A. Dahl; E. H. Carr; Louis Hartz; and from *The UNESCO Questionnaire on Ideological Conflicts Concerning Democracy.*

Group II.

Supreme Court opinions and dissenting opinions regarding apportionment.

Reynolds v. Sims
Lucas v. Colorado General Assembly

Group III.

Selected comments and documentary material pertaining to democracy, liberty, and equality.

Selected comments by R. M. MacIver; Sidney Hook; and documentary material from *Universal Declaration of Human Rights; Rights Guaranteed by the Constitution of the United States; by the Constitution of the Union of Soviet Socialist Republics; and by the Constitution of Japan.*

Group IV.

Selected observations concerning
the compatibility of democracy
and a socialized economy.

Selected observations by R. A. Dahl; J. A. Schumpeter;
N. Thomas; N. Lenin; Communist Party of the Soviet Union;
R. M. MacIver; William Ebenstein; F. A. Hayek; and H. Finer.

Group V.

Selections pertaining to anti-democratic
patterns of thought.

Selections by David Spitz; G. Mosca; and Robert Michels.

THE NATURE
OF DEMOCRACY

The UNESCO Questionnaire on Ideological Conflicts Concerning Democracy.

NOTE: *The first of the two following selections from the questionnaire indicates the reasons for the inquiry conducted by UNESCO in 1948; the second delineates the four clusters of problems with respect to which questions were sent to a variety of experts for answer. No material pertaining to the results of the inquiry is herein included. Essays selected from the materials collected in response to the questionnaire are published in R. McKeon, ed.,* Democracy in a World of Tensions *(Chicago, The University of Chicago Press, 1951).*

Selection No. 1

"The peoples of the world, laymen no less than experts, have never been more conscious of conflicts of convictions than in the years after World War II.

Ideological conflicts are present everywhere, between nations, within nations, between minds, within minds.

Few words have played a greater role in these conflicts than the word "democracy." What does it mean, connote, imply? Does it cover one and the same meaning to all and everybody, or is it just used to express whatever anybody thinks worth fighting for?

It has been the common watchword in two world wars. The victory of November, 1918, was said to be the victory of democracy. The common aim of the Allied Powers in World War II, as formulated by Roosevelt, Stalin, and Churchill at the Teheran Conference in December, 1943, was the establishment of "a world family of democratic nations." The declarations of Yalta in February and of Potsdam in August, 1945, both stressed the same principle: the Great Powers announced their intention of "meeting the political and economic problems of liberated Europe in accordance with democratic principles"; they made these principles the basis of their joint policy in Germany.

Did they mean the same by "democracy," the same by "democratic," when they used these words in these declarations? Did they only agree on the *words*, or did they agree on substance?

The events that have followed: the disagreements on elections in eastern Europe, the disagreements on the "new type democracies," the "people's democracies" established in these countries, the general disagreement within the United Nations Organization, have given ample evidence that the words did not connote any definite criteria *that could be agreed upon* in cases of concrete application of the principles laid down in the declarations of the Great Powers.

The disagreements have given rise to long series of ideological criticisms and countercriticisms; to give instances of cruder arguments it has, on the one hand, been claimed that "democracy" cannot thrive where free scope is given to racial discrimination and exploitation of toiling masses and colonial peoples, on the other, that "democracy" cannot exist where only one party takes part in elections and opposition is not tolerated.

What was the background of these violent disagreements? How were the divergencies in usage and interpretation of the word "democracy" to be clarified?

The problem is one of vast implications. It is not just a question of terminology. It has its background in contrasts of historical development, of social conditions, of political patterning, of ideological structuration, of public opinion formation, of education. It is deeply entangled in the immense cluster of problems raised by the impact of technology and industrial civilization on the lives of the peoples of the world; it is part of the general problem of world integration under conditions never before experienced in the history of mankind. It is not only a problem of philosophy, of the normative basis of the relations between the individual and the state, it is a problem of war or peace." . . . .

Selection No. 2

. . ." the inquiry will concentrate on four clusters of problems which have seemed to be among the crucial ones in the controversies so far:

First, the general problem of the ambiguity and slogan-like character of the word "democracy": Are there divergent concepts covered by the word, what are the criteria of misuse, what historical basis is there for adopting one usage as the correct one and rejecting others?

Second, the general problem of the relations between "formal" democracy as an exclusively political concept and "real" democracy as a broad social *and* political concept: Does "democracy" connote universal and equal suffrage rights only, or does it even connote other rights to equality—educational, economic ones?

Third, the problem of tolerance, of the right of opposition: Does "democracy" connote the right of any group of any opinion whatsoever to take part in political life and influence public opinion, or are there limits to such rights, and what are these? Does "democracy" necessarily imply the existence of several parties? Does "democracy" imply the duty to fight any "antidemocratic" group?

Fourth, the problem of the normative bases of the divergencies of usage and interpretation manifest in current controversies: Do the divergencies reflect irreducible conflicts of value, or do they conceal deeper agreements and forces working toward reconciliation?"

L. Lipson, *The Democratic Civilization* (New York, Oxford University Press, 1964) Excerpts, pp. 6-7.

. . . democracy has passed through many phases and vicissitudes and has appeared in several guises. Some have seen in it a revolutionary challenge to constituted authority and vested interest; a symbol of defiance, protest, and liberation; an onslaught upon privilege and class. Others have taken it for granted, accepting its existence as part of the established order into which they were born and which a placid conservatism sustained. In certain periods, democracy was a rare and curious freak to be noted and described by its contemporaries largely because it was exceptional. In others it lived only as a literary memory, recorded in the pages of historians, dramatists, and philosophers, who were mostly its critics. Democratic institutions and ideals have known both triumph and setback. After a long obsolescence, they received a second birth in the seventeenth and eighteenth centuries, throve vigorously and on the whole victoriously in the nineteenth, and in the twentieth emerged (though not unscathed) on the winning side of the two global wars in which the democratic ideal was among the issues of combat. Its opponents have included the aristocrats and oligarchs of the ancient world, the medieval nobility and its latter-day descendants, the absolute monarchs of the sixteenth and seventeenth centuries, the merchant-princes of virtually all eras since the power of the people threatened their riches, the majority of the heads of organized religions, the commanders of practically every army in the past and of most of them in the present, and the twentieth-century species of dictator, both fascist and communist. Democracy has been associated with various economies, agrarian no less than industrial, primitive no less than advanced, abundant no less than poor. . . .

When one considers how great has been the range of democracy in space and time and culture, the truth is readily apparent that no two democracies are cut to precisely the same pattern. The dissimilarities of democratic systems constitute one of the fundamental facts for analysis. . . .

. . . there is a host of contrasted institutions and procedures all of which with equal validity may be labelled democratic. The framework of the governmental structure, the processes of the party system, the meaning and priorities assigned to the different "operative ideals," [1] relations between the citizens and their officials, the character of the social order with which the political order is intertwined—on each of these major matters the democracies are markedly at variance. For instance, the democratic states include both the unitary and the federal. Some have the presidential executive, some the collegial, others the cabinet type. The party systems may comprise the minimum number of two, or extend to six and even more. Electoral methods can differ as greatly as do proportional representation, preferential voting, and single member districts with victory by a bare plurality. Democracy can be combined with highly socialized economies, which have a considerable volume of public ownership, state planning and regulation, and social services, or with an economy that retains a larger amount of unregulated capitalism and leaves a wider sphere to the private profit-seeker. The philosophies which democrats propound may place their stress on liberty, while others may emphasize equality. Some have identified democracy with individualism, others with the public interest; with minority rights, or with majority rule. Hence one learns about the nature of democracy by observing and evaluating the numerous constructions that may be placed upon a democratic philosophy, and the equally plentiful blueprints from which the machinery of a democratic state may be constructed. Comparisons must therefore be drawn not only between democratic and non-democratic systems, but also among the democracies themselves. In this way one will discover how much democracy has changed in the course of its evolution and how much it exhibits of continuity and consistency; how much may be altered without sacrifice of essentials, and just what these essentials are.

Carl L. Becker, *Modern Democracy* (New Haven, Yale University Press, 1941) Excerpts, pp. 4-12, 14-15, 26-27, 63-64.

Democracy, like liberty or science or progress, is a word with which we are all so familiar that we rarely take the trouble to ask what we mean by it. It is a term, as the devotees of semantics say, which has no "referent"—there is no precise or palpable thing or object which we all think of when the word is pronounced. On the contrary, it is a word which connotes different things to different people, a kind of conceptual Gladstone bag which, with a little manipulation, can be made to accommodate almost any collection of social facts we may wish to carry about in it. . . . We have only to stretch the concept to include any form of government supported by a majority of the people, for whatever reasons and by whatever means of expressing assent, and before we know it the empire of Napoleon, the Soviet regime of Stalin, and the Fascist systems of Mussolini and Hitler are all safely in the bag. But if this is what we mean by democracy, then virtually all forms of government are democratic, since virtually all governments, except in times of revolution, rest upon the explicit or implicit consent of the people. . . .

It would be possible . . . to define democracy either in terms of the ideal or in terms of the real form—to define it as government of the people, by the people, for the people; or to define it as government of the people, by the politicians, for whatever pressure groups can get their interests taken care of. But as a historian I am naturally disposed to be satisfied with the meaning which, in the history of politics, men have commonly attributed to the word—a meaning . . . which derives partly from the experience and partly from the aspirations of mankind. So regarded, the term democracy refers primarily to a form of government, and it has always meant government by the many as opposed to government by the one—government by the people as opposed to government by a tyrant, a dictator, or an absolute monarch. . . .

. . . the essential test of democratic government has always been this: the source of political authority must be and remain in the people and not in the ruler. A democratic government has always meant one in which the citizens, or a sufficient number of them to represent more or less effectively the common will, freely act from time to time, and according to established forms, to appoint or recall the magistrates and to enact or revoke the laws by which the community is governed. This I take to be the meaning which history has impressed upon the term democracy as a form of government. . . .

Let us . . . note the part which democracy has played in human civilization. The view, if we have been accustomed to take democratic institutions for granted, is a bit bleak and disheartening. For we see at once that in all this long time [five or six thousand years of history], over the habitable globe, the great majority of the human race has neither known nor apparently much cared for our favorite institutions. . . .

. . . taking the experience of mankind as a test, democracy has as yet had but a limited and temporary success. . . . The reason is that democratic government is a species of social luxury, at best a delicate and precarious venture which depends for success upon the validity of certain assumptions about the capacities and virtues of men, and upon the presence of certain material and intellectual conditions favorable to the exercise of these capacities and virtues. . . .

. . . until recently the means of communication were too slow and uncertain to create the necessary solidarity of interest and similarity of information over large areas. . . .

If one of the conditions essential to the success of democratic government is mobility, ease of communication, another is a certain measure of economic security. Democracy does not flourish in communities on the verge of destitution. . . .

So much for the material conditions essential for the success of democratic government. Supposing these conditions to exist, democratic government implies in addition the presence of certain capacities and virtues in its citizens. These capacities and virtues are bound up with the assumptions on which democracy rests, and are available only in so far as the assumptions are valid. The primary assumption of democratic government is that its citizens are capable of managing their own affairs. But life in any community involves a conflict of individual and class interests, and a corresponding divergence of opinion as to the measures to be adopted for the common good. The divergent opinions must be somehow reconciled, the conflict of interests somehow compromised. It must then be an assumption of democratic government that its citizens are rational creatures, sufficiently so at least to understand the interests in conflict; and it must be an assumption that they are men of good will, sufficiently so toward each other at least to make those concessions of individual and class interest required for effective workable compromises. . . .

. . . modern liberal-democracy is associated with an ideology which rests upon something more than the minimum assumptions essential to any democratic government. It rests upon a philosophy of universally valid ends and means. Its fundamental assumption is the worth and dignity and creative capacity of the individual, so that the chief aim of government is the maximum of individual self-direction, the chief means to that end the minimum of compulsion by the state. Ideally considered, means and ends are conjoined in the concept of freedom: freedom of thought, so that the truth may prevail; freedom of occupation, so that careers may be open to talent; freedom of self-government, so that no one may be compelled against his will. . . .

If . . . the democratic way of life is to survive we must distinguish the kinds of individual freedom that are essential to it from those that are unessential or disastrous. Broadly speaking, the kinds that are essential are those which the individual enjoys in his intellectual and political activities; the kinds that are unessential are the relatively unrestrained liberties he has hitherto enjoyed in his economic activities. . . .

. . . the difficult but essential task which confronts all democratic societies today may be formulated as follows: how in practice to curtail the freedom of the individual in economic enterprise sufficiently to effect that equality of opportunity and of possessions without which democracy is an empty form, and at the same time to preserve that measure of individual freedom in intellectual and political life without which it cannot exist.

W. M. McGovern, *From Luther to Hitler* (Boston, Houghton Mifflin Company, 1941) Excerpts, pp. 11-12.

Democracy, of course, means the belief that ultimate political control should rest with the citizens of the country concerned and more particularly with the numerical majority of such citizens, rather than be entrusted permanently to a single person or to any minority group. There are, of course, many different types and degrees of democracy. In some countries democracy means that the right of voting and of being elected to office is open to all adults whether male or female. In other cases women are ruled out and democracy means universal manhood suffrage. In still other cases the right to vote and hold office is limited by property or literacy tests. But even here the regime must be called democratic if ultimate control over the machinery of government rests with the bulk of the people rather than with a special minority. Under this definition, present-day England most certainly belongs to the group of democratic states, for though she retains an hereditary monarch and an hereditary House of Lords, all ultimate or final power rests with a popularly elected House of Commons.

In some few cases, as in the smaller Swiss cantons and in some of the New England townships, democracy is able to function directly, laws being passed and taxes raised at meetings attended by all citizens. In some cases, where it is impossible to hold such meetings, a large measure of this direct democratic control is exercised by means of such devices as the initiative, referendum, and recall. In still other cases no attempt is made to govern by the direct democratic process, the people ruling indirectly through elected agents and representatives; but as long as periodic elections make it possible for the people to control the machinery of government, the government must be considered democratic. In all countries which have democratic constitutions, we find that the whole basis of government rests upon certain fundamental assumptions, which have played a great part in the development of the liberal tradition. Among the more important of these fundamental assumptions is the idea that "all government must rest upon the consent of the governed." Another is the idea that "all rulers and magistrates derive their authority from the people." As a final bulwark against despotism, most democratic regimes have either tacitly or expressly adopted the doctrine of "the right of armed rebellion against a tyrannous government," or, in other words, the right to rebel in case a single person or a minority group attempts to seize or retain control over governmental institutions.

John Laird, *The Device of Government* (Cambridge, At the University Press, 1944) Excerpts, pp. 95-102.

Democracy is popular government, the people's government in some special sense. Lincoln's famous phrase 'Government *of* the people *by* the people *for* the people' would appear to define that special sense in a satisfying union of rhetoric with analysis. A relevant addition would be 'government *from* the people.'

The term 'the people' has a certain ambiguity. It may mean the politically organized community. . . . On the other hand one may think, and commonly one does think of the 'people' as the members of the community in their severalty, or even as the multitude, whence it is easy (though inaccurate) to regard them as the plebs or as the rabble.

But let us examine the force of the prepositions 'of,' 'by,' 'for' and 'from.'

Every government is the government *of* its subjects and therefore of most of the 'people' considered in their severalty. That is an analytical proposition applicable to all government. In an ideal democracy each citizen would be both ruler, in some sense, and subject, in some sense, though there would be members of the community (e.g. minors) who were only subjects. . . . In undemocratic types of government, certain members of the community are rulers but not subjects; all the rest are subjects but not rulers. Except for that there is no need to linger over the preposition 'of.'

Similarly, government *for* the people, i.e. for the people's welfare, does not effectively distinguish any one form of government from any other form. . . . In fact . . . there is nothing strange and certainly nothing self-contradictory in the conception of a benevolent despot. *Salus populi* [welfare of the people], indeed, is the nominal aim of nearly every government, and even if every human being were incurably selfish, few rulers could succeed in their selfish aims unless they appeared to be benevolent and visibly practised beneficence to support the appearance. Very likely, it is true, their beneficiaries, if ciphers, would seldom obtain their maximum benefit. If so, government *for* the people would be more likely to be for the people's benefit if it were government *by* them. That, however, is a disputable argument.

So let us turn to the force of the preposition 'by.' Only a few governments are or profess to be *by* the people. When such governments make this profession they profess to be democratic and they are democratic if the profession, instead of being a mere flourish, is a principle systematically absorbed into the texture and substance of their political order.

So understood, the meaning of democracy is that in it the people rule. This in its turn is usually taken to mean that in a democracy, unlike other forms of government, every citizen in the community is a ruler, and is not a mere subject who is ruled without ruling. In some sense this meaning of the word should be accepted. . . .

. . . if government by the people is supposed to mean government administered by all the citizens (and not in an essentially subordinate capacity) there cannot, in that sense, be government *by* the people even in a little town, to say nothing of a huge nation-state.

There is no room for such masses on the bridge of the ship of state, and if there were room, there would be little hope for the safe navigation of the vessel. . . .

In general it is the electorate, not the administration, that theorists have in mind when they speak of government *by* the people. All the citizens may be electors although not all of them are even petty administrators. All the citizens may be *equal* electors, and are so if each has but one vote. The electorate is the government *maker* or unmaker, not itself the government.

This, even if it be over-simplified, may usefully be treated as a first approximation to the theory of government *by* the people in a large political community.

Considering it so, we observe at once that the force of the preposition 'by,' as respects the electorate, is hard to separate from the force of the preposition 'from.' The citizens make and unmake their rulers, that is to say, the ruling office springs *from* the citizens. The democratic sense of government *from* the people, however, is quite specific. In a general way, as we have seen, government, if it springs neither from divine nor from 'natural' right, and if it is not imposed upon a people by a foreign conqueror, cannot very well have any source except the people. That is a much vaguer idea than the democratic making or unmaking of government by the electorate. It is still vaguer than the usual form of the modern democratic theory of the function of the electorate, namely that every citizen (if he does not die young) has the right and the duty of government-making several times during his lifetime in accordance with a definite political system in which (perhaps with insignificant exceptions) each citizen has but one vote, and the majority vote prevails.

That is the general point. In comparison it is of minor interest how many steps there are between the polls and the top of the government, whether the constituencies are on a regional basis or on an occupational basis (as they might be in a guild system or in a corporative state), whether the elected persons are to be regarded as mere transmitters of the people's voices, or as independent representatives each of whom, being elected, speaks thereafter for himself on his soul and conscience.

If the political functions of the electorate are so conceived, and if the conception is embodied in the rights and duties of the political system, government from the people, in this specifically institutional sense, is exclusively democratic. This should not be taken for granted, but I believe it can be supported by argument.

H. B. Mayo, *An Introduction to Democratic Theory* (New York, Oxford University Press, 1960) Excerpts, pp. 58-70, 97-103.

It makes sense to say that one person rules, or that a few persons do, no matter how large the state, but it makes almost no sense to say that the people rule in any modern state, in any ordinary sense of the word 'rule.' (In this sense 'rule' means to make directly the binding political decisions—or the major ones, including the decision as to what is major—and to receive the obedience). . . .

Democracy, then, as a political system must have identifiable features other than the people's actually 'governing,' to distinguish it from other methods of making public policies. The problem is to separate the accidental features from the characteristic. Some political features, such as whether the government is federal or unitary, presidential or parliamentary, unicameral or bicameral, republican or monarchical, are by general agreement accidental variations from a common type. So, too, is the kind of economic system with which the political system is associated—although this is more debatable. These and other features are not necessarily related, either in logic or practice, with features of the political system ordinarily listed as democratic. . . .

. . . a political system is democratic to the extent that the decision-makers are under effective popular control. (One should perhaps add: to the extent to which decisions are *influenced* by the people, but this is a more amorphous concept, for which allowance will be made later.) . . .

Popular control of policy-makers is then the basic feature or principle, and political systems can be classified as more or less democratic according to a number of criteria associated with popular control and designed to make it effective; only if a particular system meets the test of a substantial number of these criteria do we, by common consent, agree to call it democratic. But although the existence of democracy then becomes a matter of degree, the distinction is valid enough as we shall see, and the criteria will enable us to say in what respects and to what extent a system is democratic. . . .

DISTINGUISHING PRINCIPLES OF A DEMOCRATIC SYSTEM

Influence over decision-makers, and hence over public policies may be exercised in many ways, even in a non-democratic system. . . . But popular influence, although necessary, is not enough even if institutionalized to make a political system democratic.

1. *Popular control of policy-makers,* however, is a democratic stigmatum, and this is our first and most general principle. The one institutional embodiment of the principle universally regarded as indispensable in modern democracies is that of choosing the policymakers (representatives) at elections held at more or less regular intervals. . . .

(a) On the whole, no democratic system operates on the principle that voters directly decide public policies at elections. The control over policy is much more indirect—through the representatives. . . .

(b) The popular influence over policies, as distinct from control over policy-makers, goes on all the time and may take many institutionalized and legitimate forms. . . .

(c) Popular control by means of modern elections has only a faint resemblance to the old principle that, in some sense, authority stems from the people, and to old practices such as an elective monarchy. . . .

2. The second principle of democracy is that of *political equality,* which in turn is institutionalized as the equality of all adult citizens in voting. . . .

Political equality is complex . . . and may be broken down into several elements, consisting at least of the following:

(a) Every adult should have the vote—the familiar device of universal adult suffrage. . . .

(b) One person should have one vote—that is, there should be no plural voting.

(c) Each vote should count equally—that is, votes are not weighted in any way. . . .

(d) If every vote is to count equally, the corollary follows that the number of representatives elected should be directly proportional to the number of votes cast for them. . . . It is just at this point, however, . . . that the practice of many democracies diverges from this aspect of political equality, and often does so for very good reasons. . . .

3. The third principle may be stated either in terms of the *effectiveness of the popular control* or in terms of political freedoms. . . .

(a) To say that the voting must be effective is to say that there must be free choice, without coercion or intimidation of the voters. . . .

(b) In order that voting may be effective, it must . . . be free in another sense, i.e., at least two candidates for each position must be able to come forward if they wish. . . .

The effectiveness of popular control . . . entails a range of political freedoms. Among them are certainly the freedoms of speech, assembly, and organization [association], as well as the freedom to run for an office. . . .

4. The fourth principle is that *when the representatives are divided, the decision of the majority prevails.*

This is, in fact, the nearly universal rule for decision-making in all legislatures. . . .

The foregoing is a simplified, formal, abstract sketch of a democratic political system—its essential principles of operation for political policy-making. It concentrates upon how the binding decisions, related to government and arising from conflict and dispute, are made in the context of political freedom. In other terms, the outline concentrates upon the ways in which policy-makers get their power and authorization—their legitimacy, always a prime concern to any political theory. The principles are close enough to common usage, and to some political systems in existence, to warrant the description democratic. . . .

A working definition may be constructed from the above: a democratic political system is one in which public policies are made, on a majority basis, by representatives subject to effective popular control at periodic elections which are conducted on the principle of political equality and under conditions of political freedom. . . .

A NOTE ON THE THEORY OF REPRESENTATION

. . . I think that the idea of democratic representation—by means of free election—has crystallized around a few simple ideas.

Substantial agreement has been reached on the belief that persons as individuals, not corporate estates or 'interests' or place, are represented, although for convenience a territorial basis is usually adopted. Elections by persons, not 'interests,' is implied, I think, both by the principle of popular control of legislators and by that of equality of voting; 'interests' cannot be measured, but votes can be counted. Modern democracies have thus in the main agreed, though not without dispute, that the adult citizens should vote and be represented as persons, and not in their capacities as farmers, teachers, business men, landlords, and the like. . . .

The alternative theory, only occasionally heard now, but popularized by guild socialists in the 1920's, is that some form of 'interest' or functional representation should prevail, and votes be allocated accordingly. . . .

In summary: interest or functional representation has been rejected as the electoral basis. Instead, all democracies vote on a territorial basis, and the representatives are conceived of as representing persons.

The second idea which virtually every democracy has rejected in practice (if not in theory) is that the representatives should collectively be a kind of mirror-image or, better, a 'map to scale' of interests or opinions in the country as a whole. . . .

Now it is a familiar fact that all classes and groups in a state are not represented in the legislature in proportion to their numbers in the country. The representatives are not an occupational cross-section of the voters: lawyers and farmers, for example, are often over-represented . . . , housewives are invariably under-represented. Consequently, extensions in the suffrage have not always been matched by corresponding changes in the composition of legislatures, a fact which may help to explain a certain amount of disillusion with franchise reform. Yet—to repeat—it must be said that the microcosm view of legislatures is not a part of generally accepted democratic theory. . . .

In view of the obscurities and misleading notions of representation theory, I am inclined to think that politics would gain if we gradually dropped the word 'representative' altogether. . . . Democratic theory has little to gain from talking the language of representation, since everything necessary to the theory may be put in terms of (a) legislators (or decision-makers) who are (b) legitimated or authorized to enact public policies, and who are (c) subject or responsible to popular control at free elections.

R. M. MacIver, *The Ramparts We Guard* (New York, The Macmillan Company, 1950) Excerpts, pp. 22-29, 129, 9-11.

We hear it said that democracy means "the rule of the people." That statement clarifies nothing, for in the strict sense the people never rule. . . . You can speak of oligarchy as the rule of the few or of theocracy as the rule of the priests or of monarchy as the rule of the dynast or of dictatorship as the rule of the dictator. These statements, even if they require some qualification, are perfectly understandable and on the whole meaningful. But we cannot equally indicate the nature of democracy by saying it is the rule of the people. Still less admissable is the statement that democracy is "the rule of the masses," for the word "masses" here conveys a suggestion entirely alien to the being of democracy. It suggests the sheer division of a community into two antithetical classes, the elite on the one hand and the un-differentiated multitude on the other. Nor yet do we make the matter sufficiently clear when we say that democracy is the rule of the majority. . . .

. . . Democracy invokes the *majority principle,* not once and for all, but continuously. The majority are not a determinate body who lord it over a minority. In the democratic context the majority must always be rediscovered, must always re-emerge out of the whole. . . . Democracy involves the majority principle as a determinant of government, but the only way of invoking this principle assures to every minority certain primary rights—the liberty of opinion with all the other liberties that grow from it. If these liberties are tampered with, democracy ceases to exist. It makes no difference whether it be a majority or a minority which arrogates political liberties exclusively to itself—in either case democracy is dead. Domination by the majority becomes mass domination, which always ends quickly in the rule of the tyrant.

. . . Democracy is always seething with the movements and changes of opinion. In this flux minority opinions have their chance. New leaders arise and win a following. New movements grow and old ones' fade. Always the many are influenced by the few. But to claim that this condition is undemocratic is to be totally unrealistic.

. . . Whoever leads, whoever influences the people, it is democracy, so long as the avenue to government is free election by the majority. Democracy does not make people wise and good, it does not assure that they shall vote according to their true needs or best interests. It merely gives them the opportunity. . . .

. . . The people . . . do not and cannot govern; they control the government. In every live democracy they decide the broad march of politics. They decide whether there is to be more social legislation or less, more collectivization or somewhat more play for private enterprise, more dependence on an international system of security or more self-sufficiency and relative isolation, and so forth. They decide these issues, not one at a time but by voting for an administration favorable to one or another "platform." They decide them partly—and in the last resort—at the polls, and partly by the continuously manifested indications of public sentiment. To make decisions easier there is in every community a sense of alternative directions, marked respectively left and right, and a sway of opinion in one or the other direction. . . .

This incessant activity of popular opinion is the dynamic of democracy. . . . the citizens of a democracy are *continuously* engaged in a massive give-and-take of creative opinion-making. . . .

. . . public opinion is not formed by individuals thinking and acting in detachment from their fellows. There are trends and currents that move and swell underneath. There is contagion and response. There is a sense of direction to which many are sensitive. Often the sophisticated are less aware of it than are the run of men. Ideas take hold, goals are apprehended, no one knows how. There are deep movements that work through generations and there are surface movements that change from day to day. There is a body of opinion that coheres and cumulates. There are tides of opinion and countertides. Public opinion is an ever-changing *system* of responses to forces that are more profound and far more significant than the ephemeral appeals of propagandists and orators. At any moment it may be unstable; sometimes it is excitable and swayed by waves of emotion; but in the course of time it regains its balance and moves steadily along its course.

Hence there is much hazard for the poll-makers who claim to

measure its direction by dipping their buckets in the great sea. Their small samples are already motionless. From these they cannot project the strength of the quiet deep currents that constantly revitalize the spirit of democracy.

Perils of democracy

The perils of democracy arise from several sources. One peril springs from the sheer misunderstanding of what it means. Another proceeds from the unwillingness of men and groups to face its demands when these demands are opposed to their prejudices, their traditions, or their interests. . . . Another peril arises from the concentration of power, tempting the strong to exploit the weak. . . . An allied peril arises from the rivalries and ambitions of dominant groups, in which they become obsessed by their dividing interests and disregard the common good. . . . Another peril arises from our failure to reapply our democratic principles to changing conditions and changing needs. . . . We may, for example, falsely identify democracy with an established economic order and when that happens we are often ready to defend this order by resorting to undemocratic procedures. Or . . . we may be so convinced of the desirability of a new or reformed economic order that we are minded to abandon democratic liberties altogether to bring it about. . . . another source of danger to democracy. . . . In our own times forces are at work to break up the sense of community, of the common weal, the union one and indivisible of the citizens of a democracy. The continuous disturbance of rapid social change, the growth of specialization and the ever more elaborate organization of specialized groups . . . all these characteristics of our modern civilization have adverse influences on the solidarity of democratic peoples.

W. Lippmann, *The Phantom Public* (New York, Harcourt, Brace and Company, 1925) Excerpts, pp. 14, 41-42, 55-57, 61-62, 155.

The private citizen knows that his sovereignty is a fiction. He reigns in theory, but in fact he does not govern. . . .

The actual governing is made up of a multitude of arrangements on specific questions by particular individuals. These rarely become visible to the private citizen. Government, in the long intervals between elections, is carried on by politicians, officeholders and influential men who make settlements with other politicians, officeholders, and influential men. The mass of people see these settlements, judge them, and affect them only now and then. They are altogether too numerous, too complicated, too obscure in their effects to become the subject of any continuing exercise of public opinion.

Nor in any exact and literal sense are those who conduct the daily business of government accountable after the fact to the great mass of the voters. They are accountable only, except in spectacular cases, to the other politicians, officeholders and influential men directly interested in the particular act. . . .

The role of public opinion is determined by the fact that its relation to a problem is external. The opinion affects an opinion, but does not itself control the executive act. A public opinion is expressed by a vote, a demonstration of praise or blame, a following or a boycotting. But these manifestations are in themselves nothing. They count only if they influence the course of affairs. They influence it, however, only if they influence an actor in the affair. And it is, I believe, precisely in this secondary, indirect relationship between public opinion and public affairs that we have the clue to the limits and the possibilities of public opinion.

It may be objected at once that an election which turns one set of men out of office and installs another is an expression of public opinion which is neither secondary nor indirect. But what in fact is an election? We call it an expression of the popular will. But is it? We go into a polling booth and mark a cross on a piece of paper for one of two, or perhaps three or four names. Have we expressed our thoughts on the public policy of the United States? Presumably we have a number of thoughts on this and that with many buts and ifs and ors. Surely the cross on a piece of paper does not express them. It would take us hours to express our thoughts, and calling a vote the expression of our mind is an empty fiction.

A vote is a promise of support. It is a way of saying: I am lined up with these men, on this side. I enlist with them. I will follow. . . .

The public does not select the candidate, write the platform, outline the policy any more than it builds the automobile or acts the play. It aligns itself for or against somebody who has offered himself, has made a promise, has produced a play, is selling an automobile. The action of a group as a group is the mobilization of the force it possesses. . . .

I do not wish to labor the argument any futher than may be necessary to establish the theory that what the public does is not to express its opinions but to align itself for or against a proposal. If that theory is accepted, we must abandon the notion that democratic government can be the direct expression of the will of the people. We must abandon the notion that the people govern. Instead we must adopt the theory that, by their occasional mobilizations as a majority, people support or oppose the individuals who actually govern. We must say that the popular will does not direct continuously but that it intervenes occasionally. . . .

A false ideal of democracy can lead to disillusionment and to meddlesome tyranny. If democracy cannot direct affairs, then a philosophy which expects it to direct them will encourage people to attempt the impossible; they will fail, but that will interfere outrageously with the productive liberties of the individual. The public must be put in its place, so that it may exercise its own power, but no less and perhaps even more, so that each of us may live free of the trampling and the roar of a bewildered herd.

W. Lippmann, *The Public Philosophy* (Boston, Little, Brown and Company, 1955) Excerpt, p. 14.

. . . What then are the true boundaries of the people's power? The answer cannot be simple. But for a rough beginning let us say that the people are able to give and to withhold their consent to being governed—their consent to what the government asks of them, proposes to them, and has done in the conduct of their affairs. They can elect the government. They can remove it. They can approve or disapprove its performance. But they cannot normally initiate and propose the necessary legislation. A mass cannot govern. The people, as Jefferson said, are not "qualified to exercise themselves the Executive

Department; but they are qualified to name the person who shall exercise it. . . . They are not qualified to legislate; with us therefore they only choose the legislators."

E. E. Schattschneider, *The Semi-Sovereign People* (New York, Holt, Rinehart and Winston, 1961) Excerpts, pp. 129-142.

The classical definition of democracy as government by the people is predemocratic in its origins, based on notions about democracy developed by philosophers who never had an opportunity to see an operating democratic system. Predemocratic theories assumed that the people would take over the conduct of public affairs in a democracy and administer the government to their own advantage as simply as landowners administer their property for their own profit. Under the historical circumstances this oversimplification is easy to understand. There is less excuse for the failure of modern scholars to re-examine the traditional definition critically in the light of modern experience. . . .

It requires no research to demonstrate that it is difficult to relate the copybook maxims about democracy to the operating political system. If we start with the common definition of democracy (as government by the people), it is hard to avoid some extremely pessimistic conclusions about the feasibility of democracy in the modern world, for it is impossible to reconcile traditional concepts of what ought to happen in a democracy with the fact that an amazingly large number of people do not seem to know very much about what is going on. The significance of this kind of popular ignorance depends on what we think democracy is. . . .

We become cynical about democracy because the public does not act the way the simplistic definition of democracy says that it should act, or we try to whip the public into doing things it does not want to do, is unable to do and has too much sense to do. The crisis here is not a crisis in democracy but a crisis in theory. . . .

If we assume that the people "govern," it follows that the governing majority ought to know more than any majority has ever known or ever could know. This is the *reductio ad absurdum* of democratic theory. We cannot get out of the dilemma by (1) making a great effort to educate everyone to the point where they know enough to make these decisions nor (2) by restricting participation to the people who do know all about these matters. The first is impossible. The second is absurd because *no one* knows enough to govern by this standard. The trouble is that we have defined democracy in such a way that we are in danger of putting ourselves out of business.

There is no escape from the problem of ignorance, because *nobody knows enough to run the government*. Presidents, senators, governors, judges, professors, doctors of philosophy, editors, and the like are only a little less ignorant than the rest of us. . . .

The people are involved in public affairs by the conflict system. Conflicts open up questions for public intervention. Out of conflict the alternatives of public policy arise. Conflict is the occasion for political organization and leadership. In a free political system it is difficult to avoid public involvement in conflict; the ordinary, regular operations of the government give rise to controversy, and controversy is catching. . . .

What we are saying is that conflict, competition, leadership, and organization are the essence of democratic politics. Inherent in the operations of a democracy are special conditions which permit large numbers of people to function.

The problem is how to organize the political system so as to make the best possible use of the power of the public in view of its limitations. A popular decision bringing into focus the force of public support requires a tremendous effort to define the alternatives, to organize the discussion and mobilize opinion. The government and the political organizations are in the business of manufacturing this kind of alternatives. . . .

Above everything, *the people are powerless if the political enterprise is not competitive*. It is the competition of political organizations that provides the people with the opportunity to make a choice. Without this opportunity popular sovereignty amounts to nothing. . . .

A working definition of democracy must capitalize on the limitations of the people as well as their powers. We do this when we say that liberty and leadership are the greatest of democratic concepts. *Democracy is a competitive political system in which competing lead-*

ers and organizations define the alternatives of public policy in such a way that the public can participate in the decision-making process. The initiative in this political system is to be found largely in the government or the opposition. The people profit by this system, but they cannot, by themselves, do the work of the system. . . .

Conflict, competition, organization, leadership and responsibility are the ingredients of a working definition of democracy. Democracy is a political system in which the people have a choice among the alternatives created by competing political organizations and leaders. The advantage of this definition over the traditional definition is that it is operational, it describes something that actually happens. It describes something feasible. It does not make impossible demands on the public. . . .

The involvement of the public in politics is a natural outgrowth of the kind of conflict that almost inevitably arises in a free society. The exploitation of this situation by responsible political leaders and organizations is the essence of democracy; the socialization of conflict is the essential democratic process.

R. A. Dahl, *A Preface to Democratic Theory* (Chicago, University of Chicago Press, 1956) Excerpts, pp. 131-134.

I have shown both that elections are a crucial device for controlling leaders and that they are quite ineffective as indicators of majority preference. These statements are really not in contradiction. A good deal of traditional democratic theory leads us to expect more from national elections than they can possibly provide. We expect elections to reveal the "will" or the preferences of a majority on a set of issues. This is one thing elections rarely do, except in an almost trivial fashion. Despite this limitation the election process is one of two fundamental methods of social control which, operating together, make governmental leaders so responsive to non-leaders that the distinction between democracy and dictatorship still makes sense. The other method of social control is continuous political competition among individuals, parties, or both. Elections and political competition do not make for government by majorities in any very significant way, but they vastly increase the size, number, and variety of minorities whose preferences must be taken into account by leaders in making policy choices. I am inclined to think that it is in this characteristic of elections—not minority rule but minorities rule—that we must look for some of the essential differences between dictatorships and democracies.

But there is another characteristic of elections that is important for our inquiry. If the majority rarely rules on matters of specific policy, nevertheless the specific policies selected by a process of "minorities rule" probably lie most of the time within the bounds of consensus set by the important values of the politically active members of the society, of whom the voters are a key group. . . . For politicians subject to elections must operate within the limits set both by their own values, as indoctrinated members of the society, and by their expectations about what policies they can adopt and still be re-elected.

In a sense, what we ordinarily describe as democratic "politics" is merely the chaff. It is the surface manifestation, representing superficial conflicts. Prior to politics, beneath it, enveloping it, restricting it, conditioning it, is the underlying consensus on policy that usually exists in the society among a predominant portion of the politically active members. Without such a consensus no democratic system would long survive the endless irritations and frustrations of elections and party competition. With such a consensus the disputes over policy alternatives are nearly always disputes over a set of alternatives that have already been winnowed down to those within the broad area of basic agreement. . . .

That some minorities will frustrate and in that sense tyrannize over others is inherent in a society where people disagree, that is, in human society. But if frustration is inherent in human society, dictatorship is not. However, if there is anything to be said for the processes that actually distinguish democracy (or polyarchy) from dictatorship, it is not discoverable in the clear-cut distinction between government by a majority and government by a minority. The distinction comes much closer to being one between government by a minority and government by *minorities*. As compared with the political processes of a dictatorship, the characteristics of polyarchy greatly extend the number, size, and diversity of the minorities whose preferences will influence the outcome of governmental decisions. Furthermore, these characteristics evidently have a reciprocal influence on a number of key aspects of politics: the kinds of leaders recruited, the legitimate and illegitimate types of political activity, the range and kinds of policies open to leaders, social processes for information and communication—indeed upon the whole ethos of the society. It is in these and other effects more than in the sovereignty of the majority that we find the values of a democratic process.

E. H. Carr, *The New Society* (New York, St. Martin's Press, Inc., 1957) Excerpts, pp. 61-62, 74-76.

Modern democracy, as it grew up and spread from its focus in western Europe over the past three centuries, rested on three main propositions: first, that the individual conscience is the ultimate source of decisions about what is right and wrong; second, that there exists between different individuals a fundamental harmony of interests strong enough to enable them to live peacefully together in society; third, that where action has to be taken in the name of society, rational discussion between individuals is the best method of reaching a decision on that action. Modern democracy is, in virtue of its origins, individualist, optimistic and rational. The three main propositions on which it is based have all been seriously challenged in the contemporary world. . . .

From the conception of democracy as a select society of free individuals, enjoying equal rights and periodically electing to manage the affairs of society, a small number of their peers, who deliberate together (the assumption being that the course which appeals to the majority is likely to be the most rational), we have passed to the current reality of mass democracy. The typical mass democracy of today is a vast society of individuals, stratified by widely different social and economic backgrounds into a series of groups or classes, enjoying equal political rights the exercise of which is organized through two or more closely integrated political machines called parties. Between the parties and individual citizens stand an indeterminate number of entities variously known as unions, associations,

Reprinted by permission of Macmillan & Company, Ltd., and St. Martin's Press, Inc.

lobbies or pressure-groups devoted to the promotion of some economic interest, or of some social or humanitarian cause in which keen critics usually detect a latent and perhaps unconscious interest. At the first stage of the democratic process, these associations and groups form a sort of exchange and mart where votes are traded for support of particular policies; the more votes such a group controls the better its chance of having its views incorporated in the party platform. At the second stage, when these bargains have been made, the party as a united entity "goes to the country" and endeavors by every form of political propaganda to win the support of the unattached voter. At the third stage, when the election has been decided, the parties once more dispute or bargain together, in the light of the votes cast, on the policies to be put into effect; the details of procedure at this third stage differ considerably in different democratic countries in accordance with varying constitutional requirements and party structures. What is important to note is that the first and third stages are fierce matters of bargaining. At the second stage, where the mass persuasion of the electorate is at issue, the methods employed now commonly approximate more and more closely to those of commercial advertisers, who on the advice of modern psychologists, find the appeal to fear, envy or self-aggrandizement more effective than the appeal to reason. . . . We have returned to a barely disguised struggle of interest-groups in which the arguments used are for the most part no more than a rationalization of the interests concerned, and the role of persuasion is played by carefully calculated appeals to the irrational subconscious. . . .

. . . mass democracy is a new phenomenon—a creation of the last half century—which it is inappropriate and misleading to consider in terms of the philosophy of Locke or of the liberal democracy of the nineteenth century. . . . To speak today of the defence of democracy as if we were defending something which we knew and had possessed for many decades or many centuries is self-deception and sham.

It is no answer to point to institutions that have survived from earlier forms of democracy. . . . The criterion must be sought not in the survival of traditional institutions, but in the question where power resides and how it is exercised. In this respect democracy is a matter of degree. Some countries today are more democratic than others. But none is perhaps very democratic, if any high standard of democracy is applied. Mass democracy is a difficult and hitherto largely unchartered territory; and we should be nearer the mark, and should have a far more convincing slogan, if we spoke of the need, not to defend democracy, but to create it.

Louis Hartz, "Democracy: Image and Reality," W. N. Chambers and R. H. Salisbury, eds., *Democracy Today, Problems and Prospects* (New York, Collier Books, 1962) Excerpts, pp. 25-30.

The system of democracy works by virtue of certain processes which its theory never describes, to which, indeed, its theory is actually hostile. But we identify the system with the theory, as if we actually lived by the ancient Jeffersonian image of democracy we cherish, so that when we are confronted with some of the practices which make democracy work we become terrified that the system is breaking up. . . .

Democracy has always worked through group coercion, crowd psychology, and economic power, yet for fifty years these factors have sent a tremor through democratic hearts. It would be absurd, of course, to argue that none of these factors poses a problem for the democratic process. Quite obviously they all do. The tyranny of party and group, if carried beyond a certain point, can begin to nullify the decision of an electorate. Mass opinion, if it reaches a point where it is completly manipulable by a monopolistic force, will also make a sham of the democratic system. And a powerful economic minority clearly has certain bounds within which it must function if democracy is to retain its meaning. But it is one thing to define these problems as problems of "excess," of the necessary machinery of the democratic world somehow getting out of hand, and it is quite another to define them as an apocalyptic "exposure" of democratic institutions. They do indeed expose our theory, which has room for none of them, but they do not expose the real processes by which democracy has always worked.

. . . during the last half century, with respect to domestic factors, we have had a surplus of pessimistic excitement about the "fate of democratic institutions," and . . . this in turn derives from the discovery of things which challenge the image of democracy more than they do its *practice*. But how does such a situation come about? How can it happen that the theory of a system will leave out so much of the real machinery by which it lives? And why should men so confuse the theory with the machinery that they are led in the end to suffer unreal anxieties? . . .

The truth is, no modern political system as it has risen to power has ever developed an image which corresponds to the real procedures by which it works. Nor has this been due to any trick, any conscious hypocrisy of mind. It has been due to the inevitable perspectives of political controversy, which compel a system to define itself in terms of the one it seeks to undermine. Its image of itself is a negation of what it seeks to destroy. Thus Marxism, instead of being a picture of socialist society, the nature of which we are only now beginning to discover, is a negative picture of capitalism. And in the same sense the doctrine of liberal democracy, instead of being a description of democratic life, is a negative description of life in the old European world that democracy destroyed. Locke, Rousseau, and Bentham are in this sense not "theorists of democracy" at all: they are inverted theorists of the "corporate society" of the Seventeenth and Eighteenth centuries.

Once we go back to that society, it is clear enough why the democratic image these men gave us should be hostile to half of the machinery that was later invented in order to make democracy work. The points at which they assailed the old corporate system were precisely the points at which that machinery was destined to appear: this is one of the crucial correlations involved in our whole problem, the link between the institutions of the corporate world that the classical thinkers denounced and the new inventions of the democratic age that they did not bother to mention. Seeking to emancipate men from the rigid pluralism of church, guild, and province, those thinkers were bound to be "individualists." How could they say, even if they understood the fact, that democracy itself would function through a new pluralism of associations, parties, and groups? Anxious to shatter the claims of revelation, to dissolve the hierarchies based on the notion of mass incompetence, they were bound to be "rationalists." Could they say also that the electorate of a large state, if only to unify itself sufficiently to function, would have to forge a common opinion largely through the use of stereotypes and symbols, and that herein would lie the possibilities of manipulation? Nor is the issue less clear with respect to economic power. The men who gave us our image of democracy were associated with the rise of the middle class, and where there has been no such class democracy has had its difficulties. But seeking to shatter the rule of another older class they could not fail to be universalists, to form an image of pure "equality."

Thus Locke, Bentham, and Jefferson were bound to coin clichés which contradicted half of the institutional reality which has made them triumph in the modern world. The bond between the old institutions of the corporate age and the new institutions of the democratic age, a bond of group pluralism, mass emotion, and elite rule, had, in the nature of things, to remain as hidden as possible. This does not mean, of course, that democracy is really the same as the dying feudalism of the Seventeenth and Eighteenth centuries, that no progress in the direction of individualism, real popular decision, and the equal state has actually taken place. . . . So what happens in the case of an ascendant social and political system is that it strikes in fact some middle ground between the blazing negative ideals of its origin and the operational necessities of actual life. As a living thing it turns out to be a mad anomaly, a set of ideals half realized through institutions which contradict them, which no one has ever described. And it is always productive, at a certain stage in its later history, of a crowd of thinkers who suddenly discover that no one has ever described it. This is the age of "realism," which mixes with new anxiety a vast amount of empirical research.

But why should the facts be so hard to face? Why, if we see ourselves as we have always been, should we feel that our existence is suddenly threatened? There is really nothing mysterious about this, nothing excessively subtle. We have projected into the real world the moral difficulties we have actually experienced in perceiving the realities of democratic life. . . .

On the world plane, especially, where democracy meets Fascism and Communism, our current mood has great operational relevance. For these ideologies are utopian, have behind them the driving negative images that democracy had in the day of its origin out of the feudal order. Strictly speaking this was not true of Fascism. Negative it was, a revolt against the whole Enlightenment complex which produced both democracy and Communism, but negative it remained until the end. Communism, however, is a different matter. Rooted itself in the Enlightenment, its battle against capitalism has produced even more vivid promises of emancipation than those produced by democracy in its struggle against the old order: statelessness, abundance, the end of all natural coercion. . . .

Communism is itself subject to the same process of disenchantment that democracy has experienced, the same principle of rising realism, the same crisis of anxiety. And because its negative ideals are in fact broader than those of democracy, and in certain areas its institutions are a more glaring contradiction of them, its shock of disenchantment is bound to be even more severe than any we have sustained. . . . There is mounting evidence to prove that Communism is susceptible to an even more frightful version of the unillusionment we have experienced, the hidden anticlimax which the Enlightenment imposes on all its children.

APPORTIONMENT

Reynolds v. Sims, 377 U. S. 533, 12 L ed 2d 506 (1964).

Selections from the opinion of the Supreme Court delivered by Mr. Chief Justice Warren and from the dissenting opinion of Mr. Justice Harlan. The Court upheld the ruling of the Federal District Court for the Middle District of Alabama that the existing and two legislatively proposed plans for the apportionment of seats in the two houses of the Alabama Legislature were unconstitutional under the Equal Protection Clause of the Constitution of the United States.

PORTIONS OF MR. CHIEF JUSTICE WARREN'S OPINION:

Undeniably the Constitution of the United States protects the right of all qualified citizens to vote, in state as well as in federal elections. A consistent line of decisions by this Court in cases involving attempts to deny or restrict the right of suffrage has made this indelibly clear. It has been repeatedly recognized that all qualified voters have a constitutionally protected right to vote, . . . and to have their votes counted, ... The right to vote can neither be denied outright, . . . nor destroyed by alteration of ballots, . . . nor diluted by ballot-box stuffing, ... Racially based gerrymandering, . . . and the conducting of white primaries, . . . both of which result in denying to some citizens their right to vote, have been held to be constitutionally impermissible. And history has seen a continuing expansion of the scope of the right of suffrage in this country. The right to vote freely for the candidate of one's choice is of the essence of a democratic society, and any restrictions on that right strike at the heart of representative government. And the right of suffrage can be denied by a debasement or dilution of the weight of a citizen's vote just as effectively as by wholly prohibiting the free exercise of the franchise.

In *Baker v. Carr*, 369 U.S. 186 . . . , we held that a claim asserted under the Equal Protection Clause challenging the constitutionality of a State's apportionment of seats in its legislature, on the ground that the right to vote of certain citizens was effectively impaired since debased and diluted, in effect presented a justiciable controversy subject to adjudication by the federal courts. . . .

In *Gray v. Sanders*, 372 U.S. 368, . . . , we held that the Georgia county unit system, applicable in state-wide primary elections, was unconstitutional since it resulted in a dilution of the weight of the votes of certain Georgia voters merely because of where they resided. After indicating that the Fifteenth and Nineteenth Amendments prohibit a State from overweighting or diluting votes on the bases of race or sex, we stated:

"How then can one person be given twice or ten times the voting power of another person in a state-wide election merely because he lives in a rural area or because he lives in the smallest rural county? Once the geographical unit for which a representative is to be chosen is designated, all who participate in the election are to have an equal vote whatever their race, whatever their sex, whatever their occupation, whatever their income, and wherever their home may be in that geographical unit. This is required by the Equal Protection Clause of the Fourteenth Amendment. The concept of 'we the people' under the Constitution vizualizes no preferred class of voters but equality among those who meet the basic qualifications. The idea that every voter is equal to every other voter in his State, when he casts his ballot in favor of one of several competing candidates, underlies many of our decisions."

Continuing, we stated that "there is no indication in the Constitution that homesite or occupation affords a permissible basis for distinguishing between qualified voters within the State." And finally, we concluded: "The conception of political equality from the Declaration of Independence, to Lincoln's Gettysburg Address, to the Fifteenth, Seventeenth, and Nineteenth Amendments can mean only one thing—one person, one vote." . . .

In *Wesberry v. Sanders*, 376 U.S. 1, . . . we held that attacks on the constitutionality of congressional districting plans enacted by state legislatures do not present nonjusticiable questions and should not be dismissed generally for "want of equity." We determined that the constitutional test for the validity of congressional districting schemes was one of substantial equality of population among the various districts established by a state legislature for the election of members of the Federal House of Representatives.

In that case we decided that an apportionment of congressional seats which "contracts the value of some votes and expands that of others" is unconstitutional, since "the Federal Constitution intends that when qualified voters elect members of Congress each vote be given as much weight as any other vote. . . ." We concluded that the constitutional prescription for election of members of the House of Representatives "by the people," construed in its historical context, "means that as nearly as is practicable one man's vote in a congressional election is to be worth as much as another's." We further stated:

"It would defeat the principle solemnly embodied in the Great Compromise—equal representation in the House for equal numbers of the people—for us to hold that, within the States, legislatures may draw the lines of congressional districts in such a way as to give some voters a greater voice in choosing a Congressman than others."

We found further, in Wesberry, that "our Constitution's plain objective" was that "of making equal representation for equal numbers of people the fundamental goal. . . ." We concluded by stating:

"No right is more precious in a free country than that of having a voice in the election of those who make the laws under which, as good citizens, we must live. Other rights, even the most basic, are illusory if the right to vote is undermined. Our Constitution leaves no room for classification of people in a way that unnecessarily abridges this right." . . .

. . . Wesberry clearly established that the fundamental principle of representative government in this country is one of equal representation for equal numbers of people, without regard to race, sex, economic status, or place of residence within a State. Our problem, then, is to ascertain, in the instant cases, whether there are any constitutionally cognizable principles which would justify departures from the basic standard of equality among voters in the apportionment of seats in state legislatures. . . .

. . . Undoubtedly, the right of suffrage is a fundamental matter in a free and democratic society. Especially since the right to exercise the franchise in a free and unimpaired manner is preservative of other basic civil and political rights, any alleged infringement of the right of citizens to vote must be carefully and meticulously scrutinized. . . .

Legislators represent people, not trees or acres. Legislators are elected by voters, not farms or cities or economic interests. As long as ours is a representative form of government, and our legislatures are those instruments of government elected directly by and directly representative of the people, the right to elect legislators in a free and unimpaired fashion is a bedrock of our political system. It could hardly be gainsaid that a constitutional claim had been asserted by an allegation that certain otherwise qualified voters had been entirely prohibited from voting for members of their state legislature. And, if a State should provide that the votes of citizens in one part of the State should be given two times, or five times, or 10 times the weight of votes of citizens in another part of the State, it could hardly be contended that the right to vote of those residing in the disfavored areas had not been effectively diluted. It would appear extraordinary to suggest that a State could be constitutionally permitted to enact a law providing that certain of the State's voters could vote two, five, or 10 times for their legislative representatives, while voters living elsewhere could vote only once. And it is inconceivable that a state law to the effect that, in counting votes for legislators, the votes of citizens in one part of the State would be multiplied by two, five, or 10, while the votes of persons in another area would be counted only at face value, could be constitutionally sustainable. Of course, the effect of state legislative districting schemes which give the same number of representatives to unequal numbers of constituents is identical. Overweighting and overvaluation of the votes of those living here has the certain effect of dilution and undervaluation of the votes of those living there. The resulting discrimination against those individual voters living in disfavored areas is easily demonstrable mathematically. Their right to vote is simply not the same right to vote as that of those living in a favored part of the State. Two, five, or 10 of them must vote before the effect of their voting is equivalent to that of their favored neighbor. Weighting the votes of citizens differently, by any method or means, merely because of where they happen to reside, hardly seems justifiable. One must be ever aware that the Constitution forbids "sophisticated as well as simple-minded modes of discrimination." . . .

State legislatures are, historically, the fountainhead of representative government in this country. . . . But representative government is in essence self-government through the medium of elected representatives of the people, and each and every citizen has an inalienable right to full and effective participation in the political processes of his State's legislative bodies. Most citizens can achieve this participation only as qualified voters through the election of legislators to represent them. Full and effective participation by all citizens in state government requires, therefore, that each citizen have an equally effective voice in the election of members of his state legislature. Modern and viable state government needs, and the Constitution demands, no less.

Logically, in a society ostensibly grounded on representative government, it would seem reasonable that a majority of the people of a State could elect a majority of that State's legislators. To conclude differently, and to sanction minority control of state legislative bodies, would appear to deny majority rights in a way that far surpasses any possible denial of minority rights that might otherwise be thought to result. Since legislatures are responsible for enacting laws by which all citizens are to be governed, they should be bodies which are collectively responsive to the popular will. And the concept of equal protection has been traditionally viewed as requiring the uniform treatment of persons standing in the same relation to the governmental action questioned or challenged. With respect to the allocation of legislative representation, all voters, as citizens of a State, stand in the same relation regardless of where they live. Any suggested criteria for the differentiation of citizens are insufficient to justify any discrimination, as to the weight of their votes, unless relevant to the permissible purposes of legislative apportionment. Since the achieving of fair and effective representation for all citizens is concededly the basic aim of legislative apportionment, we conclude that the Equal Protection Clause guarantees the opportunity for equal participation by all voters in the election of state legislators. Diluting the weight of votes because of place of residence impairs basic constitutional rights under the Fourteenth Amendment just as much as invidious discriminations based upon factors such as race, . . . or economic status, ... Our constitutional system amply provides for the protection of minorities by means other than giving them majority control of state legislatures. And the democratic ideals of equality and majority rule, which have served this Nation so well in the past, are hardly of any less significance for the present and the future.

We are told that the matter of apportioning representation in a state legislature is a complex and many-faceted one. We are advised that States can rationally consider factors other than population in apportioning legislative representatives. We are admonished not to restrict the power of the States to impose differing views as to political philosophy on their citizens. We are cautioned about the dangers of entering into political thickets and mathematical quagmires. Our answer is this: a denial of constitutionally protected rights demands judicial protection; our oath and our office require no less of us. . . .

To the extent that a citizen's right to vote is debased, he is that much less a citizen. The fact that an individual lives here or there is not a legitimate reason for overweighting or diluting the efficacy of his vote. The complexions of societies and civilizations change, often with amazing rapidity. A nation once primarily rural in character becomes predominantly urban. Representation schemes once fair and equitable become archaic and outdated. But the basic principle of representative government remains, and must remain, unchanged—the weight of a citizen's vote cannot be made to depend on where he lives. Population is, of necessity, the starting point for consideration and the controlling criterion for judgment in legislative apportionment controversies. A citizen, a qualified voter, is no more nor no less so because he lives in the city or on the farm. This is the clear and strong command of our Constitution's Equal Protection Clause. . . . The Equal Protection Clause demands no less than substantially equal legislative representation for all citizens, of all places as well as of all races.

We hold that, as a basic constitutional standard, the Equal Protection Clause requires that the seats in both houses of a bicameral state legislature must be apportioned on a population basis. Simply stated, an individual's right to vote for state legislators is unconstitutionally impaired when its weight is in a substantial fashion diluted when compared with votes of citizens living in other parts of the State. . . . We . . . find the federal analogy inapposite and irrelevant to state legislative districting schemes. . . .

The system of representation in the two Houses of the Federal Congress is one ingrained in our Constitution, as part of the law of the land. It is one conceived out of compromise and concession indispensable to the establishment of our federal republic. Arising from unique historical circumstances, it is based on the consideration that in establishing our type of federalism a group of formerly independent States bound themselves together under one national government. Admittedly, the original 13 states surrendered some of their sovereignty in agreeing to join together "to form a more perfect Union." . . .

Political subdivisions of States—counties, cities, or whatever—never were and never have been considered as sovereign entities. Rather, they have been traditionally regarded as subordinate governmental instrumentalities created by the State to assist in the carrying out of state governmental functions. . . .

Since we find the so-called federal analogy inapposite to a consideration of the constitutional validity of state legislative apportionment schemes, we necessarily hold that the Equal Protection Clause requires both houses of a state legislature to be apportioned on a population basis. The right of a citizen to equal representation and to have his vote weighted equally with those of all other citizens in the election of members of one house of a bicameral state legislature would amount to little if States could effectively submerge the equal-population principle in the apportionment of seats in the other house. If such a scheme were permissible, an individual citizen's ability to exercise an effective voice in the only instrument of state government directly representative of the people might be almost as effectively thwarted as if neither house were apportioned on a population basis. Deadlock between the two bodies might result in compromise and concession on some issues. But in all too many cases the more probable result would be frustration of the majority will through minority veto in the house not apportioned on a population basis, stemming directly from the failure to accord adequate overall legislative representation to all of the State's citizens on a nondiscriminatory basis. In summary, we can perceive no constitutional difference, with respect to the geographical distribution of state legislative representation, between the two houses of a bicameral state legislature.

We do not believe that the concept of bicameralism is rendered anachronistic and meaningless when the predominant basis of representation in the two state legislative bodies is required to be the same —population. A prime reason for bicameralism, modernly considered, is to insure mature and deliberate consideration of, and to prevent precipitate action on, proposed legislative measures. Simply because the controlling criterion for apportioning representation is required to be the same in both houses does not mean that there will be no differences in the composition and complexion of the two bodies. Different constituencies can be represented in the two houses. One body could be composed of single-member districts while the other could have at least some multimember districts. The length of terms of the legislators in the separate bodies could differ. The numerical size of the two bodies could be made to differ, even significantly, and the geographical size of districts from which legislators are elected could also be made to differ. And apportionment in one house could be arranged so as to balance off minor inequities in the representation of certain areas in the other house. In summary, these and other factors could be, and are presently in many States, utilized to engender differing complexions and collective attitudes in the two bodies of a state legislature, although both are apportioned substantially on a population basis.

By holding that as a federal constitutional requisite both houses of a state legislature must be apportioned on a population basis, we mean that the Equal Protection Clause requires that a State make an honest and good faith effort to construct districts, in both houses of its legislature, as nearly of equal population as is practicable. We realize that it is a practical impossibility to arrange legislative districts so that each one has an identical number of residents, or citizens, or voters. Mathematical exactness or precision is hardly a workable constitutional requirement. . . .

For the present, we deem it expedient not to attempt to spell out any precise constitutional tests. What is marginally permissible in one State may be unsatisfactory in another, depending on the particular circumstances of the case. Developing a body of doctrine on a case-by-case basis appears to us to provide the most satisfactory means of arriving at detailed constitutional requirements in the area of state legislative apportionment. . . . Thus, we proceed to state here only a few rather general considerations which appear to us to be relevant.

A State may legitimately desire to maintain the integrity of various political subdivisions, insofar as possible, and provide for compact districts of contiguous territory in designing a legislative apportionment scheme. Valid considerations may underlie such aims. Indiscriminate districting, without any regard for political subdivision or natural or historical boundary lines, may be little more than an open invitation to partisan gerrymandering. Single-member districts may be the rule in one State, while another State might desire to achieve some flexibility by creating multimember or floterial districts. Whatever the means of accomplishment, the overriding objective must be substantial equality of population among the various districts, so that the vote of any citizen is approximately equal in weight to that of any other citizen in the State.

History indicates, however, that many States have deviated, to a greater or lesser degree, from the equal-population principle in the apportionment of seats in at least one house of their legislatures. So long as the divergences from a strict population standard are based on legitimate considerations incident to the effectuation of a rational state policy, some deviations from the equal-population principle are constitutionally permissible with respect to the apportionment of seats in either or both of the two houses of a bicameral state legislature. But neither history alone, nor economic or other sorts of group interests, are permissible factors in attempting to justify disparities from population-based representation. Citizens, not history or economic interests, cast votes. Considerations of area alone provide an insufficient justification for deviations from the equal-population principle. Again, people, not land or trees or pastures, vote. Modern developments and improvements in transportation and communication make rather hollow, in the mid-1960's, most claims that deviations from population-based representation can validly be based solely on geographical considerations. Arguments for allowing such deviations in order to insure effective representation for sparsely settled areas and to prevent legislative districts from becoming so large that the availability of access of citizens to their representatives is impaired are today, for the most part unconvincing.

A consideration that appears to be of more substance in justifying some deviations from population-based representation in state legislatures is that of insuring some voice to political subdivisions, as political subdivisions. Several factors make more than insubstantial claims that a State can rationally consider according political subdivisions some independent representation in at least one body of the state legislature, as long as the basic standard of equality of population among districts is maintained. Local governmental entities are frequently charged with various responsibilities incident to the operation of state government.

In many States much of the legislature's activity involves the enactment of so-called local legislation, directed only to the concerns of particular political subdivisions. And a State may legitimately desire to construct districts along political subdivision lines to deter the possibilities of gerrymandering. However, permitting deviations from population-based representation does not mean that each local governmental unit or political subdivision can be given separate representation, regardless of population. Carried too far, a scheme of giving at least one seat in one house to each political subdivision (for example, to each county) could easily result, in many States, in a total subversion of the equal-population principle in that legislative body. This would be especially true in a State where the number of counties is large and many of them are sparsely populated, and the number of seats in the legislative body being apportioned does not significantly exceed the number of counties. Such a result, we conclude, would be constitutionally impermissible. And careful judicial scrutiny must of course be given, in evaluating state apportionment schemes, to the character as well as the degree of deviations from a strict population basis. But if, even as a result of a clearly rational state policy of according some legislative representation to political subdivisions, population is submerged as the controlling consideration in the apportionment of seats in the particular legislative body, then the right of all of the State's citizens to cast an effective and adequately weighted vote would be unconstitutionally impaired. . . .

That the Equal Protection Clause requires that both houses of a state legislature be apportioned on a population basis does not mean that States cannot adopt some reasonable plan for periodic revision of their apportionment schemes. Decennial reapportionment appears to be a rational approach to readjustment of legislative representation in order to take into account population shifts and growth. . . .

PORTIONS OF MR. JUSTICE HARLAN'S DISSENTING OPINION.

Today's holding is that the Equal Protection Clause of the Fourteenth Amendment requires every State to structure its legislature so that all the members of each house represent substantially the same number of people; other factors may be given play only to the extent that they do not significantly encroach on this basic "population" principle. Whatever may be thought of this holding as a piece of political ideology—and even on that score the political history and practices of this country from its earliest beginnings leave wide room for debate,

. . . —I think it demonstrable that the Fourteenth Amendment does not impose this political tenet on the States or authorize this Court to do so.

The Court's constitutional discussion . . . is remarkable . . . for its failure to address itself at all to the Fourteenth Amendment as a whole or to the legislative history of the Amendment pertinent to the matter at hand. Stripped of aphorisms, the Court's argument boils down to the assertion that appellees' right to vote has been invidiously "debased" or "diluted" by systems of apportionment which entitle them to vote for fewer legislators than other voters, an assertion which is tied to the Equal Protection Clause only by the constitutionally frail tautology that "equal" means "equal."

Had the Court paused to probe more deeply into the matter, it would have found that the Equal Protection Clause was never intended to inhibit the States in choosing any democratic method they pleased for the apportionment of their legislatures. This is shown by the language of the Fourteenth Amendment taken as a whole, by the understanding of those who proposed and ratified it, and by the political practices of the States at the time the Amendment was adopted. It is confirmed by numerous state and congressional actions since the adoption of the Fourteenth Amendment, and by the common understanding of the Amendment as evidenced by subsequent constitutional amendments and decisions of this Court before *Baker v. Carr*, . . . made an abrupt break with the past, in 1962.

The failure of the Court to consider any of these matters cannot be excused or explained by any concept of "developing" constitutionalism. It is meaningless to speak of constitutional "development" when both the language and history of the controlling provisions of the Constitution are wholly ignored. Since it can, I think, be shown beyond doubt that state legislative apportionments, as such, are wholly free of constitutional limitations, save such as may be imposed by the Republican Form of Government Clause . . . , the Court's action now bringing them within the purview of the Fourteenth Amendment amounts to nothing less than an exercise of the amending power by this Court. . . .

The Court relies exclusively on that portion of ¶1 of the Fourteenth Amendment which provides that no State shall "deny to any person within its jurisdiction the equal protection of the laws," and disregards entirely the significance of ¶2, which reads:

"Representatives shall be apportioned among the several States according to their respective numbers counting the whole number of persons in each State, excluding Indians not taxed. *But when the right to vote at any election for* the choice of electors for President and Vice President of the United States, Representatives in Congress, *the executive and Judicial officers of a State, or the members of the Legislature thereof, is denied* to any of the male inhabitants of such State, being twenty-one years of age, and citizens of the United States, *or in any way abridged*, except for participation in rebellion, or other crime, the basis of representation therein shall be reduced in the proportion which the number of such male citizens shall bear to the whole number of male citizens twenty-one years of age in such State." (Emphasis added.)

The Amendment is a single text. It was introduced and discussed as such in the Reconstruction Committee, which reported it to the Congress. It was discussed as a unit in Congress and proposed as a unit to the States, which ratified it as a unit. A proposal to split up the Amendment and submit each section to the States as a separate amendment was rejected by the Senate. Whatever one might take to be the application to these cases of the Equal Protection Clause if it stood alone, I am unable to understand the Court's utter disregard of the second section which expressly recognizes the States' power to deny "or in any way" abridge the right of their inhabitants to vote for "the members of the State Legislature," and its express provision of a remedy for such denial or abridgment. The comprehensive scope of the second section and its particular reference to the state legislatures precluded the suggestion that the first section was intended to have the result reached by the Court today. If indeed the words of the Fourteenth Amendment speak for themselves, as the majority's disregard of history seems to imply, they speak as clearly as may be against the construction which the majority puts on them. But we are not limited to the language of the Amendment itself.

[*Mr. Justice Harlan then reviews the proposal and ratification of the Amendment and developments in the years following 1868.*]

Since the Court now invalidates the legislative apportionments in six States, and has so far upheld the apportionment in none, it is scarcely necessary to comment on the situation in the States today, which is, of course, as fully contrary to the Court's decision as is the record of every prior period in this Nation's history. As of 1961, the Constitutions of all but 11 States, roughly 20% of the total, recognized bases of apportionment other than geographic spread of population, and to some extent favored sparsely populated areas by a variety of devices, ranging from straight area representation or guaranteed minimum area representation to complicated schemes of the kind exemplified by the provisions of New York's Constitution of 1894. . . .

In this summary of what the majority ignores, note should be taken of the Fifteenth and Nineteenth Amendments. The former prohibited the States from denying or abridging the right to vote "on account of race, color, or previous condition of servitude." The latter . . . added sex to the prohibited classifications. . . .

. . . If constitutional amendment was the only means by which all men and, later, women, could be guaranteed the right to vote at all, even for *federal* officers, how can it be that the far less obvious right to a particular kind of apportionment of *state* legislatures—a right to which is opposed a far more plausible conflicting interest of the State than the interest which opposes the general right to vote—can be conferred by judicial construction of the Fourteenth Amendment? Yet, unless one takes the highly implausible view that the Fourteenth Amendment controls methods of apportionment but leaves the right to vote itself unprotected, the conclusion is inescapable that the Court has, for purposes of these cases, rejected the Fifteenth and Nineteenth Amendments to the same limbo of constitutional anachronisms to which the second section of the Fourteenth Amendment has been assigned. . . .

The Court's elaboration of its new "constitutional" doctrine indicates how far—and how unwisely—it has strayed from the appropriate bounds of its authority. The consequence of today's decision is that in all but the handful of States which may already satisfy the new requirements the local District Court or, it may be, the state courts, are given blanket authority and the constitutional duty to supervise apportionment of the State Legislatures. It is difficult to imagine a more intolerable and inappropriate interference by the judiciary with the independent legislatures of the States. . . .

. . . Predictions once made that the courts would never have to face the problem of actually working out an apportionment have proved false. This Court, however, continues to avoid the consequences of its decisions, simply assuring us that the lower courts "can and . . . will work out more concrete and specific standards." . . . Deeming it "expedient" not to spell out "precise constitutional tests," the Court contents itself with stating "only a few rather general consideration." . . .

Although the Court—necessarily, as I believe—provides only generalities in elaboration of its main thesis, its opinion nevertheless fully demonstrates how far removed these problems are from fields of judicial competence. Recognizing that "indiscriminate districting" is an invitation to "partisan gerrymandering," . . . the Court nevertheless excludes virtually every basis for the formation of electoral districts other than "indiscriminate districting." In one or another of today's opinions, the Court declares it unconstitutional for a State to give effective consideration to any of the following in establishing legislative districts:

(1) history;

(2) "economic or other sorts of group interests";

(3) area;

(4) geographical considerations;

(5) a desire "to insure effective representation for sparsely settled areas";

(6) "availability of access of citizens to their representatives";

(7) theories of bicameralism (except those approved by the Court);

(8) occupation;

(9) "an attempt to balance urban and rural power";

(10) the preference of a majority of voters in the State.

So far as presently appears, the *only* factor which a State may consider, apart from numbers, is political subdivisions. But even "a clearly rational state policy" recognizing this factor is unconstitutional if "population is submerged as the controlling consideration. . . ."

I know of no principle of logic or practical or theoretical politics, still less any constitutional principle, which establishes all or any of these exclusions. Certain it is that the Court's opinion does not establish them. So far as the Court says anything at all on this score, it says only that "legislators represent people, not trees or acres," . . . ; that "citizens, not history or economic interests, cast votes," . . . ; that "people, not land or trees or pastures, vote," . . . All this may be conceded. But it is surely equally obvious, and, in the context of elections, more meaningful to note that people are not ciphers and that legislators can represent their electors only by speaking for their interests—economic, social, political—many of which do reflect the place where the electors live. The Court does not establish, or indeed even attempt to make a case for the proposition that conflicting interests within a State can only be adjusted by disregarding them when voters are grouped for purposes of representation.

With these cases the Court approaches the end of the third round set in motion by the complaint filed in *Baker v. Carr*. What is done today deepens my conviction that judicial entry into this realm is profoundly ill-advised and constitutionally impermissible. As I have said before, . . . I believe that the vitality of our political system, on which in the last analysis all else depends, is weakened by reliance on the judiciary for political reform; in time a complacent body politic may result.

These decisions also cut deeply into the fabric of our federalism. . . . no thinking person can fail to recognize that the aftermath of these cases, however desirable it may be thought in itself, will have been achieved at the cost of a radical alteration in the relationship between the States and the Federal Government, more particularly the Federal judiciary. . . .

Finally, these decisions give support to a current mistaken view of the Constitution and the constitutional function of this Court. This view, in a nutshell, is that every major social ill in this country can find its cure in some constitutional "principle," and that this Court should "take the lead" in promoting reform when other branches of government fail to act. The Constitution is not a panacea for every blot upon the public welfare, nor should this Court, ordained as a judicial body, be thought of as a general haven for reform movements. The Constitution is an instrument of government, fundamental to which is the premise that in a diffusion of governmental authority lies the greatest promise that this Nation will realize liberty for all its citizens. This Court, limited in function in accordance with that premise, does not serve its high purpose when it exceeds its authority, even to satisfy justified impatience with the slow workings of the political process. For when, in the name of constitutional interpretation, the Court *adds* something to the Constitution that was deliberately excluded from it, the Court in reality substitutes its view of what should be so for the amending process.

Lucas v. Colorado General Assembly, 377 U.S. 713, 12 L ed 2d 632 (1964).

Selections from the opinion of the Supreme Court delivered by Mr. Chief Justice Warren and from the dissenting opinion of Mr. Justice Clark. The Court reversed a decision of the Federal District Court for the District of Colorado which upheld the validity of an apportionment scheme established by a 1962 amendment of the Colorado Constitution which had been adopted by the voters of Colorado.

PORTIONS OF MR. CHIEF JUSTICE WARREN'S OPINION:

At the November 1962 general election, the Colorado electorate adopted proposed Amendment No. 7 by a vote of 305,700 to 172,725 and defeated proposed Amendment No. 8 by a vote of 311,749 to 149,822. Amendment No. 8, rejected by a majority of the voters, prescribed an apportionment plan pursuant to which seats in both houses of the Colorado Legislature would purportedly be apportioned on a population basis. Amendment No. 7, on the other hand, provided for the apportionment of the House of Representatives on the basis of population, but essentially maintained the existing apportionment in the Senate, which was based on a combination of population and various other factors. . . .

Amendment No. 7 provides for the establishment of a General Assembly composed of 39 senators and 65 representatives, with the State divided geographically into 39 senatorial and 65 representative districts, so that all seats in both houses are apportioned among single-member districts. . . .

Senatorial apportionment, under Amendment No. 7, involves little more than adding four new Senate seats and distributing them to four populous counties in the Denver area, and in substance perpetuates the existing senatorial apportionment scheme. Counties containing only 33.2% of the State's total population elect a majority of the 39-member Senate under the provisions of Amendment No. 7. . . .

Several aspects of this case serve to distinguish it from the other cases involving state legislative apportionment also decided this date. Initially, one house of the Colorado Legislature is at least arguably apportioned substantially on a population basis under Amendment No. 7 and the implementing statutory provisions. Under the apportionment schemes challenged in the other cases, on the other hand, clearly neither of the houses in any of the state legislatures is apportioned sufficiently on a population basis so as to be constitutionally sustainable. Additionally, the Colorado scheme of legislative apportionment here attacked is one adopted by a majority vote of the Colorado electorate almost contemporaneously with the District Court's decision on the merits in this litigation. Thus, the plan at issue did not result from prolonged legislative inaction. . . .

As appellees have correctly pointed out, a majority of the voters in every county of the State voted in favor of the apportionment scheme embodied in Amendment No. 7's provisions, in preference to that contained in proposed Amendment No. 8, which, subject to minor deviations, would have based the apportionment of seats in both houses on a population basis. . . .

Finally, this case differs from the others decided this date in that the initiative device provides a practicable political remedy to obtain relief against alleged legislative malapportionment in Colorado. An initiated measure proposing a constitutional amendment or a statutory enactment is entitled to be placed on the ballot if the signatures of 8% of those voting for the Secretary of State in the last election are obtained. No geographical distribution of petition signers is required. Initiative and referendum has been frequently utilized throughout Colorado's history. . . .

In *Reynolds v. Sims* . . . , we held that the Equal Protection Clause requires that both houses of a bicameral state legislature must be apportioned substantially on a population basis. Of course, the court below assumed, and the parties apparently conceded, that the Colorado House of Representatives, under the statutory provisions enacted by the Colorado Legislature in early 1963 pursuant to Amendment No. 7's dictate that the legislature should create 65 House districts "as nearly equal in population as may be," is now apportioned sufficiently on a population basis to comport with federal constitutional requisites. We need not pass on this question, since the apportionment of Senate seats, under Amendment No. 7, clearly involves departures from population-based representation too extreme to be constitutionally permissible, and there is no indication that the apportionment of the two houses of the Colorado General Assembly, pursuant to the 1962 constitutional amendment, is severable. We therefore conclude that the District Court erred in holding the legislative apportionment plan embodied in Amendment No. 7 to be constitutionally valid. Under neither Amendment No. 7's plan, nor, of course, the previous statutory scheme, is the overall legislative representation in the two houses of the Colorado Legislature sufficiently grounded on population to be constitutionally sustainable under the Equal Protection Clause.

Except as an interim remedial procedure justifying a court in staying its hand temporarily, we find no significance in the fact that a nonjudicial, political remedy may be available for the effectuation of asserted rights to equal representation in a state legislature. Courts sit to adjudicate controversies involving alleged denials of constitutional rights. . . .

. . . An individual's constitutionally protected right to cast an equally weighted vote cannot be denied even by a vote of a majority of a State's electorate, if the apportionment scheme adopted by the voters fails to measure up to the requirements of the Equal Protection Clause. Manifestly, the fact that an apportionment plan is adopted in a popular referendum is insufficient to sustain its constitutionality or to induce a court of equity to refuse to act. . . . "One's right to life, liberty, and property . . . and other fundamental rights may not be submitted to vote; they depend on the outcome of no elections." A citizen's constitutional rights can hardly be infringed simply because a majority of the people choose that it be. We hold that the fact that a challenged legislative apportionment plan was approved by the electorate is without federal constitutional significance, if the scheme adopted fails to satisfy the basic requirements of the Equal Protection Clause, as delineated in our opinion in *Reynolds v. Sims*. And we conclude that the fact that a practicably available political remedy, such as the initiative and referendum, exists under state law provides justification only for a court of equity to stay its hand temporarily while recourse to such a remedial device is attempted or while proposed initiated measures relating to legislative apportionment are pending and will be submitted to the State's voters at the next election. . . .

. . . appellees' argument, accepted by the court below, that the apportionment of the Colorado Senate, under Amendment No. 7, is rational because it takes into account a variety of geographical, historical, topographic and economic considerations fails to provide an adequate justification for the substantial disparities from population-based representation in the allocation of Senate seats to the disfavored populous areas. And any attempted reliance on the so-called federal analogy is factually as well as constitutionally without merit.

Since the apportionment of seats in the Colorado Legislature, under the provisions of Amendment No. 7, fails to comport with the requirements of the Equal Protection Clause, the decision below must be reversed. . . .

PORTIONS OF MR. JUSTICE CLARK'S DISSENTING OPINION:

. . . I have some additional observations with reference to this case.

The parties concede that the Colorado House of Representatives is now apportioned "as nearly equal in population as may be." The Court does not disturb this stipulation though it seems to accept it in niggardly fashion. . . . But the Court strikes down Colorado's apportionment, which was adopted by the majority vote of every political subdivision in the State, because the Senate's majority is elected by 33.2% of the population, a much higher percentage than that which elects a majority of the Senate of the United States.

I refuse to interfere with this apportionment for several reasons. First, Colorado enjoys the initiative and referendum system which it often utilizes and which, indeed, produced the present apportionment. As a result of the action of the Legislature and the use of the initiative and referendum, the State Assembly has been reapportioned eight times since 1881. This indicates the complete awareness of the people of Colorado to apportionment problems and their continuing efforts to solve them. The courts should not interfere in such a situation. . . . Next, . . . there are rational and most persuasive reasons for some deviations in the representation in the Colorado Assembly. The State has mountainous areas which divide it into four regions, some parts of which are almost impenetrable. There are also some depressed areas, diversified industry and varied climate, as well as enormous recreational regions and difficulties in transportation. These factors give rise to problems indigenous to Colorado, which only its people can intelligently solve. This they have done in the present apportionment.

Finally, I cannot agree to the arbitrary application of the "one man, one vote" principle for both houses of a State Legislature. In my view, if one house is fairly apportioned by population (as is admitted here) then the people should have some latitude in providing, on a rational basis, for representation in the other house. The Court seems to approve the federal arrangement of two Senators from each State on the ground that it was a compromise reached by the framers of our Constitution and is a part of the fabric of our national charter. But what the Court overlooks is that Colorado, by an overwhelming vote, has likewise written the organization of its legislative body into its Constitution, and our dual federalism requires that we give it recognition. After all, the Equal Protection Clause is not an algebraic formula. Equal protection does not rest on whether the practice assailed "results in some inequality" but rather on whether "any state of facts reasonably can be conceived that would sustain it"; and one who attacks it must show "that it does not rest upon any reasonable basis, but is essentially arbitrary." . . . Certainly Colorado's arrangement is not arbitrary. On the contrary, it rests on reasonable grounds which, as I have pointed out, are peculiar to that State. It is argued that the Colorado apportionment would lead only to a legislative stalemate between the two houses, but the experience of Congress completely refutes this argument. Now in its 176th year, the federal plan has worked well. It is further said that in any event Colorado's apportionment would substitute compromise for the legislative process. But most legislation is the product of compromise between the various forces acting for and against its enactment.

In striking down Colorado's plan of apportionment, the Court, I believe, is exceeding its powers under the Equal Protection Clause; it is invading the valid functioning of the procedures of the States, and thereby is committing a grievous error which will do irreparable damage to our federal-state relationship. I dissent.

DEMOCRACY, LIBERTY, AND EQUALITY

R. M. MacIver, *The Ramparts We Guard* (New York, The Macmillan Company, 1950) Excerpts, pp. 12-21, 125-127.

. . . there are many kinds of liberty and many kinds of equality. Some liberties are hard to reconcile with others, and some are totally obnoxious to others. Some kinds of equality are at war with others, some kinds are incompatible with any social order and some in particular are incompatible with democracy. . . .

The confusion of democracy and equality has been baneful in the past, and still is common among us. Democracy confers certain rights *equally* on all men—it does not do the impossible, make them equal in skill or intelligence or position or power of influence or authority. In none of these respects are men ever equal nor can any kind of government ever make them equal. . . . Equality by itself is no ideal thing. If all men were equally wretched, equally poor, or equally powerful, the equality would be no boon. . . . In a slave state all men, except the slave-drivers, are equal in servitude. In this sense men may be more equal under a totalitarian regime than under a democracy. . . . If men say they want to be free and equal their demand for freedom puts a limit on their demand for equality. Democracy, by assuring men of fundamental rights, makes them equal thereby in respect of the exercise of these rights. They are equal before the law, they are equal as citizens, equal as voting units, equally free to speak their minds and to organize in pursuit of their interests. . . . Beyond certain limits equality and liberty are opposed. . . . Any attempt to achieve equality in wealth for all citizens would surely result in the most extreme totalitarianism. To keep men equal in wealth, in spite of their unequal abilities and varying aptitudes, would require a degree of all-round regimentation vastly surpassing anything that dynast or tyrant or dictator has hitherto accomplished. . . .

. . . there are two kinds of equality that come squarely within the scope of democracy. One is the equality of civil rights, including the right to count equally with everyone else in the determination of government. . . . The other is the equality of opportunity. This equality lies in the ethos, the spirit, of democracy, not in its mere form. Therefore it has to be won by the progressive legislation approved by democratic peoples. It is the fulfillment of the *logic* of the democratic constitution. . . .

The widespread confusion concerning the relation of democracy to equality is an aspect of deeper confusion concerning democracy and individualism. Democracy gives a new status to the individual, that is, to every person as a person. He is invested with active as well as *passive rights*. He is protected against power and he is endowed with power, the power to share equally with every other citizen in the creation of government. But these rights of the individual do not presume his independence of other men.

. . . They do not separate his affairs from the affairs of other men, so that he can conduct his affairs without concern for theirs, without regard for the effect on theirs. They do not convey the right to deny the law or to resist the law. . . . He can claim no rights the exercise of which is demonstrably injurious to his fellow men. . . .

Democracy . . . does not set up "the liberty of the individual" but the liberty of the citizen. His rights as a person are incorporated in his citizenship . . . all these rights do not sum up to the loose generalization, "the liberty of the individual" . . . liberties of any sort, and not least the liberties guaranteed under democracy, themselves depend on regulation and restraint. . . .

In the political context equality is asserted as a right, as a demand, not as a fact. In other words it is a claim that existing inequalities be removed. But what kind of existing inequalities and on what ground? There is inequality everywhere in human society. And to complicate the situation there are endless *differences*, differences of interest, differences of disposition, differences of taste, differences of outlook, that cannot be called inequalities. There are other differences, differences of intelligence, of strength, of health, of fortitude, of endurance, and so forth, that are properly named inequalities, but often it is hard to draw the line between inequalities and mere differences. And it is still more difficult to say how far inequalities of the kind just mentioned are themselves inherent in human nature and how far they are responsive to socially determined conditions.

What then, in this welter of differences and inequalities, is meant by the assertion of equality as a right? It must mean one or more of three things, one, that *equality of treatment* should be established for all citizens, perhaps for all men, two, that *equality of opportunity* should be thus provided, and three, that *equality of equipment* should somehow be instituted.

(1) *Equality of Treatment* is in the strictest sense identity of treatment. But in some relations that would be ridiculous, in others obviously undesirable. Should the judge exact the same fine for the same offense from the beggar and from the millionaire? Or even the same percentage of their income? But again there are relations in which equality of treatment is regarded as desirable, inequality as offensive. The police, for example, should not be allowed to bully people who are poor or humble, nor should these be denied in the law-courts equality of consideration with the prosperous or influential. And whenever we speak of "human rights" we think of certain fundamental securities, immunities, and liberties that should be assured alike to all men.

When then should men be accorded equality of treatment, in the strict sense, and when different treatment? What is it we want here? To what principle do we appeal? Surely not to the dead mechanics of equality but to the living value of fairness, *equity*. Equity transcends and abrogates the monotonous arithmetic of equality. . . . Equity makes law flexible, rational, ethical. To treat men equitably we must often treat them differently, according to their situation and their need. The goal is not equality as such but the provision for all of the social conditions under which they can enjoy as much well-being as possible, thus fulfilling their own lives.

(2) Here we arrive at *equality of opportunity*. . . . That all men should be as free as possible to develop their capacities, that intrinsic merit should not be blocked by needless material obstacles or by social discrimination—here is a principle that has a strong and clear appeal. Moreover, it is a principle that does not involve the mechanical cutting up of distributable goods into equal portions. Instead, it requires the provision of social facilities of many kinds, so that each may move according to his capacity toward the particular goal of his own choice.

(3) At the other extreme stands the last of our trio, *equality of equipment*. It is the most soulless and the most dangerous of all the claims made in the name of equality. For now the abstract notion of equality asserts itself as a right. Purely for its own sake it bids men divide all things equally. It offers no explanation why unequal men should possess equal things. What is the goal? What is the benefit to society? It is a grossly materialistic principle, for it is utterly inapplicable not only to spiritual and intellectual goods but also to the most double-edged of all the possessions of men—power over other men. Indeed, the tragic irony of this blind faith in abstract equality is that to achieve its objective would ruthlessly endow the engineers of its program with a deadly and all-embracing power before which all other inequalities shrink into insignificance.

We have given here only the most rudimentary analysis of a very complicated theme. But it may suffice to justify the argument . . . that the confusion of equality with democracy is full of peril.

Sidney Hook, "Naturalism and Democracy." From Y. H. Krikorian, ed., *Naturalism and the Human Spirit* (New York, Columbia University Press, 1944) Excerpts, pp. 48-51.

. . . we may say that a democratic state is one in which the basic decisions of government rest upon the freely given consent of the governed. This obviously is only a beginning. For as soon as we begin to investigate the conditions which must be present before we grant that a state lives up to this principle, we are carried beyond the sphere of political considerations into the domain of ethics. Thus, if information has been withheld or withdrawn before consent is assessed; if the opposition is muzzled or suppressed so that consent is as unanimous as a totalitarian plebiscite; or if economic sanctions are threatened against a section of the community in the event that consent takes one form or another, we declare that the "spirit" or "logic" or "rationale" of democracy is absent from its political forms. If birth does not give divine right, neither do numbers. We are all acquainted with situations in which we say that a political democracy has traduced its own ideals. Whenever we criticize existing states which conform to the political definition of democracy on the ground that they are not democratic enough; whenever we point out that Athenian democracy was limited only to free men or that in some parts of the American South it is limited only to white men, or that in some countries it is limited only to men, we are invoking a broader principle of democracy as a controlling reference in our judgments of comparison. This principle is an ethical one.

What is this principle of ethical democracy? It is the principle of equality—an equality, not of status or origin, but of opportunity, relevant functions, and social participation. The enormous literature and bitter controversy which center around the concept of equality indicate that it is only a little less ambiguous than the concept of democracy. It is necessary, therefore, to block it off from some current notions before developing the argument.

1. The principle of equality is not a *description* of fact about men's physical or intellectual natures. It is a *prescription* of policy for treating men.

2. It is not a prescription for treating men in identical ways who are unequal in their physical or intellectual nature. It is a policy of equality of concern or consideration for men whose different needs may require differential treatment.

3. It is not a mechanical policy of equal opportunity for everyone at any time and in all respects. . . . It is equality of opportunity for all individuals to develop whatever personal and socially desirable talents they possess and to make whatever unique contributions their capacities permit.

4. It is not a demand for absolute uniformity of living conditions or even for arithmetically equal compensation for socially useful work. It demands that when the productive forces of a society make possible the gratification of basic human needs (which are, of course, historical variables), no one should be deprived of necessities in order to provide others with luxuries.

5. It is not a policy of restricting the freedom of being different or becoming different. It is a policy of *encouraging* the freedom to be different, restricting only the exercise of freedom which converts talents or possessions into a monopoly that frustrates the emergence of other free personalities.

6. It is not a demand that all people be leaders or that none should be. It does demand that the career of leadership, like other careers, be open to all whose natural or acquired talents qualify them; that everyone have a say in the process of selecting leaders; that the initiative of leaders operate within a framework of basic laws; and that these laws in turn ultimately rest upon the freely given consent of the persons who constitute the community.

7. It does not make the assumption of sentimental humanitarianism that all men are naturally good. It does assume that men, treated as equals in a community of persons, may become better. The emphasis upon respect for the personality of all individuals, the attitude which treats the personality, not as something fixed, but as a growing, developing pattern, is unique to the philosophy of democracy.

What I have been trying to show is that the logic of the democrat's position compels him to go beyond the limited conception of political democracy—the equality of freedom—to a broader attitude extending to those other phases of social existence that bear upon the effective exercise of equality of freedom. . . .

It is clear that the principle of equality, like any principle of justice, cannot by itself determine what is specifically right or good in each concrete case. But whatever the right is discovered to be, from the point of view of democracy it is the result of an analysis which considers equally the needs of all the persons involved in the situation; and, furthermore, whatever the good is, it becomes better to the extent that it is shared among other members of the community. It is also clear that in concrete situations there will be conflicts between various demands for equality and that in negotiating these conflicts the methods of intelligence are indispensable for a functioning of democracy. If "naturalism" and "scientific empiricism" be generic terms for the philosophic attitude which submits all claims of fact and value to test by experience, then scientific empiricism as a philosophy is more congenial to a democratic than to an antidemocratic community, for it brings into the open light of criticism the interests in which moral values and social institutions are rooted.

Universal Declaration of Human Rights: adopted by the General Assembly of the United Nations, December 10, 1948.

Preamble

Whereas recognition of the inherent dignity and of the equal and inalienable rights of all members of the human family is the foundation of freedom, justice and peace in the world,

Whereas disregard and contempt for human rights have resulted in barbarous acts which have outraged the conscience of mankind, and the advent of a world in which human beings shall enjoy freedom of speech and belief and freedom from fear and want has been proclaimed as the highest aspiration of the common people,

Whereas it is essential, if man is not to be compelled to have recourse, as a last resort, to rebellion against tyranny and oppression, that human rights should be protected by the rule of law,

Whereas it is essential to promote the development of friendly relations between nations,

Whereas the peoples of the United Nations have in the Charter reaffirmed their faith in fundamental human rights, in the dignity and worth of the human person and in the equal rights of men and women and have determined to promote social progress and better standards of life in larger freedom,

Whereas Member States have pledged themselves to achieve, in cooperation with the United Nations, the promotion of universal respect for and observance of human rights and fundamental freedoms,

Whereas a common understanding of these rights and freedoms is of the greatest importance for the full realization of this pledge,

Now therefore the GENERAL ASSEMBLY proclaims

This Universal Declaration of Human Rights as a common standard of achievement for all peoples and all nations, to the end that every individual and every organ of society, keeping this Declaration constantly in mind, shall strive by teaching and education to promote respect for these rights and freedoms and by progressive measures, national and international, to secure their universal and effective recognition and observance, both among the peoples of Member States themselves and among the peoples of territories under their jurisdiction.

Article 1

All human beings are born free and equal in dignity and rights. They are endowed with reason and conscience and should act towards one another in a spirit of brotherhood.

Article 2

Everyone is entitled to all the rights and freedoms set forth in this Declaration, without distinction of any kind, such as race, colour, sex, language, religion, political or other opinion, national or social origin, property, birth or other status. Furthermore, no distinction shall be made on the basis of the political, jurisdictional or international status of the country or territory to which a person belongs, whether it be independent, trust, non-self-governing or under any other limitation of sovereignty.

Article 3

Everyone has the right to life, liberty and security of person.

Article 4

No one shall be held in slavery or servitude; slavery and the slave trade shall be prohibited in all their forms.

Article 5

No one shall be subjected to torture or to cruel, inhuman or degrading treatment or punishment.

Article 6

Everyone has the right to recognition everywhere as a person before the law.

Article 7

All are equal before the law and are entitled without any discrimination to equal protection of the law. All are entitled to equal protection against any discrimination in violation of this Declaration and against any incitement to such discrimination.

Article 8

Everyone has the right to an effective remedy by the competent national tribunals for acts violating the fundamental rights granted him by the constitution or by law.

Article 9

No one shall be subject to arbitrary arrest, detention or exile.

Article 10

Everyone is entitled in full equality to a fair and public hearing by an independent and impartial tribunal, in the determination of his rights and obligations and of any criminal charge against him.

Article 11

(1) Everyone charged with a penal offence has the right to be presumed innocent until proved guilty according to law in a public trial at which he has had all the guarantees necessary for his defence.

(2) No one shall be held guilty of any penal offence on account of any act or omission which did not constitute a penal offence, under national or international law, at the time when it was committed. Nor shall a heavier penalty be imposed than the one that was applicable at the time the penal offence was committed.

Article 12

No one shall be subjected to arbitrary interference with his privacy, family, home or correspondence, nor to attacks upon his honour and reputation. Everyone has the right to the protection of the law against such interference or attacks.

Article 13

(1) Everyone has the right to freedom of movement and residence within the borders of each state.

(2) Everyone has the right to leave any country, including his own, and to return to his country.

Article 14

(1) Everyone has the right to seek and to enjoy in other countries asylum from persecution.

(2) This right may not be invoked in the case of prosecutions genuinely arising from non-political crimes or from acts contrary to the purposes and principles of the United Nations.

Article 15

(1) Everyone has the right to a nationality.

(2) No one shall be arbitrarily deprived of his nationality nor denied the right to change his nationality.

Article 16

(1) Men and women of full age, without any limitation due to race,

nationality or religion, have the right to marry and to found a family. They are entitled to equal rights as to marriage, during marriage and at its dissolution.

(2) Marriage shall be entered into only with the free and full consent of the intending spouses.

(3) The family is the natural and fundamental group unit of society and is entitled to protection by society and the State.

Article 17

(1) Everyone has the right to own property alone as well as in association with others.

(2) No one shall be arbitrarily deprived of his property.

Article 18

Everyone has the right to freedom of thought, conscience and religion; this right includes freedom to change his religion or belief, and freedom, either alone or in community with others and in public or private, to manifest his religion or belief in teaching, practice, worship and observance.

Article 19

Everyone has the right to freedom of opinion and expression; this right includes freedom to hold opinions without interference and to seek, receive and impart information and ideas through any media and regardless of frontiers.

Article 20

(1) Everyone has the right to freedom of peaceful assembly and association.

(2) No one may be compelled to belong to an association.

Article 21

(1) Everyone has the right to take part in the government of his country, directly or through freely chosen representatives.

(2) Everyone has the right of equal access to public service in his country.

(3) The will of the people shall be the basis of the authority of government; this will shall be expressed in periodic and genuine elections which shall be by universal and equal suffrage and shall be held by secret vote or by equivalent free voting procedures.

Article 22

Everyone, as a member of society, has the right to social security and is entitled to realization, through national effort and international co-operation and in accordance with the organisation and resources of each State, of the economic, social and cultural rights indispensable for his dignity and the free development of his personality.

Article 23

(1) Everyone has the right to work, to free choice of employment, to just and favourable conditions of work and to protection against unemployment.

(2) Everyone, without discrimination, has the right to equal pay for equal work.

(3) Everyone who works has the right to just and favourable remuneration insuring for himself and his family an existence worthy of human dignity, and supplemented, if necessary, by other means of social protection.

(4) Everyone has the right to form and to join trade unions for the protection of his interests.

Article 24

Everyone has the right to rest and leisure, including reasonable limitation of working hours and periodic holidays with pay.

Article 25

(1) Everyone has the right to a standard of living adequate for the health and well-being of himself and of his family, including food, clothing, housing and medical care and necessary social services, and the right to security in the event of unemployment, sickness, disability, widowhood, old age or other lack of livelihood in circumstances beyond his control.

(2) Motherhood and childhood are entitled to special care and assistance. All children, whether born in or out of wedlock, shall enjoy the same social protection.

Article 26

(1) Everyone has the right to education. Education shall be free, at least in the elementary and fundamental stages. Elementary education shall be compulsory. Technical and professional education shall be made generally available and higher education shall be equally accessible to all on the basis of merit.

(2) Education shall be directed to the full development of the human personality and to the strengthening of respect for human rights and fundamental freedoms. It shall promote understanding, tolerance, and friendship among all nations, racial or religious groups, and shall further the activities of the United Nations for the maintenance of peace.

(3) Parents have a prior right to choose the kind of education that shall be given to their children.

Article 27

(1) Everyone has the right to freely participate in the cultural life of the community, to enjoy the arts and to share in scientific advancement and its benefits.

(2) Everyone has the right to the protection of the moral and material interests resulting from any scientific, literary or artistic production of which he is the author.

Article 28

Everyone is entitled to a social and international order in which the rights and freedoms set forth in this Declaration can be fully realized.

Article 29

(1) Everyone has duties to the community in which alone the free and full development of his personality is possible.

(2) In the exercise of his rights and freedoms, everyone shall be subject only to such limitations as are determined by law solely for the purpose of securing due recognition and respect for the rights and freedoms of others and of meeting the just requirements of morality, public order and the general welfare in a democratic society.

(3) These rights and freedoms may in no case be exercised contrary to the purposes and principles of the United Nations.

Article 30

Nothing in this Declaration may be interpreted as implying for any State, group or person any right to engage in any activity or to perform any act aimed at the destruction of any of the rights and freedoms set forth herein.

Rights Guaranteed by the Constitution of the United States.

ARTICLE I.

Section 2. 1. The House of Representatives shall be composed of members chosen every second year by the people of the several States, and the electors in each State shall have the qualifications requisite for electors of the most numerous branch of the State legislature.

Section 6. 1. [Senators and Representatives] shall in all cases, except treason, felony, and breach of the peace, be privileged from arrest during their attendance at the session of their respective Houses, and in going to and returning from the same; and for any speech or debate in either House, they shall not be questioned in any other place.

Section 9. 2. The privilege of the writ of *habeas corpus* shall not be suspended, unless when in cases of rebellion or invasion the public safety may require it.

3. No bill of attainder or *ex post facto* law shall be passed.

Section 10. 1. No State shall . . . pass any bill of attainder, *ex post facto* law, or law impairing the obligation of contracts, or grant any title of nobility.

ARTICLE III.

Section 2. 3. The trial of all crimes, except in cases of impeachment, shall be by jury; and such trial shall be held in the State where the said crimes shall have been committed; but when not committed within any State, the trial shall be at such place or places as the Congress may by law have directed.

Section 3. 1. Treason against the United States shall consist only in levying war against them, or in adhering to their enemies, giving them aid and comfort. No person shall be convicted of treason unless on the testimony of two witnesses to the same overt act, or on confession in open court.

2. The Congress shall have the power to declare the punishment of treason, but no attainder of treason shall work corruption of blood, or forfeiture except during the life of the person attained.

ARTICLE IV.

Section 2. 1. The citizens of each State shall be entitled to all privileges and immunities of citizens in the several States.

Section 4. The United States shall guarantee to every State in this Union a republican form of government, and shall protect each of them against invasion; and on application of the legislature, or of the executive (when the legislature cannot be convened) against domestic violence.

AMENDMENT I.

Congress shall make no law respecting an establishment of religion, or prohibiting the free exercise thereof; or abridging the freedom of speech, or of the press; or the right of the people peaceably to assemble, and to petition the government for a redress of grievances.

AMENDMENT II.

A well regulated militia, being necessary to the security of a free State, the right of the people to keep and bear arms, shall not be infringed.

AMENDMENT III.

No soldier shall, in time of peace be quartered in any house, without the consent of the owner, nor in time of war, but in a manner to be prescribed by law.

AMENDMENT IV.

The right of the people to be secure in their persons, houses, papers, and effects, against unreasonable searches and seizures, shall not be violated, and no warrants shall issue, but upon probable cause, supported by oath or affirmation, and particularly describing the place to be searched and the persons or things to be seized.

AMENDMENT V.

No person shall be held to answer for a capital, or otherwise infamous crime, unless on a presentment or indictment of a grand jury, except in cases arising in the land or naval forces, or in the militia, when in actual service in time of war or public danger; nor shall any person be subject for the same offense to be twice put in jeopardy of life or limb; nor shall be compelled in any criminal case to be a witness against himself, nor be deprived of life, liberty, or property, without due process of law; nor shall private property be taken for public use without just compensation.

AMENDMENT VI.

In all criminal prosecutions, the accused shall enjoy the right to a speedy and public trial, by an impartial jury of the State and district wherein the crime shall have been committed, which district shall have been previously ascertained by law, and to be informed of the nature and cause of the accusation; to be confronted with the witnesses against him; to have compulsory process for obtaining witnesses in his favor, and to have the assistance of counsel for his defense.

AMENDMENT VII.

In suits at common law, where the value in controversy shall exceed twenty dollars, the right of trial by jury shall be preserved, and no fact tried by a jury shall be otherwise reexamined in any court of the United States, than according to the rules of the common law.

AMENDMENT VIII.

Excessive bail shall not be required, nor excessive fines imposed, nor cruel and unusual punishments inflicted.

AMENDMENT IX.

The enumeration in the Constitution of certain rights shall not be construed to deny or disparage others retained by the people.

AMENDMENT X.

The powers not delegated to the United States by the Constitution, nor prohibited by it to the States, are reserved to the States respectively, or to the people.

AMENDMENT XIII.

Section 1. Neither slavery nor involuntary servitude, except as punishment for crime whereof the party shall have been duly convicted, shall exist within the United States, or any place subject to their jurisdiction.

Section 2. Congress shall have power to enforce this article by appropriate legislation.

AMENDMENT XIV.

Section 1. All persons born or naturalized in the United States, and subject to the jurisdiction thereof, are citizens of the United States and of the State wherein they reside. No State shall make or enforce any law which shall abridge the privileges or immunities of citizens of the United States; nor shall any State deprive any person of life, liberty, or property, without due process of law; nor deny to any person within its jurisdiction the equal protection of the laws.

Section 2. Representatives shall be apportioned among the several States according to their respective numbers, counting the whole number of persons in each State, excluding Indians not taxed. But when the right to vote at any election for the choice of electors for President and Vice President of the United States, representatives in Congress, the executive and judicial officers of a State, or the members of the legislature thereof, is denied to any of the male inhabitants of such State, being twenty-one years of age, and citizens of the United States, or in any way abridged, except for participation in rebellion, or other crime, the basis of representation therein shall be reduced in the proportion which the number of such male citizens shall bear to the whole number of male citizens twenty-one years of age in such State.

Section 5. The Congress shall have the power to enforce, by appropriate legislation, the provisions of this article.

AMENDMENT XV.

Section 1. The right of citizens of the United States to vote shall not be denied or abridged by the United States or by any State on account of race, color, or previous condition of servitude.

Section 2. The Congress shall have power to enforce this article by appropriate legislation.

AMENDMENT XIX.

The right of citizens of the United States to vote shall not be denied or abridged by the United States or by any State on account of sex.

The Congress shall have power by appropriate legislation to enforce the provisions of this article.

AMENDMENT XXIV.

Section 1. The right of citizens of the United States to vote in any primary or other election for President or Vice President, for electors for President or Vice President, or for Senator or Representative in Congress, shall not be denied or abridged by the United States or any State by reason of failure to pay any poll tax or other tax.

Section 2. The Congress shall have power to enforce this article by appropriate legislation.

Constitution of the Union of Soviet Socialist Republics.

Chapter X

FUNDAMENTAL RIGHTS AND DUTIES OF CITIZENS

ARTICLE 118.

Citizens of the U.S.S.R. have the right to work, that is, the right to guaranteed employment and payment for their work in accordance with its quantity and quality.

The right to work is ensured by the socialist organization of the national economy, the steady growth of the productive forces of Soviet society, the elimination of the possibility of economic crises, and the abolition of unemployment.

Article 119.

Citizens of the U.S.S.R. have the right to rest and leisure.

The right to rest and leisure is ensured by the establishment of an eight-hour day for industrial, office, and professional workers, the reduction of the working day to seven or six hours for arduous trades and to four hours in shops where conditions of work are particularly arduous; by the institution of annual vacations with full pay for industrial, office, and professional workers, and by the provision of a wide network of sanitoria, holiday homes and clubs for the accommodation of the working people.

Article 120.

Citizens of the U.S.S.R. have the right to maintenance in old age and also in case of sickness or disability.

This right is ensured by the extensive development of social insurance of industrial, office, and professional workers at state expense, free medical service for the working people, and the provision of a wide network of health resorts for the use of the working people.

Article 121.

Citizens of the U.S.S.R. have the right to education.

This right is ensured by universal and compulsory elementary education; by free education up to and including the seventh grade; by a system of state stipends for students of higher educational establishments who excel in their studies; by instruction in schools being conducted in the native language, and by the organization in the factories, state farms, machine and tractor stations, and collective farms of free vocational, technical and agronomic training for the working people.

Article 122.

Women in the U.S.S.R. are accorded equal rights with men in all spheres of economic, government, cultural, political and other public activity.

The possibility of exercising these rights is ensured by women being accorded an equal right with men to work, payment for work, rest and leisure, social insurance and education, and by state protection of the interests of mother and child, state aid to mothers of large families and unmarried mothers, maternity leave with full pay, and the provision of a wide network of maternity homes, nurseries, and kindergartens.

ARTICLE 123.

Equality of rights of citizens of the U.S.S.R., irrespective of their nationality or race, in all spheres of economic, government, cultural, political and other public activity, is an indefeasible law.

Any direct or indirect restriction of the rights of, or, conversely, the establishment of any direct or indirect privileges for, citizens on account of their race or nationality, as well as any advocacy of racial or national exclusiveness or hatred and contempt, are punishable by law.

ARTICLE 124.

In order to ensure to citizens freedom of conscience, the church in the U.S.S.R. is separated from the state, and the school from the church. Freedom of religious worship and freedom of anti-religious propaganda is recognized for all citizens.

ARTICLE 125.

In conformity with the interests of the working people, and in order to strengthen the socialist system, the citizens of the U.S.S.R. are guaranteed by law:

(a) freedom of speech;
(b) freedom of the press;
(c) freedom of assembly, including the holding of mass meetings;
(d) freedom of street processions and demonstrations.

These civil rights are ensured by placing at the disposal of the working people and their organizations printing presses, stocks of paper, public buildings, the streets, communications facilities and other material requisites for the exercise of these rights.

ARTICLE 126.

In conformity with the interests of the working people, and in order to develop the organizational initiative and political activity of the masses of the people, citizens of the U.S.S.R. are guaranteed the right to unite in public organizations: trade unions, co-operative societies, youth organizations, sport and defence organizations, cultural, technical and scientific societies; and the most active and politically-conscious citizens in the ranks of the working class, working peasants and working intelligentsia voluntarily unite in the Communist Party of the Soviet Union, which is the vanguard of the working people in their struggle to build communist society and is the leading core of all organizations of the working people, both public and state.

ARTICLE 127.

Citizens of the U.S.S.R. are guaranteed inviolability of the person. No person may be placed under arrest except by decision of a court or with the sanction of a procurator.

ARTICLE 128.

The inviolability of the homes of citizens and privacy of correspondence are protected by law.

ARTICLE 129.

The U.S.S.R. affords the right of asylum to foreign citizens persecuted for defending the interests of the working people, or for scientific activities, or for struggling for national liberation.

ARTICLE 130.

It is the duty of every citizen of the U.S.S.R. to abide by the Constitution of the Union of Soviet Socialist Republics, to observe the laws, to maintain labour discipline, honestly to perform public duties, and to respect the rules of socialist intercourse.

ARTICLE 131.

It is the duty of every citizen of the U.S.S.R. to safeguard and fortify public, socialist property as the sacred and inviolable foundation of the Soviet system, as the source of the wealth and might of the country, as the source of the prosperity and culture of all the working people.

Persons committing offences against public, socialist property are enemies of the people.

ARTICLE 132.

Universal military service is law.

Military service in the Armed Forces of the U.S.S.R. is an honourable duty of the citizens of the U.S.S.R.

ARTICLE 133.

To defend the country is the sacred duty of every citizen of the U.S.S.R. Treason to the Motherland—violation of the oath of allegiance, desertion to the enemy, impairing the military power of the state, espionage—is punishable with all the severity of the law as the most heinous of crimes.

The Constitution of Japan

Chapter III. RIGHTS AND DUTIES OF THE PEOPLE

ARTICLE 10.

The conditions necessary for being a Japanese national shall be determined by law.

ARTICLE 11.

The people shall not be prevented from enjoying any of the fundamental human rights. These fundamental human rights guaranteed to the people by this Constitution shall be conferred upon the people of this and future generations as eternal and inviolate rights.

ARTICLE 12.

The freedoms and rights guaranteed to the people by this Constitution shall be maintained by the constant endeavor of the people, who shall refrain from any abuse of these freedoms and rights and shall always be responsible for utilizing them for the public welfare.

ARTICLE 13.

All of the people shall be respected as individuals. Their right to life, liberty, and the pursuit of happiness shall, to the extent that it does not interfere with the public welfare, be the supreme consideration in legislation and in other governmental affairs.

ARTICLE 14.

All of the people are equal under the law and there shall be no discrimination in political, economic, or social relations, because of race, creed, sex, social status, or family origin.

Peers and peerage shall not be recognized.

No privilege shall accompany any award of honor, decoration, or any distinction, nor shall any such award be valid beyond the life-time of the individual who now holds or hereafter may receive it.

ARTICLE 15.

The people have the inalienable right to choose their public officials and to dismiss them.

All public officials are servants of the whole community and not of a group thereof.

Universal adult suffrage is guaranteed with regard to the election of public officials.

In all elections, secrecy of the ballot shall not be violated. A voter shall not be answerable, publicly or privately, for the choice he has made.

ARTICLE 16.

Every person shall have the right of peaceful petition for the redress of damage, for the removal of public officials, for the enactment, repeal, or amendment of laws, ordinances, or regulations and for other matters; nor shall any person be in any way discriminated against for sponsoring such a petition.

ARTICLE 17.

Every person may *sue* for redress as provided by law from the State or a public entity, in case he has suffered damage through illegal act of any public official.

ARTICLE 18.

No person shall be held in bondage of any kind. Involuntary servitude, except as punishment for crime, is prohibited.

ARTICLE 19.

Freedom of thought and conscience shall not be violated.

ARTICLE 20.

Freedom of religion is guaranteed to all. No religious organization shall receive any privileges from the State, nor exercise any political authority.

No person shall be compelled to take part in any religious act, celebration, rite, or practice.

The State and its organs shall refrain from religious education or any other religious activity.

ARTICLE 21.

Freedom of assembly and association as well as speech, press, and all other forms of expression are guaranteed.

No censorship shall be maintained, nor shall the secrecy of any means of communication be violated.

ARTICLE 22.

Every person shall have freedom to choose and change his residence and to choose his occupation to the extent that it does not interfere with the public welfare.

Freedom of all persons to move to a foreign country and to divest themselves of their nationality shall be inviolate.

ARTICLE 23.

Academic freedom is guaranteed.

ARTICLE 24.

Marriage shall be based only on the mutual consent of both sexes and it shall be maintained through mutual cooperation with the equal rights of husband and wife as a basis.

With regard to choice of spouse, property rights, inheritance, choice of domicile, divorce, and other matters pertaining to marriage and the family, laws shall be enacted from the standpoint of individual dignity and the essential equality of the sexes.

ARTICLE 25.

All people shall have the right to maintain the minimum standards of wholesome and cultured living.

In all spheres of life, the State shall use its endeavors for the promotion and extension of social welfare and security, and of public health.

ARTICLE 26.

All people shall have the right to receive an equal education correspondent to their ability, as provided by law.

All people shall be obligated to have all boys and girls under their protection receive ordinary education as provided for by law. Such compulsory education shall be free.

ARTICLE 27.

All people shall have the right and the obligation to work.

Standards for wages, hours, rest, and other working conditions shall be fixed by law.

Children shall not be exploited.

ARTICLE 28.

The right of workers to organize and to bargain and act collectively is guaranteed.

ARTICLE 29.

The right to own or to hold property is inviolable.

Property rights shall be defined by law, in conformity with the public welfare.

Private property may be taken for public use upon just compensation therefor.

ARTICLE 30.

The people shall be liable to taxation as provided by law.

ARTICLE 31.

No person shall be deprived of life or liberty, nor shall any other criminal penalty be imposed, except according to procedure established by law.

ARTICLE 32.

No persons shall be denied the right of access to the courts.

ARTICLE 33.

No person shall be apprehended except upon warrant issued by a competent judicial officer which specifies the offense with which the person is charged, unless he is apprehended, the offense being committed.

ARTICLE 34.

No person shall be arrested or detained without being at once informed of the charges against him or without the immediate privilege of counsel; nor shall he be detained without adequate cause; and upon demand of any person such cause must be immediately shown in open court in his presence and the presence of his counsel.

ARTICLE 35.

The right of all persons to be secure in their homes, papers, and effects against entries, searches, and seizures shall not be impaired except upon warrant issued for adequate cause and particularly describing the place to be searched and things to be seized, or except as provided by Article 33.

Each search or seizure shall be made upon separate warrant issued by a competent judicial officer.

ARTICLE 36.

The infliction of torture by any public officer and cruel punishments are absolutely forbidden.

ARTICLE 37.

In all criminal cases the accused shall enjoy the right to a speedy and public trial by an impartial tribunal.

He shall be permitted full opportunity to examine all witnesses, and he shall have the right of compulsory process for obtaining witnesses on his behalf at public expense.

At all times the accused shall have the assistance of competent counsel who shall, if the accused is unable to secure the same by his own efforts, be assigned to his use by the State.

ARTICLE 38.

No person shall be compelled to testify against himself.

Confession made under compulsion, torture, or threat, or after prolonged arrest or detention shall not be admitted in evidence.

No person shall be convicted or punished in cases where the only proof against him is his own confession.

ARTICLE 39.

No person shall be held criminally liable for an act which was lawful at the time it was committed, or of which he has been acquitted, nor shall he be placed in double jeopardy.

ARTICLE 40.

Any person, in case he is acquitted after he has been arrested or detained, may sue the State for *redress* as provided by law.

Chapter X. SUPREME LAW

ARTICLE 97.

The fundamental human rights by this Constitution guaranteed to the people of Japan are fruits of the age-old struggle of man to be free; they have survived the many exacting tests for durability and are conferred upon this and future generations in trust, to be held for all time inviolate.

GROUP IV

COMPATIBILITY OF DEMOCRACY AND A SOCIALIZED ECONOMY

R. A. Dahl, *Modern Political Analysis* (Englewood Cliffs, N.J., Prentice-Hall, Inc., 1963) Excerpts, pp. 7-9.

Many people indiscriminately apply terms like "democracy," "dictatorship," "capitalism," and "socialism" to both political and economic systems. This tendency to confuse political with economic systems stems from the lack of a standardized set of definitions, from ignorance of the historical origins of these terms, and probably in some cases from a desire to exploit a highly favorable or unfavorable term like democracy or dictatorship in order to influence attitudes about economic systems.

It follows from what we have already said, however, that the political aspects of an institution are not the same as its economic aspects. Historically, the terms "democracy" and "dictatorship" have usually referred to political systems, whereas "capitalism" and "socialism" have referred to economic institutions. From the way the terms have been used historically, these definitions might be appropriate. (1) A democracy is a political system in which the opportunity to participate in decisions is widely shared among all adult citizens. (2) A dictatorship is a political system in which the opportunity to participate in decisions is restricted to a few. (3) Capitalism is an economic system in which most major economic activities are per-

© Copyright 1963, by Prentice-Hall, Inc. Reprinted by permission of Prentice-Hall, Inc.

fórmed by privately owned and controlled firms. (4) Socialism is an economic system in which most major activities are performed by agencies owned and controlled by the government.

Each pair of terms rests on a dichotomy, and dichotomies are often rather unsatisfactory. In fact, many political systems are neither wholly democratic nor wholly dictatorial; and in many economic systems private and governmental operations are mixed together in all sorts of complex ways. . . . remember that the distinction between an economic system and a political system is indispensable to clear thinking.

No matter what terms we use, the two aspects of social life—the political and the economic—are different. However, like the central nervous system and the circulatory system in an animal, these two aspects are also interrelated. But the way in which the two aspects are related cannot be determined by definition alone: Empirical inquiry is necessary.

The failure to distinguish between a definition and an empirical proposition is common in political analysis. Yet nothing can be shown to be true or false about the real world of politics (or economics) simply by definition. A definition is, so to speak, a proposed treaty governing the use of terms. A sentence that employs such terms, however, contains an *empirical proposition* if it purports to say something about the world we experience. Whether the proposition is true or false depends on the degree to which the proposition and the real world correspond.

This point can be illustrated by considering the relation between economic and political systems. Assuming that we use these terms as they were defined a moment ago, four relationships would be logically possible.

	The political system is:	The economic system is:
I	A Democracy	Capitalism
II	A Democracy	Socialism
III	A Dictatorship	Capitalism
IV	A Dictatorship	Socialism

None of these combinations is a logical absurdity. None is excluded by definition. Whether each combination actually does exist, or is likely to exist, can only be determined by studying actual political and economic systems. Is it true, as advocates of capitalism sometimes argue, that in industrial nations democracy could not exist without a capitalist economy? Is it true, as Lenin and other communists have argued, that a capitalist economy can exist only under a political dictatorship? Although questions like these are not always easy to answer, in principle we can do so only by examining all (or a fair sample) of past and present political and economic systems to see what combinations do or probably could exist. We *cannot* answer these questions by debating definitions.

J. A. Schumpeter, *Capitalism, Socialism, and Democracy*, 3rd ed. (New York, Harper & Brothers Publishers, 1950) Excerpts, pp. 269, 296-301.

I think that most students of politics have by now come to accept the criticisms leveled at the classical doctrine of democracy. . . . I also think that most of them agree, or will agree before long, in accepting another theory which is much truer to life and at the same time salvages much of what sponsors of the democratic method really mean by this term. . . .

It will be remembered that our chief troubles about the classical theory centered in the proposition that "the people" hold a definite and rational opinion about every individual question and that they give effect to this opinion—in a democracy—by choosing "representatives" who will see to it that that opinion is carried out. Thus the selection of representatives is made secondary to the primary purpose of the democratic arrangement which is to vest the power of deciding political issues in the electorate. Suppose we reverse the roles of these two elements and make the deciding of issues by the electorate secondary to the election of the men who are to do the deciding. To put it differently, we now take the view that the role of the people is to produce a government, or else an intermediate body which in turn will produce a national executive or government. And we define: the democratic method is that institutional arrangement for arriving at political decisions in which individuals acquire the power to decide by means of a competitive struggle for the people's vote. . . .

. . . historically, the modern democracy rose along with capitalism, and in causal connection with it. But the same holds true for democratic practice: democracy in the sense of our theory of competitive leadership presided over the process of political and institutional change by which the bourgeoisie reshaped, and from its own point of view rationalized, the social and political structure that preceded its ascendancy: the democratic method was the political tool of that reconstruction. . . .

Whether or not democracy is one of those products of capitalism which are to die out with it is of course another question. . . .

The ideology of classical socialism is the offspring of bourgeois ideology. In particular, it fully shares the latter's rationalist and utilitarian background and many of the ideas and ideals that entered the classical doctrine of democracy. So far as this goes, socialists in fact experienced no difficulty whatever in appropriating this part of the bougeois inheritance and in making out a case for the proposition that those elements of the classical doctrine which socialism is unable to absorb—the emphasis on protection of private property for instance—are really at variance with its fundamental principles. Creeds of this kind could survive even in entirely non-democratic forms of socialism and we may trust the scribes and pharisees to bridge by suitable phrases any gap there may be between creed and practice. But it is the practice that interests us—the fate of democratic practice as interpreted by the doctrine of competitive leadership. And so, . . . the real question is again how well or ill socialism qualifies for the task of making the democratic method function should it attempt to do so.

The essential point to grasp is this. No responsible person can view with equanimity the consequences of extending the democratic method, that is to say the sphere of "politics," to all economic affairs. Believing that democratic socialism means precisely this, such a person will naturally conclude that democratic socialism must fail. But this does not necessarily follow. . . . extension of the range of public management does not imply corresponding extension of the range of political management. Conceivably, the former may be extended so as to absorb a nation's economic affairs while the latter still remains within the boundaries set by the limitations of the democratic method.

It does follow however that in socialist society these limitations will raise a much more serious problem. For socialist society lacks the automatic restrictions imposed upon the political sphere by the bourgeois scheme of things. Moreover, in socialist society it will no longer be possible to find comfort in the thought that the inefficiencies of political procedure are after all a guarantee of freedom. Lack of efficient management will spell lack of bread. However, the agencies that are to operate the economic engine . . . may be so organized and manned as to be sufficiently exempt in the fulfillment of their current duties from interference by politicians or, for that matter, by fussing citizens' committees or by their workmen. That is to say, they may be sufficiently removed from the atmosphere of political strife as to display no inefficiencies other than those associated with the term Bureaucracy. . . .

. . . In a sense . . . the present-day forms and organs of democratic procedure are as much the outgrowth of the structure and issues of the bourgeois world as is the fundamental principle of democracy itself. But this is no reason why they should have to disappear along with capitalism. General elections, parties, parliaments, cabinets and prime ministers may still prove to be the most convenient instruments for dealing with the agenda that the socialist order may reserve for political decision. The list of these agenda will be relieved of all those items that at present arise from the clash of private interests and from the necessity of regulating them. Instead there will be new ones. There will be such questions to decide as what the volume of investment should be or how existing rules for the distribution of the social product should be amended and so on. General debates about efficiency, investigation committees of the type of the English Royal Commissions would continue to fulfill their present functions.

Thus the politicians in the cabinet, and in particular the politician at the head of the Ministry of Production, would no doubt assert the influence of the political element, both by their legislative measures concerning the general principles of running the economic engine and by their power to appoint which could not be entirely absent or entirely formal. But they need not do so to an extent incompatible with efficiency. . . .

I have emphasized that democracy cannot be expected to function satisfactorily unless the vast majority of the people in all classes are resolved to abide by the rules of the democratic game and that this in turn implies that they are substantially agreed on the fundamentals of their institutional structure. At present the latter condition fails to be fulfilled. So many people have renounced, and so many more are going to renounce, allegience to the standards of capitalist society that on this ground alone democracy is bound to work with increasing friction. At the stage visualized however, socialism may remove the rift. It may reestablish agreement as to the tectonic principles of the social fabric. If it does, then the remaining antagonisms will be exactly of the kind with which the democratic method is well able to cope.

N. Thomas, "Rethinking Socialism," *The Virginia Quarterly Review*, Vol. XXXIV (Winter, 1958) Excerpts, pp. 45-46, 52.

Socialism is the doctrine and movement which hold that the practice of freedom, equality, and fraternity require conscious planning to establish and maintain efficient and democratic controls both of natural resources and of great aggregations of tools and skills for the common good, rather than for private profit. In general, natural resources and great basic industries of an oligarchic type should be publicly owned, and on that basis democratically controlled. In planning and social ownership the state must be a principal agent but a democratic state concerned to act as the powerful servant and not the arbitrary master of individuals who comprise it. . . .

I am socialist because I believe that democratic socialism as I have . . . defined it in word and deed, however far from perfection, has offered incomparably the best existent philosophy of social action looking toward achievement of a universal fellowship of men and nations dedicated to freedom, cooperation, equality of right, and the use of their marvelous technical powers for life and abundance for all, rather than for war and destruction. A socialist philosophy and attitude will not automatically solve our problems; it offers at once inspiration and intellectual basis for their solution.

N. Lenin, *The State and Revolution* (1917): as published in *The Essential Left* (New York, Barnes & Noble, Inc., 1961) Excerpts, Chapter V, 2, pp. 224-227.

In capitalist society, under the conditions most favourable to its development, we have a more or less complete democracy in the form of a democratic republic. But this democracy is always bound by the narrow framework of capitalist exploitation, and, consequently, always remains, in reality, a democracy only for the minority, only for the possessing classes, only for the rich. Freedom in capitalist society always remains more or less the same as it was in the ancient Greek republics, that is, freedom for the slave owners. The modern wage-slaves, in virtue of the conditions of capitalist exploitation, remain to such an extent crushed by want and poverty that they 'cannot be bothered with democracy,' have 'no time for politics'; that, in the ordinary peaceful course of events, the majority of the population is debarred from participating in public political life. . . .

Democracy for an insignificant minority, democracy for the rich—that is the democracy of capitalist society. If we look more closely into the mechanism of capitalist democracy, everywhere—in the so-called 'petty' details of the suffrage (the residential qualifications, the exclusion of women, etc.), in the technique of the representative institutions, in the actual obstacles to the right of meeting (public buildings are not for the 'poor'), in the purely capitalist organization of the daily press, etc.,—on all sides we shall see restrictions upon restrictions of Democracy. These restrictions, exceptions, exclusions, obstacles for the poor, seem slight—especially in the eyes of one who has himself never known want, and has never lived in close contact with the oppressed classes in their herd life, and nine-tenths, if not

Reprinted by permission of Barnes & Noble, Inc. and George Allen & Unwin, Ltd.

ninety-nine hundredths, of the bourgeois publicists and politicians are of this class! But in their sum these restrictions exclude and thrust out the poor from politics and from an active share in democracy. Marx splendidly grasped the *essence* of capitalist democracy, when . . . he said that the oppressed are allowed, once every few years to decide which particular representatives of the oppressing class are to represent and repress them in Parliament.

But from this capitalist democracy . . . progress does not march along a simple, smooth and direct path to 'greater and greater democracy,' as the Liberal professors and the lower middle-class Opportunists would have us believe. No, progressive development—that is, towards Communism—marches through the dictatorship of the proletariat; and cannot do otherwise, for there is no one else who can *break the resistance* of the exploiting capitalists, and no other way of doing it.

And the dictatorship of the proletariat—that is, the organization of the advance-guard of the oppressed as the ruling class, for the purpose of crushing the oppressors—cannot produce merely an expansion of democracy. *Together* with an immense expansion of democracy—for the first time becoming democracy for the poor, democracy for the people, and not democracy for the rich folk—the dictatorship of the proletariat will produce a series of restrictions of liberty in the case of the oppressors, exploiters, and capitalists. We must crush them in order to free humanity from wage-slavery; their resistance must be broken by force. It is clear that where there is suppression there must be violence, and there cannot be liberty or democracy. . . .

Democracy for the vast majority of the nation, and the suppression by force—that is, the exclusion from democracy—of the exploiters and oppressors of the nation: this is the modification of democracy which we shall see during the *transition* from Capitalism to Communism.

Only in Communist Society, when the resistance of the capitalists has finally been broken, when the capitalists have disappeared, when there are no longer any classes (that is, when there is no difference between the members of society in respect of their social means of production), *only then* 'does the State disappear *and one can speak of freedom.*' Only then will be possible and will be realized a really full democracy, a democracy without any exceptions. And only then will democracy itself begin to wither away in virtue of the simple fact that, freed from capitalist slavery, from the innumerable horrrors, savagery, absurdities and infamies of capitalist exploitation, people will gradually *become* accustomed to the observation of the elementary rules of social life, known for centuries, repeated for thousands of years in all sermons. They will become accustomed to their observance without force, without constraint, without subjection, without the *special apparatus* for compulsion which is called the State. . . .

Thus, in capitalist society, we have a democracy that is curtailed, wretched, false; a democracy only for the rich, for the minority. The dictatorship of the proletariat, the period of transition to Communism, will, for the first time, produce a democracy for the people, for the majority, side by side with the necessary suppression of the minority constituted by the exploiters. Communism alone is capable of giving a really complete democracy, and the fuller it is the more quickly will it become unnecessary and wither away of itself.

Programme of the Communist Party of the Soviet Union, Part One, V, paragraphs 14, 23-25 (1961).

The struggle for democracy is a component of the struggle for socialism. The more profound the democratic movement, the higher becomes the level of the political consciousness of the masses and the more clearly they see that only socialism clears for them the way to genuine freedom and well-being. . . .

. . . whatever the form in which the transition from capitalism to socialism is effected, that transition can come about only through revolution. However varied the forms of a new, people's state power in the period of socialist construction, their essence will be the same —*dictatorship of the proletariat,* which represents genuine democracy, democracy for the working people.

A bourgeois republic, however democratic, however hallowed by slogans purporting to express the will of the people or nation as a whole, or extra-class will, inevitably remains in practice—owing to the existence of private capitalist ownership of the means of production—a dictatorship of the bourgeoisie, a machine for the exploitation and suppression of the vast maporily of the working people by a handful of capitalists. In contrast to the bourgeoisie, which conceals the class character of the state, the working class does not deny the class character of the state.

The dictatorship of the proletariat is a dictatorship of the overwhelming majority over the minority; it is directed against the exploiters, against the oppression of peoples and nations, and is aimed at abolishing all exploitation of man by man. The dictatorship of the proletariat expresses not only the interests of the working class, but also those of all working people; its chief content is not violence but creation, the building of a new, social-society, and the defense of its gains against the enemies of socialism.

R. M. MacIver, *The Ramparts We Guard* (New York, The Macmillan Company, 1950) Excerpts, pp. 137, 129-130.

DEMOCRACY AND CAPITALISM. The association of democracy and capitalism is in the first instance an historical one. Democracy developed with the rise of a middle class, and the middle class became greatly strengthened with the growth of industry and consequently of capital, which became mainly a middle class acquisition. Under feudalism the middle class was too small and weak to challenge the ruling class. It was the power acquired by the middle class, particularly through their industrial achievements, that finally overthrew the close-knit monarchical absolutism that supervened on the decay of the feudal order.

The current antithesis between the socialist state and the capitalist state is, however, misleading. The true distinction is between socialist states in the full sense, that is, states which have nationalized the whole apparatus of production, and socio-capitalist states, that is, states which combine an area of collectivism with an area of private production and exchange. Every modern state, outside the communist system, is socio-capitalist, the mixture being everywhere different and always changing. The trend of socio-capitalist states has been toward a higher degree of collectivism. . . .

Observe that socialism of a non-revolutionary or non-Marxist type —for example, the type once promoted by Robert Owen or that sponsored today by, say Norman Thomas or by the British Labor Party—can logically maintain the compatibility of socialism and democracy, whereas the Marxist type can not. The logic of Marxism is invincibly anti-democratic, and the slogans of democracy are used by it in a propagandist way, whether it be to decry the "sham democracy" of other systems or to assert the "true democracy" of its own.

William Ebenstein, *Today's Isms*, 3rd ed. (Englewood Cliffs, N.J., Prentice-Hall, Inc., 1961) Excerpts, pp. 125-127, 202-203, 205-206, 208-209, 228.

TWO CONCEPTIONS OF DEMOCRACY

When a representative of the United States, Britain, or France talks about democracy, he frequently means the very opposite of what a Russian or Chinese communist has in mind when he uses the same term. Thus at the end of World War II, when the United States, Britain, France, and the Soviet Union occupied Germany, one of their chief objectives was the democratization of Germany. At first all four powers wholeheartedly agreed on the objective, but it soon became evident that the Russian concept was entirely different from the Anglo-American-French understanding of democracy.

The western powers took the view that bringing democracy to Germany meant free elections; a free press; freedom of political association; freedom of religion, thought, and speech; equality before the law; the right to oppose the government; the right to choose one's job; the right to form free trade unions; the right to move freely within one's country, go abroad temporarily, or emigrate permanently; and—in a general way—the right of every person to develop his mental and moral faculties to the fullest possible extent.

Above all, *freedom from fear* is basic in the western concept of democracy. No society can be called free unless its citizens feel safe from unwarranted intrusion into their affairs by governmental authorities.

This aspect of democracy has been most aptly described in this way; in a free country, a knock at the door early in the morning means the milkman is there; in a totalitarian country, the same knock might mean the secret police are there, come to snatch a man from his home and family and to jail, exile, or execute him without trial or due process of law.

The communist conception of democratizing Germany was entirely different from the western. In the first place, when the communist speaks of democracy, he has in mind, not government *of* the people, nor government *by* the people, but, as a leading Soviet philosopher puts it, "whether this or that policy is carried out in the interests of the people, in the interests of its overwhelming majority, or in the interests of its minority." (G. F. Aleksandrov, *The Pattern of Soviet Democracy*, 1948)

Which doctrine reveals whether government is carried out *in the interests of the people?* Marxism, Leninism-Stalinism. Who interprets this doctrine correctly? The Communist Party. Who in the Communist Party determines the party line? The Presidium, a group of a dozen men or so. Who in the Presidium determines its general policy? The communist dictator. . . .

. . . communists call the essentials of democracy—freedom of speech, press, and association, equality before the law, and all the other fundamental democratic rights and liberties—*formal* democracy, as compared with the *real* democracy of communism, in which the means of production are owned by the state. In this communist conception, the traditional democratic freedoms assume a new meaning. . . .

SOCIALISM AND DEMOCRACY

The link between democracy and socialism is the most important single element in socialist thought and policy. Looking at the history of socialism, it can be quickly seen that *successful socialist movements have grown up only in nations with strong democratic traditions,* such as Great Britain, Scandinavia, Holland, Belgium, Switzerland, Australia, New Zealand and, more recently, Israel.

The reason for this parallelism is simple. Where democratic, constitutional government is generally accepted, socialists can concentrate on their specific program, overambitious as that program may seem, namely: to create more opportunity for the underprivileged classes; to end inequality based on birth rather than service; to open the horizons of education to all the people; to eliminate discriminatory practices based on sex, religion, race, or social class; to regulate and reorganize the economy for the benefit of the whole community; to maintain full employment; to provide adequate social security for the sick, unemployed, and aged; to re-plan the layout of towns and cities; to tear down the slums and build new houses; to provide medical facilities for everybody, irrespective of the size of his purse; and finally, to rebuild society on the foundation of cooperation in lieu of competition, incentive, and profit.

All these goals of democratic socialism have one thing in common: *to make democracy more real by broadening the application of democratic principles from the political to the nonpolitical areas of society.* . . .

. . . socialist parties have fought an uphill and generally losing struggle in nations in which democracy is not a living thing, but an aspiration, a hope, an idea yet to be realized. . . .

SOCIALISM VERSUS COMMUNISM

Socialism and communism are not two of a kind, but represent two incompatible ways of thought and life, as incompatible as liberalism and totalitarianism.

There are several factors of irreconcilable antagonism between socialists and communists. First, *communists* seek to bring about the end of capitalism by a single act of *revolutionary upheaval and civil war. Socialists,* on the other hand, adhere to *strict constitutional procedures;* they seek power by ballots, rather than bullets, and, once in office, they know they are not in for keeps, but are subject to be voted out in the next election. . . .

In the crucial issue of public ownership, the gap that separates socialists from communists is unbridgeable. Communists visualize the transition from capitalist enterprise to public ownership as sudden and complete. . . . In contrast, socialists do not believe that the transition from capitalism to public ownership of the means of production can be either sudden or complete. Most socialists believe in the instalment plan. Public ownership of the means of production is being built up gradually, by instalments; if one phase works, then the next will be tackled. . . .

There is another vital difference with regard to public ownership. Communists seek to transfer all means of production, distribution, and exchange to the state, leaving to the individual only the free discretion over consumer goods. Communists insist on *total nationalization*, because their dogma tells them that publicly owned property is always preferable to private enterprise.

By contrast, socialists seek to work out a set of empirical principles that will indicate in a *particular* instance whether a specific *industry or service* is to be transferred to public ownership and control. The socialists' criterion may be that the industry under examination is a monopoly (such as gas and light, telephone, and other utilities tend to become); or that the industry is sick (as the British coal industry was before its nationalization); or that the industry, although neither inefficient nor monopolistic, is of such vital importance to the national economy in peace and war that it seems socially undesirable to leave its operation in private hands (the British iron and steel industry was nationalized on these grounds). . . .

Today, there is not a single socialist party in the world, nor a single socialist leader of repute and responsibility still adhering to the old formula of nationalizing *all* the means of production, distribution, and exchange. In July 1951, the Socialist International, speaking for over thirty socialist parties throughout the world, adopted a program that specifically rejected the older doctrine of total nationalization, and conceded that socialist planning is compatible with private ownership in agriculture, handicrafts, retail trade, and small and medium-sized industries.

F. A. Hayek, *The Road to Serfdom* (Chicago, The University of Chicago Press, 1944) Excerpts, pp. 88-100.

Most planners who have seriously considered the practical aspects of their task have little doubt that a directed economy must be run on more or less dictatorial lines. That the complex system of inter-related activities, if it is to be consciously directed at all, must be directed by a single staff of experts, and that ultimate responsibility and power must rest in the hands of a commander-in-chief whose actions must not be fettered by democratic procedure, is too obvious a consequence of underlying ideas of central planning not to command fairly general assent. The consolation our planners offer us is that this authoritarian direction will apply "only" to economic matters. . . .

. . . the assurance people derive from this belief that the power which is exercised over economic life is a power over matters of secondary importance only, and which makes them take lightly the threat to the freedom of our economic pursuits, is altogether unwarranted. It is largely a consequence of the erroneous belief that there are purely economic ends separate from the other ends of life. Yet, apart from the pathological case of the miser, there is no such thing. The ultimate ends of the activities of reasonable beings are never economic. Strictly speaking, there is no "economic motive" but only economic factors conditioning our striving for other ends. What in ordinary language is misleadingly called the "economic motive" means merely the desire for general opportunity, the desire for power to achieve unspecified ends. . . .

The authority directing all economic activity would control not merely the part of our lives which is concerned with inferior things; it would control the allocation of the limited means for all our ends. And whoever controls all economic activity controls the means for all our ends and must therefore decide which are to be satisfied and which not. This is really the crux of the matter. Economic control is not merely control of a sector of human life which can be separated from the rest; it is the control of the means for all our ends. And whoever has sole control of the means must also determine which ends are to be served, which values are to be rated higher and which lower—in short, what men should believe and strive for. Central planning means that the economic problem is to be solved by the community instead of the individual; but this involves that it must also be the community, or rather its representatives, who must decide the relative importance of the different needs.

The so-called economic freedom which the planners promise us means precisely that we are to be relieved of the necessity of solving our own economic problems and that the bitter choices which this often involves are to be made for us. Since under modern conditions we are for almost everything dependent on means which our fellow-men provide, economic planning would involve direction of almost the whole of our life. There is hardly an aspect of it, from our primary needs to our relations with our family and friends, from the nature of our work to the use of our leisure, over which the planner would not exercise his "conscious control." . . .

Our freedom of choice in a competitive society rests on the fact that, if one person refuses to satisfy our wishes, we can turn to another. But if we face a monopolist we are at his mercy. And an authority directing the whole economic system would be the most powerful monopolist conceivable. While we need probably not be afraid that such an authority would exploit this power in the manner in which a private monopolist would do so, while its purpose would presumably not be the extortion of maximum financial gain, it would have complete power to decide what we are to be given and on what terms. It would not only decide what commodities and services were to be available and in what quantities; it would be able to direct their distribution between districts and groups and could, if it wished, discriminate between persons to any degree it liked. If we remember why planning is advocated by most people, can there be much doubt that this power would be used for the ends of which the authority approves and to prevent the pursuit of ends which it disapproves? . . .

. . . the claim that a planned economy would produce a substantially larger output than the competitive system is being progressively abandoned by most students of the problem. Even a good many economists with socialist views who have seriously studied the problems of central planning are now content to hope that a planned society will equal the efficiency of a competitive system; they advocate planning no longer because of its superior productivity but because it will enable us to secure a more just and equitable distribution of wealth. This is, indeed, the only argument for planning which can be seriously pressed. It is indisputable that if we want to secure a distribution of wealth which conforms to some predetermined standard, if we want consciously to decide who is to have what, we must plan the whole economic system. But the question remains whether the price we should have to pay for the realization of somebody's ideal of justice is not bound to be more discontent and more oppression than was ever caused by the much-abused free play of economic forces. . . .

It is often said that political freedom is meaningless without economic freedom. This is true enough, but in a sense almost opposite from that in which the phrase is used by our planners. The economic freedom which is the prerequisite of any other freedom cannot be the freedom from economic care which the socialists promise us and which can be obtained only by relieving the individual at the same time of the necessity and of the power of choice; it must be the freedom of our economic activity which, with the right of choice, inevitably also carries the risk and the responsibility of that right.

H. Finer, *Road to Reaction* (Boston, Little, Brown and Company, 1946) Excerpts, pp. 221-228. Reprint edition by Quadrangle Books (1963).

There are two kinds of freedom. One is merely the absence of obstruction; it is essential; but it may be consistent with mere passivity. The second kind of freedom is strength or power, the ability to take action, or self-expression. . . .

Men have no freedom worth mentioning when they have no possibility of exercising their faculties and energy as they feel they must. Freedom in this dynamic sense cannot come to men, in all the abundance potential in our time, unless they collectively manage a large proportion of the social resources and economic equipment. The present economic waste by mismanagement is enormous; it is nothing but lost or unexploited strength; it constitutes a loss of freedom to many.

If the present economic system could unfailingly guarantee to rule out luck, force, fraud, misrepresentation, absentee ownership, the unmerited inheritance of wealth and therefore of irresponsible power; secure the equalization of educational opportunity and expunge unfair economic advantages; keep wide open the door to talent in every occupation; assure the dissolution of all monopolies; compel the pure, equal, and instantaneous transmission of economic information to all producers and consumers, and make certain that scientific discoveries were immediately applied for the benefit of all, it would be a noble

Reprinted by permission of the author.

experiment to try private enterprise with relatively little governmental supplement for another fifty years—provided all started equal.

The inherent inability to make these changes is only too amply admitted by the managers of the present system in whispered candor among friends, and in not infrequent mutual recrimination. . . .

If the maximum freedom for all is to be available, then the maximum of economic welfare must be sought for all. This is not to confuse welfare and freedom. Economic welfare is a factor in freedom which requires property and income to allow men to realize their desires, and to substantiate the exercise of opportunity, faculties, and energies. There is a labyrinthine interfusion of welfare and freedom. These are not merely concrete things, that is pots and pans and the right to reside where one likes, but concepts that are significant in the degree we *feel* them to be. . . .

There is no knowing exactly what fusion of welfare and freedom will suit the individual except by experience and trial. The pattern which will suit him will be found en route, not at the beginning of a long and unending adventure. Every economic system is a stage, not a fate. . . . The nineteenth century was not the beginning—nor the end, much as some economists may believe it to be. . . . The future of individual good, then, is deeply involved in the whole long future of government. For it is in their own government that men can find the collective strength which will assure them of individual liberty. Popular self-government alone can marshal the power, that is the knowledge, the authority, and the ubiquity, to uphold the claims of all men to a satisfying admixture of wealth and freedom. . . . The freedom of our time cannot possibly be an entire freedom from government, it can only be a freedom within government. The principal issue is to make sure that government is so constituted and conducted that it furnishes the prospect of advance according to the will of the majority and keeps the way back as well as the way forward continuously negotiable.

All men desire security as well as freedom. It is obvious that security guarantees freedom, for it is a safeguard against constraint by the irrational circumstances of the economy and by the managerial infirmities of economic individualists who are in possession of the productive machinery of society. Security is freedom to the extent that income offers the effective power to choose a way of action. . . .

. . . we have arrived at a technique and spirit of democratic government never equalled in human history, because there were never before such vast and dense agglomerations of human beings; never such a diffusion of knowledge and moral and practical wisdom; never such means of rapid communication among the people themselves and their myriad groupings. . . .

Society as a whole, acting through its rationally constituted and deputed organs, is in a far better position than at any time in history to move forward to the collective management of many spheres of social life. When men attain to such a responsibility they certainly acquire freedom. This does not mean a government over all and everything. Society is now so able because what was known before only to individuals is now better known to social institutions, and can be even better known still through its own arrangements for the promotion and advancement of knowledge. Again, what was hitherto willed by individuals severally, and showed shortcomings in the consequent welfare for all, can be better willed and fulfilled by the social agents of all men freely choosing their purposes and deputies. The organs for fact-finding, analysis, interpretation, and the graduated and discriminating expression of popular approval and disapproval, were, in their contemporary quality, never before dreamed of. Finally, the organs of external control are sound and trustworthy.

Hence we have no reason to be afraid of our social strength, or the strength we care to lend to the government, or of the freedom we obtain as the result of using it through the organized medium—the social manager—which is government. . . .

Abundance will be better obtained by far more confidence in the management by social administration of sectors of the national economy. The competitive system is irredeemably caught in the dark, tangled wood of its own egoisms, hostilities, frictions, and rigidities, the inevitable product of its own premises—egoism, and therefore severity; insecurity, and therefore fear and therefore offensive and defensive measures for its own security. Power, not being socially responsible, is abused in such a system, and limits the production of goods for private advantage. . . .

The regulator and producer of abundance and justice is public freedom, and this also creates those private felicities and security which constitute private freedom, in the sense of the capacity for continuous initiative. Public freedom unreservedly demands free association, election and recall of government, freedom of speech, writing, opinion, and opposition. It is within these that men learn their responsibility that marches with their endowment of authority, the common sense and tact of more than everyday affairs. . . . Free government has truly come of age, and offers, to the millions upon millions whose minds and characters have never yet been given the opportunity to contribute to the common good, a broad avenue of advancement.

ANTI-DEMOCRATIC THOUGHT

David Spitz, *Patterns of Anti-Democratic Thought* (New York, The Macmillan Company, 1949) Excerpts, Chapter I.

. . . the democratic state is seen to contain at least two central ingredients that crucially set it apart from all other forms of state. One is the free play of conflicting opinions. The other is the constitutional responsibility of the rulers to the ruled. . . . democracy . . . completely and ineluctably depends on the unrestrained organization of opposing views, . . . democracy makes conflict of ideas the very basis of the state. Through this primary liberty of opinion those who temporarily sit on the thrones of power are held accountable to those over whom that power is exercised, and men, free to speak their individual minds and to organize the more effectively to express their divergent beliefs, share equally as citizens in the formulation of the general conditions under which they are to live. . . .

. . . the doctrines of anti-democratic thought are, simply, those ideas which deny the possibility or challenge the desirability of democracy: the first by insisting that the free play of conflicting opinions *cannot* have any fundamental impact on the policy and composition of government; the second by urging that the free play of conflicting opinions *should not* have any fundamental impact on the policy and composition of government. Anti-democratic theories would, further, and in consequence, argue that rulers could not or should not be rendered responsible to those over whom they rule: that the few rather than the many must or should command the instruments of political power, that minorities rather than majorities must or should prevail. . . .

. . . the vital difference between the democratic and the oligarchic conceptions. In the one case opinion is free; in the other it may be controlled. In democracy this free opinion makes and unmakes governments, influences and shapes the broad channels of public policy. In oligarchy, whether opinion be free or restricted, it is indeterminative as a primary force in the political process. It may be invoked formally to sustain the party or group in power; it does not direct or immediately influence them. Democracy, and democracy alone, depends for its survival on the free operation of opposing views. Oligarchy recognizes but one view, that of the rulers. Here is the crucial demarcation of democratic from oligarchical thought. . . .

. . . the doctrines of anti-democratic thought may be classified, broadly, . . . into two major headings: (a) the impossibility of democracy, and (b) the undesirability of democracy. Under the first of these headings we include all those doctrines that hold democracy to be impossible of attainment because, whether we will it or not, political power always resides in the hands of a few, a ruling class. This ruling class does not . . . rest on the acquiescence of the people; it does not move with the changing tides of opinion. It rules, and rules irresponsibly, in accordance with the necessary dictates of unalterable imperatives. This, say the theorists of this school, is the way political power has always been determined; it is the way it is determined today; so, they conclude, it is the way—and the only way—that political power will be determined in the future.

Of the several expressions of this doctrine two are pre-eminent. . . . One is the theory of the ruling class as organizational necessity. In this view, . . . democracy is held to be impossible because of certain organizational imperatives inherent in the social structure. Every society . . . is organized in a particular way, and in the process of organization some one factor or characteristic becomes central. Those who control this key factor . . . control the organization, and those who control the organization are held to be the masters of that society. . . .

The second and somewhat more diversified argument against the possibility of democracy is the theory of the ruling class as conspiracy of power. In this construction . . . it is not the organization of the social order but the quality of men that is the decisive factor. Those who rule are not so much a class as they are a clique, a group of power-holding or power-seeking men who conjoin force with ambition, deceit with the will-to-dominate. . . . they ruthlessly employ [their unique qualities] in an irresistable drive for power that will give them control of the state and therewith the benefits of that control. . . .

Under our second major heading, the undesirability of democracy, we include all those doctrines that accept the possibility of the democratic state but reject as undesirable its operation and its consequences. . . .

Democracy, according to the theorists of this view . . . , is the rule of the average man; and the average man, it is held, is plainly an irrational and incompetent man. He is . . . a mediocrity, and as such cannot be expected to judge wisely of the numerous and complex affairs of state. To entrust to this average man . . . the great and small everyday issues of government, is to ensure irrationality and incompetence of decision. Only where the determination of policy is restricted to wise and competent rulers, it is argued, can the greatness and well-being of the state be secured. Where it is not, where, as in democracy, the mediocrity of the many overthrows the superior leadership of the few, inefficiency and incoherence inescapably follow. This . . . is the nature and result of democracy. It is the denial of wisdom and the institutionalization of decline. . . .

G. Mosca, *The Ruling Class* (New York, McGraw-Hill Book Company, 1939) Excerpts, pp. 50-53, 153-157, 395, 411-417, 474.

Among the constant facts and tendencies that are to be found in all political organizations, one is so obvious that it is apparent to the most casual eye. In all societies—from societies that are very meagerly developed and have barely attained the dawnings of civilization, down to the most advanced and powerful societies—two classes of people appear—a class that rules and a class that is ruled. The first class, always the less numerous, performs all political functions, monopolizes power and enjoys the advantages that power brings, whereas the second, the more numerous class, is directed and controlled by the first, in a manner that is now more or less legal, now more or less arbitrary and violent, and supplies the first, in appearance at least, with material means of subsistence and with the instrumentalities that are essential to the vitality of the political organism.

In practical life we all recognize the existence of this ruling class. . . . We all know that, in our own country, whichever it may be, the management of public affairs is in the hands of a minority of influential persons, to which management, willingly or unwillingly, the majority defer. . . .

Whatever the type of political organization, pressures arising from the discontent of the masses who are governed, from the passions by which they are swayed, exert a certain amount of influence on the policies of the ruling, the political class. . . .

. . . granting that the discontent of the masses might succeed in deposing a ruling class, inevitably . . . there would have to be another organized minority within the masses themselves to discharge the functions of a ruling class. Otherwise all organization, and the whole social structure, would be destroyed.

From the point of view of scientific research the real superiority of the concept of the ruling, or political, class lies in the fact that the varying structure of ruling classes has a preponderant importance in determining the political type, and also the level of civilization, of the different peoples. . . .

. . . What Aristotle called a democracy was simply an aristocracy of fairly broad membership. . . . Later on the modern democratic theory, which had its source in Rousseau, took its stand upon the concept that the majority of the citizens in any state can participate, and in fact *ought* to participate, in its political life, and the doctrine of popular sovereignty still holds sway over many minds in spite of the fact that modern scholarship is making it increasingly clear that democratic, monarchical and aristocratic principles function side by side in every political organism. . . .

. . . If it is easy to understand that a single individual cannot command a group without finding within the group a minority to support him, it is rather difficult to grant, as a constant and natural fact, that minorities rule majorities, rather than majorities minorities. But that is one of the points—so numerous in all the other sciences—where the first impression one has of things is contrary to what they are in reality. In reality the dominion of an organized minority, obeying a single impulse, over the unorganized majority is inevitable. . . .

Many doctrines that advocate liberty and equality . . . are summed up and given concrete form in the theory that views universal suffrage as the foundation of all sound government. It is commonly believed that the only free, equitable and legitimate government is a government that is based upon the will of the majority, the majority by its vote delegating its powers for a specified length of time to men who represent it. Down to a few generations ago—and even today in the eyes of many writers and statesmen—all flaws in representative government were attributed to incomplete or mistaken applications of the principles of representation and suffrage. . . .

. . . the assumption that the elected official is the mouthpiece of the majority of his electors is as a rule not consistent with the facts; . . .

What happens in other forms of government—namely, that an organized minority imposes its will on the disorganized majority—happens also and to perfection, whatever the appearance to the contrary, under the representative system. When we say that the voters "choose" their respresentatives, we are using a language that is very inexact. The truth is that the representative *has himself elected* by the voters, and, if that phrase should seem too inflexible and too harsh to fit some cases, we might qualify it by saying that *his friends have him elected.* In elections, as in all other manifestations of social life, those who have the will and, especially, the moral, intellectual and material *means* to force their will upon others take the lead over the others and command them. . . .

. . . In practice, . . . the representative system results not at all in government by the majority; it results in the participation of a certain number of social values in the guidance of the state, in the fact that many political forces which in an absolute state, a state ruled by a bureaucracy alone, would remain inert and without influence upon government become organized and so exert influence on government. . . .

Into [representative assemblies] the most disparate political forces and elements make their way, and the existence of a small independent minority is often enough to control the conduct of a large majority and, especially, to prevent the bureaucratic organization from becoming omnipotent. But when, beyond being organs of discussion and publicizing, assemblies come to concentrate all the prestige and power of legitimate authority in their own hands, as regularly happens in parliamentary governments, then . . . the whole administrative and judiciary machine falls prey to the irresponsible and anonymous tyranny of those who win in the elections and speak in the name of the people, and we get one of the worst types of political organization that the real majority in a modern society can possibly be called upon to tolerate. . . .

. . . the term "democratic" seems . . . suitable for the tendency which aims to replenish the ruling class with elements deriving from the lower classes, and which is always at work, openly or latently and with greater or lesser intensity, in all political organisms. "Aristocratic" we would call the opposite tendency, which also is constant and varies in intensity, and which aims to stabilize social control and political power in the descendants of the class that happens to hold possession of it at the given historical moment. . . .

. . . in systems where everybody, or almost everybody, can vote—the chief task of the various party organizations into which the ruling class is divided is to win the votes of the more numerous classes, which are necessarily the poorest and most ignorant. These classes ordinarily live in submission to a government which often they do not care for, and the aims and workings of which more often still they do not understand. . . .

The democratic tendency—the tendency to replenish ruling classes from below—is constantly at work with greater or lesser intensity in all human societies. At times the rejuvenation comes about in rapid or violent ways. More often, in fact normally, it takes place through a slow and gradual infiltration of elements from the lower into the higher classes. . . .

But every time the democratic movement has triumphed, in part or in full, we have invariably seen the aristocratic tendency come to life again through efforts of the very men who had fought it and sometimes had proclaimed its suppression. . . .

. . . Confining oneself to the political field, one has to admit the great benefits which constitute the undying glory of the nineteenth century as a result of the very illusions that guided it. To be sure, majority government and absolute political equality, two of the mottoes that the century inscribed on its banners, were not achieved, because they could not be achieved, and the same may be said of fraternity. But the ranks of the ruling classes have been held open. The barriers that kept individuals of the lower classes from entering the higher have been either removed or lowered, and the development of the old absolutist state into the modern representative state has made it possible for almost all political forces, almost all social values, to participate in the political management of society.

Robert Michels, *Political Parties* (New York, Dover Publications, Inc., 1959) Excerpts, pp. 1-11, 377, 390, 400-408.

The most restricted form of oligarchy, absolute monarchy, is founded upon the will of a single individual. . . . One commands, all others obey. The will of one single person can countervail the will of the nation, and even today we have a relic of this in the constitutional monarch's right of veto. . . .

At the antipodes of the monarchical principle, in theory, stands democracy, denying the right of one over others. *In abstracto*, it makes all citizens equal before the law. It gives to each one of them the possibility of ascending to the top of the social scale, and thus facilitates the way for the rights of the community, annulling before the law all privileges of birth, and desiring that in human society the struggle for preeminence should be decided solely in accordance with individual capacity. . . .

Our age has destroyed once for all the ancient and rigid forms of aristocracy, has destroyed them, at least, in certain important regions of political constitutional life. Even conservatism assumes at times a democratic form. Before the assaults of the democratic masses it has long since abandoned its primitive aspect, and loves to change its disguise. . . .

. . . The fundamental principle of modern monarchy (hereditary monarchy) is absolutely irreconcilable with the principles of democracy, even when these are understood in the most elastic sense. Caesarism is still democracy, or may at least still claim the name,

Reprinted by permission of Dover Publications.

when it is based upon the popular will; but automatic monarchy, never.

We may sum up the argument by saying that in modern party life aristocracy gladly presents itself in democratic guise, whilst the substance of democracy is permeated with aristocratic elements. On the one side we have aristocracy in a democratic form, and on the other democracy with an aristocratic content.

The democratic external form which characterizes the life of political parties may readily veil from superficial observers the tendency towards aristocracy, or rather towards oligarchy, which is inherent in all party organization. . . .

In theory, the principle of social and democratic parties is the struggle against oligarchy in all its forms. The question therefore arises how we are to explain the development in such parties of the very tendencies against which they have declared war. . . .

Whilst the majority of the socialist schools believe that in a future more or less remote it will be possible to attain to a genuinely democratic order, and whilst the greater number of those who adhere to aristocratic political views consider that democracy, however dangerous to society, is at least realizable, we find in the scientific world a conservative tendency voiced by those who deny resolutely and once for all that there is any such possibility. . . .

[Sociological phenomena] would seem to prove beyond dispute that society cannot exist without a "dominant" or "political" class, and that the ruling class, whilst its elements are subject to a frequent partial renewal, nevertheless constitutes the only factor of sufficiently durable efficacy in the history of human development. According to this view, the government, or, if the phrase be preferred, the state, cannot be anything other than the organization of a minority. . . . The majority is thus permanently incapable of self-government. Even when the discontent of the masses culminates in a successful attempt to deprive the bourgeoisie of power, this is after all, so Mosca contends, effected only in appearance; always and necessarily there springs from the masses a new organized minority which raises itself to the rank of a governing class. Thus the majority of human beings, in a condition of eternal tutelage, are predestined by tragic necessity to submit to the dominion of a small minority, and must be content to constitute the pedestal of an oligarchy.

The principle that one dominant class inevitably succeeds to another, and the law deduced from that principle that oligarchy is, as it were, a preordained form of the common life of great social aggregates, far from conflicting with or replacing the materialist conception of history, completes that conception and reinforces it. There is no essential contradiction between the doctrine that history is the record of a continued series of class struggles and the doctrine that class struggles invariably culminate in the creation of new oligarchies which undergo fusion with the old. . . .

Leadership is a necessary phenomenon in every form of social life. Consequently it is not the task of science to inquire whether this phenomenon is good or evil, or predominantly one or the other. But there is great scientific value in the demonstration that every system of leadership is incompatible with the most essential postulates of democracy. We are now aware that the law of the historic necessity of oligarchy is primarily based upon a series of facts of experience. . . .

. . . the principal cause of oligarchy in the democratic parties is to be found in the technical indispensability of leadership. . . .

. . . the fundamental sociological law of political parties . . . may be formulated in the following terms: "It is organization which gives birth to the dominion of the elected over the electors, of the mandatories over the mandators, of the delegates over the delegators. Who says organization, says oligarchy."

Every party organization represents an oligarchical power grounded upon a democratic basis. We find everywhere electors and elected. Also we find everywhere that the power of the elected leaders over the electing masses is almost unlimited. The oligarchical structure of the building suffocates the basic democratic principle. That which IS OPPRESSES THAT WHICH OUGHT TO BE. For the masses, this essential difference between the reality and the ideal remains a mystery. . . .

The formation of oligarchies within the various forms of democracy is the outcome of organic necessity, and consequently affects every organization, be it socialist or even anarchist. . . . The supremacy of the leaders in the democratic and revolutionary parties has to be taken into account in every historic situation present and to come, even though only a few and exceptional minds will be fully conscious of its existence. The mass will never rule except *in abstracto*. Consequently the question we have to discuss is not whether ideal democracy is realizable, but rather to what point and in what degree democracy is desirable, possible, and realizable at a given moment. . . .

Nothing could be more anti-scientific than the supposition that as soon as socialists have gained possession of governmental power it will suffice for the masses to exercise a little control over their leaders to secure that the interests of these leaders shall coincide perfectly with the interests of the led. . . .

The objective immaturity of the mass is not a mere transitory phenomenon which will disappear with the progress of democratization [on the day following the establishment of socialism.] On the contrary, it derives from the very nature of the mass as mass, for this, even when organized, suffers from an incurable incompetence for the solution of the diverse problems which present themselves for solution— because the mass *per se* is amorphous and therefore needs division of labour, specialization, and guidance. . . .

In the present work . . . it seemed necessary to lay considerable stress upon the pessimistic aspect of democracy which is forced on us by historical study. We had to inquire whether, and within what limits democracy must remain purely ideal, possessing no other value than that of a moral criterion which renders it possible to appreciate the varying degrees of that oligarchy which is immanent in every social regime. . . .

The defects inherent in democracy are obvious. It is none the less true that as a form of social life we must choose democracy as the least of evils. . . .

The democratic currents of history resemble successive waves. They break ever on the same shoal. They are ever renewed. This enduring spectacle is simultaneously encouraging and depressing. When democracies have gained a certain stage of development, they undergo a gradual transformation, adopting the aristocratic spirit, and in many cases also the aristocratic forms, against which at the outset they struggled so fiercely. Now new accusers arise to denounce the traitors; after an era of glorious combats and of inglorious power, they end by fusing with the old dominant class; whereupon once more they are in their turn attacked by fresh opponents who appeal to the name of democracy. It is probable that this cruel game will continue without end.

1. Democratic Myths and Democratic Realities
2. The Need for Leadership in a Democracy
3. Why Democracy Rather Than Authoritarianism?
4. Qualifications for Voting in the United States
5. Comparison of Rights Guaranteed in the Constitution of the United States and in the Constitution of the Union of Soviet Socialist Republics
6. Comparison of Rights Guaranteed in the Constitution of the United States and in the Constitution of Japan
7. The Difference Between Representation and Representative Government
8. The Case for Functional Representation
9. Types of Socialized Economy
10. The Case for Capitalism
11. The Case for Socialism
12. Differences Between Socialism and Communism
13. Lenin's Conception of Democracy
14. The Compatibility of Democracy and Socialism
15. The Importance of Freedom of Speech for Democracy
16. Why Freedom of Association Is Essential to Democracy
17. The Good and Evil Aspects of Pressure Politics
18. The Relative Importance of Liberty and Equality
19. The Kinds of Equality Essential to Democracy
20. The Functions of Political Parties in a Democracy
21. Authoritarian Government: Its Nature and Claimed Merits
22. The Criteria of Democracy
23. The Principal Menaces to Democracy
24. Why War Is a Menace to Democracy
25. Principles of Representation and Methods of Apportionment
26. Various Meanings of "Democracy"
27. The Impossibility of Democracy
28. The Undesirability of Democracy

29. The Future of Democracy
30. Public Opinion: Its Nature and Its Significance in the Governmental Process
31. Cabinet-Parliamentary Government
32. The Doctrines of Separation of Powers and Checks and Balances
33. Rigged Elections
34. Social Liberty Distinguished from Legal Liberty
35. Criticism of the Supreme Court's Ruling that Both Houses of a State Legislature Must be Based on the Principle of Apportionment According to Population
36. Restrictions on Freedom of Speech Are a Menace to Democracy
37. Denial of Freedom of Speech to Subversives Is Consistent with Democratic Principles
38. Democratic Doctrine Requires Freedom of Speech for Anti-Democratic Groups
39. The Few Always Rule
40. Majority Rule Is a Fiction
41. Property-Owning Qualifications for Voting Are Undemocratic
42. The Age Qualification for Voting Should Be Eighteen
43. The Inseparability of Rights and Duties
44. The Meaning of "Social Democracy"
45. The Interests of Individuals and Their Relation to Place of Residence
46. Majority-Choice Election Methods
47. Proportional Representation as a Method of Election
48. The Importance of Methods of Nomination
49. Freedom of Religion and Democracy
50. Freedom of the Press: Is it Essential to Democracy?
51. Voting Qualifications Which Conflict with Democratic Doctrine
52. The Role of the People in the Democratic Process of Government
53. Conditions Essential to the Effective Enjoyment of Legal Liberties

54. Elites: Their Distinguishing Characteristics
55. In Democracies, A Two-Party Situation Is Preferable to a Multiple-Party Situation
56. Administrative Officials Should Be Appointed Rather than Elected
57. Equality of Treatment May Be Unfair
58. Ways and Means of Influencing Government in a Democracy
59. Majority Rule Menaces Minority Rights
60. The Democratic Process of Government Safeguards Minority Rights
61. Judicial Review Is Undemocratic
62. The Meaning of "Free Elections"
63. A One-Party System Is Undemocratic
64. The Relative Importance of the Various Criteria of Democratic Government
65. Democracy Requires Short Terms of Office for Elective Officials
66. Majority Rule Seldom Occurs in a Democracy
67. A Community-Minded People Is Essential to the Successful Functioning of Democratic Government
68. Both Democratic and Authoritarian Governments Resort to Coercion
69. The Relationship Between Democracy and Federalism
70. Factors Determinative of the Survival of Democracy
71. The Line of Demarcation Between Democracy and Authoritarianism Fluctuates
72. Different Types of Authoritarianism
73. The Nature of Totalitarianism
74. Democracy Promotes Individuality
75. The Relationship Between Forms of Government and World Peace
76. Democracy Requires a Population-Based Apportionment of Representatives
77. The Strictly Equal Representation of Areas, Regardless of Population, Is by no Means Indicative of Authoritarianism

78. Government by Minorities, Rather than Majority Rule, Usually Occurs in Democracies
79. Different Theories Concerning the Duties of an Elected Representative
80. The Comparative Importance of Nomination Methods and Modes of Election
81. The Tactics Resorted to by Pressure Groups in Order to Gain Their Objectives
82. The Nature and Consequences of Gerrymandering
83. Illiteracy and Poverty Prevent the Attainment of Genuinely Democratic Government
84. Liberty Requires a Government of Law Rather than a Government of Men
85. Liberty Without Law Is Unattainable
86. Democracy Requires Acceptance of the Results of Elections
87. Appointment of the Chief Executive, Rather than Popular Election of this Official, Fails to Warrant the Conclusion That Authoritarian Government Exists
88. Democracy Requires Adequate Sources of Information for the People
89. The Manipulation of Public Opinion by Officials Is a Menace to Democracy
90. Why Democracies Fail

INDEX

312

NOTES

NOTES

NOTES

NOTES

NOTES

NOTES

NOTES

NOTES

NOTES

NOTES

NOTES

NOTES